W9-ADK-662

PEASANT UPRISINGS IN JAPAN
of the
TOKUGAWA PERIOD

By
HUGH BORTON, Ph.D.

Second Edition
With a New Introduction

PARAGON BOOK REPRINT CORP.
New York
1968

Library of Congress Catalogue Card Number: 68-54192

An unaltered and unabridged reprint of the work first published in 1938, in Vol. XVI of The Transactions of the Asiatic Society of Japan (Second Ser.)

Manufactured in the United States of America
by Arno Press, Inc., New York, N. Y. 10017

PEASANT UPRISINGS

IN JAPAN

OF THE TOKUGAWA PERIOD

By

HUGH BORTON, Ph.D.

To My Father

and

To My Wife

This work was presented in partial fulfillment for the degree of Doctor of Philosophy at the Rijksuniversiteit, Leiden, Holland, and through their permission is printed in its present revised form.

INTRODUCTION

I am naturally pleased to have my study of peasant uprisings in Japan during the two hundred and sixty years of the Tokugawa Period reprinted by Paragon Books. The appearance of the reprint just at this time is particularly fortunate. Interest among Japanese historians in these and other types of uprisings and disturbances has increased notably since World War II. Many leftist writers have considered them as manifestations of the struggle of the oppressed masses against the despotic power of the feudal system in accord with Marx's materialistic interpretation of history.

On the other hand, there seems to be little new evidence to justify this interpretation. The general thesis which is elaborated below is that these uprisings were largely separate, disconnected incidents in which the farmers demanded improvement in their economic status or elimination of unjust local officials or feudal barons. Except in a few cases, such as the famous uprising of Ōshio Heihachirō in Ōsaka in 1837 which was against corruption and the high price of rice (see below p. 93 ff), there was no concerted effort made to develop a national, anti-government movement or to force a change in the feudal system. This position is supported by Professor Aoki Koji in his recently published, exhaustive and definitive work on this whole subject. He points out that the uprisings are obviously significant examples of dissatisfaction with the existing social structure and its oppressive conditions. He also notes that during the two periods of greatest economic distress and famine from 1783-1787 and 1833-1837, the uprisings were widespread and most numerous but still largely separate and uncoordinated. Thereafter the farm population became divided into two groups, the large and small peasants, and thus the uprisings no longer involved the entire rural community of a province or even a single domain, thus losing their effectiveness.

Finally, Professor Aoki argues quite cogently that even though the uprisings reached their highest peak for a single year in 1866, the year before the downfall of the Tokugawa dictatorship and the beginning of the Meiji Restoration, they were not the cause of this change in government. He notes that even though these uprisings in 1866 produced a consciousness among the peasants which was a potential threat to the feudal regime, the Meiji Restoration developed independently of the peasants. The Restoration was directed against the danger of foreign pressure threatening the semi-colonization of Japan and against the Tokugawa regime because of its inability to govern effectively. It was brought about by a coup d'etat within the Imperial Palace and the farmers found themselves victims of changes engineered and perpetrated by members of the ruling class of warriors. (See Aoki Koji, *Hyakushō Ikki no Nenjiteki Kenkyū* (A Study by years of Peasant Uprisings) Tōkyō, Shinseisha, 1966, pp. 10 ff.) The power to rule had shifted from one group of leading warriors (the Tokugawa) to the Emperor and the group of Western Clans which supported him. There was no overthrow of the ruling warrior class, no rise of the peasants to power and no radical change in their conditions.

In the preface to the original edition, written over thirty years ago, I emphasized that the actual number of known uprisings in the Tokugawa period was determined by the material which had thus far been discovered. Then, as now, new materials were constantly being uncovered so that the total number of incidents was continually increasing. At that time, Professor Kokusho Iwao and his collaborators at Kyoto University had discovered over a thousand separate incidents making an annual average of 3.8. In a later publication, his total figure was raised to over 1600. As a result of extensive research, Professor Aoki is now able to list 1,809 uprisings with a yearly average of 10.1. He also records over three hundred disturbances in the cities and towns, many of them rice riots, and nearly seven hundred incidents in the villages.

But the actual number of occurrences of these uprisings is not as important as the question of whether or not recent research has discovered any basic differences with the information presented below on such problems as their causes, the peak years in which they occurred, the general geographical areas where they broke out most frequently and the types that developed. In general, the answer appears to be that no new striking changes can be discerned. On the other hand, Professor Aoki has clarified many aspects of the subject. For example, he notes that the formation of the farm villages in the seventeenth century afforded a new opportunity for the farmers to develop bands or groups and to protest collectively against many abuses and hardships. As a consequence of this new social change, there was a marked increase in the number of peasant uprisings. Similarly, it is no mere coincidence that the severity and number of them increased in the mid-eighteenth century just at a time when the government of the Tokugawa dictatorship and the other feudal barons were facing economic difficulties. When the ruling-class warriors, whose wealth was measured in terms of rice income, increased pressure on the farmers to produce more and the peasants had already reached their maximum production capacity, some sort of outbursts were likely to result.

Furthermore, Professor Aoki has clarified the definition of the various types of uprisings. He lists six different types: desertion *(chōsan)*, legal complaint *(shūso)*, appeal to higher authority *(osso)*, mob appeal *(gōso)*, uprising *(bōdō)* and mob destruction (*uchikowashi*). As for desertion, this method was most prevalent in the early part of the period and involved peasants moving elsewhere in the hopes of improving their lot. As the law forbade such action, the feudal barons would dispatch their officials to capture the fugitives and bring them back to their farms. As the whole feudal structure was based on what the peasant was able to produce, the authorities were reluctant to punish the peasant simply for desertion. They were glad enough to have him back producing more rice. (See below p. 30). In some cases, however, these desertions turned into full-fledged uprisings (See below p. 144 ff.) The second category, legal complaints (*shūso*) refers to those cases where the farmers appealed directly to their immediate superiors, the village officials or the representatives of the feudal barons. So long as the uprising remained in this category, those participating, including the leaders, usually were not punished.

By far the largest majority of these uprisings fall into the last four categories, all of which took violent form and carried heavy penalties for the leaders, if not for many of the participants. In the appeals to higher authority *(osso)* the band or group consciously avoided going to the village officials but attempted to present their complaints directly to the head of the fief or to a high official of the Tokugawa government. The mob appeal *(gōso)* followed the same procedure as the previous type but, as the name implies, was composed on an unruly mob. "An uprising" (*bōdō*) is defined as being even more violent and often included large numbers of angry peasants armed with bamboo spears, clubs and farm implements. If provoked, or if their demands were not considered favorably, these uprisings would develop into the last and most violent type, namely, mob destruction or *uchikowashi.* These last two categories were most prevalent throughout times of famine and extreme hardship and towards the latter part of the Tokugawa Period. (See below p. 16).

Professor Aoki has not only collected a vast amount of new material in his work referred to above but presented it in an extremely useful manner. His study begins with the year 1590 and ends with 1867, while my study is from 1603 to 1867. His book is really two volumes in one. The first third is explanatory text, supplemented by useful diagrams and charts. The last two-thirds is composed entirely of three chronological tables: a) peasant uprisings in rural areas, b) those in the towns and cities and c) those in the villages. These tables also contain the following information for each incident: geographical location, feudal fief involved, extent, causes, demands of the participants and the sources on which this information is based.

Some of the early works on peasant uprisings listed in the bibliography of this reprint have either been extensively revised or enlarged. For example, Professor Kokusho Iwao published an enlarged and supplementary edition of his "Study of Peasant Uprisings" under the title *Hyakushō Ikki no Kenkyū Zokuhen* (Tōkyō, Minerva Shobo, 1959). The four volumes of source materials which he planned to publish seem never to have materialized (See below p. xi). The other great pre-war authority on this subject, Professor Ono Takeo, has had his *Hyakushō Ikki Sōdan* (Materials on Peasant Uprisings) reprinted without changes in a postwar edition.

A considerable amount of new material, in addition to Aoki's work cited above, has appeared in the postwar years. For example, when the Historical Research Bureau of Kyōto University published its *Nihon Kindai Shi Jiten* (Modern Japanese Historical Dictionary), in 1958, it included a chronological chart of peasant uprisings from 1830-1867. The material for this chart was based on research undertaken by Kyōto University's Agricultural History Center. Other works include: Tamura Eitarō, *Kindai Nihon Nōmin Undō Shiron* (Historical Treatise on the Japanese Peasant Movement), Tōkyō, Getsuyō Shobo, 1948 and Hayashi Motoi, *Hyakushō Ikki no Dentō* (Tradition in Peasant Uprisings), Tōkyō, Miraisha, 1955. For the latter part of the Tokugawa Period and after the Meiji Restoration see Aoki Koji, *Meiji Nōmin Sōjō no Nenjiteki Kenkyū* (Peasant Revolts, A study by Years of the Meiji Period), Tōkyō, Shinseisha, 1967; Aoki Keiichirō, *Nihon Nōmin Undō Shi* (A History of the Peasant Movement in Japan), 6 vol., Tōkyō, Hyōron Shinsha, 1958-62.

In conclusion, I regret that the contingencies connected with this reprint edition made it impossible to incorporate into the body of the text the invaluable information which has appeared in the past thirty years. On the other hand, I am grateful for this opportunity to add the material mentioned above and hope the reader will find it adds to the value of the original study.

Hugh Borton

East Asian Institute
Columbia University,
July 1, 1968

TABLE OF CONTENTS

PREFACE

For some time having had an interest in the development of Japan of the Tokugawa Period (1603–1868), yet realizing the wealth of material facing any student of contemporary or older Japan, it seemed wiser to the author to select a specific study for investigation. As there have recently appeared various studies and documents for research in Peasant Uprisings of the Tokugawa Period, and as little material has appeared in European languages, the following work has been undertaken, as much from an historic as from an economic viewpoint.

Although a special bibliography, both Japanese and European, has been appended to this work, a brief bibliographical note may be of assistance at this point. In the first place, the two most competent Japanese scholars in the field of study of peasant uprisings are Professor Takeo Ono, of Hōsei University, Tokyo, and Professor Iwao Kokushō, of Kyoto Imperial University. Both these men have not only been collecting and editing source material, but have made valuable comparative studies. The most important primary sources, for studies especially during the Tokugawa Period, include Ono, Takeo: *Hyakushō Ikki Sōdan;* and Honjo, E., editor, *Kinsei Shakai Keizai Sōsho,* especially Volumes I, X, and XI. Various source materials are also contained in the local district and prefectural histories, *Gunshi* and *Kenshi,* filled with primary sources, usually arranged chronologically and edited by competent scholars under the auspices of these various localities. There are still a few unpublished MSS. on the subject in the library of the Shiryō Hensanjo of Tokyo Imperial University, but as Professor Kokushō is now compiling a four volume work on source materials of peasant uprisings in Japan, most of the important documents will be included in that study. For an excellent comparative study, the reader is referred to

Professor Kokushō's *Hyakushō Ikki no Kenkyū.* However, due to the fact that the actual number of occurrences of these uprisings is directly dependent on the discovery of new materials, and is increasing monthly, the charts in this work are less valuable than those published in October 1935 by Mr. Hidenosuke Numazaki, a collaborator of Professor Kokushō, in *Hyakushō Ikki Chōsa Hōkokusho,* or *Report on the investigation of peasant uprisings.*

Unfortunately the materials are much more limited in western languages. Dr. Takekoshi devotes one chapter to "The resistance of the agricultural classes," in the third volume of his *Economic aspects of the history of the civilization of Japan,* and Professor Eijirō Honjo mentions the problem in his recent work, *The social and economic history of Japan.* The only article dealing directly with a peasant uprising is a translation by Professor J. Rahder of an uprising in Kurume, Kyushu, in 1754, entitled "Record of Kurume Uprising," *Acta Orientalia,* Vol. XIV. For general reference purposes, an excellent bibliography on Japanese economic writings is found in Professor Honjo's, *Nihon Keizaishi Bunken.*

A few technicalities in the treatment of the material should be mentioned. In the first place, the following study of peasant uprisings of the Tokugawa Period does not attempt to be a strictly linguistic work. Rather than devote time and energy on a few specific incidents with a detailed linguistic explanation, it seemed better to attempt a general survey of the problem, although accuracy has been attempted in translation of specific demands of the peasants. Here, however, exact renderings of the texts are extremely difficult due to the ambiguity and terseness of these demands on the one hand, and the constant use of technical terms on the other. Here particularly, no one is more aware of the possibility of errors and mistakes in translation than is the author.

No attempt has been made to transform the dates of the uprisings into the exact western chronological equivalent. All Japanese studies thus far have given the Japanese chronology and a change to exact month and day, western style, would not only be extremely laborious, but in this case, unnecessary to an understanding of the problem. Those wishing to know the exact western equivalent for any dates mentioned in the text can easily do so by reference to Bramsen, William, "Japanese chronology, calendars, and chronological tables," a supplement to Vol. XXXVII of the *Transactions of the Asiatic Society of Japan,* 1910. Japanese terms, for which there is no exact equivalent in English, have been retained in many cases such as *daikan,* (an intendant in charge of a domain), *Bakufu,* (the peculiar military form of government of the Tokugawa family), *shōya,* (a village official) and the like. Their meaning is explained when they first appear in the text, and all technical terms appear in the glossary. To some, the unnecessary biographical references in the footnotes, to the lords of the various domains, may seem cumbersome, but as such information is extremely scarce in European languages, and rarely found in any single Japanese work, such treatment seems justifiable. For those who find continual reference to Japanese proper names laborious, and who are interested only in a general outline of the subject, the author would recommend perusal of Chapters I-III inclusive, and for a typical uprising, that in Ōmi in 1842, which is treated in Chapter VI. The remainder of the work is a detailed account of peasant uprisings as they appeared in the Tokugawa Era.

The author wishes to take this opportunity to thank those various institutions, scholars and friends, both Occidental and Oriental, that have made this work possible. He is primarily indebted to the continued interest of Professor Evarts B. Greene of Columbia University and to that institution and the American Council of Learned Societies, of Washington, D. C., which have made his studies abroad possible, and to Professor J. J. L. Duyvendak, to whom, among other things, he is especially indebted for valuable advice in planning those studies. He wishes to express his gratitude to Professor Zennosuke Tsuji of the Shiryō Hensanjo of Tokyo Imperial University, not only for permission to use some of their MSS., but also for his friendly advice and interest. To Messrs. Abe and

Okayama, the author is indebted for their efforts on his behalf in discovering inaccessible materials and for their patience and assistance with some of the more difficult texts; and to Professors Kokushō and Ono for their kind permission to use their valuable works. And lastly, to Leiden University for permission to present this thesis in mimeographed form as partial requirement for the Ph. D. degree of that University, prior to its publication in the *Transactions of the Asiatic Society of Japan;* and to my promoter, Dr. J. Rahder, whose instruction, encouragement and assistance, have been as valuable as they have been abundant and conscientious, the author is profoundly grateful.

Moorestown, N. J.
March 23rd, 1937. Hugh Borton

ABBREVIATIONS

The following abbreviations have been used:

Harvard Journal of Asiatic Studies	H.J.A.S.
Journal of the American Oriental Society	J.A.O.S.
Transactions of the Asiatic Society of Japan	T.A.S.J.

CHAPTER I.

INTRODUCTION

The recent developing interest of the Japanese scholarly world in the study of peasant uprisings in Japan, especially those of the Tokugawa Period (1603-1868), and those centering around the Meiji Restoration of 1868, warrants that notice should be taken by the West of this work. The time has come to consider Japan—at least feudal Japan from 1600 to 1868—not as a country hermetically sealed from outside influence nor as a country whose central government was so powerful that all was serene within. That modern scholars have already disovered over a thousand uprisings in Japan during a period a little over two hundred and fifty years, justifies the statement that, "the decentralization of power of the agricultural districts held its own against the principle of centralization of power of the Tokugawa government."[1] Any study, therefore of such widespread social unrest should help to point out the fact that the regime had characteristics within itself which lead to its inevitable collapse. Perhaps this unrest added impetus to the breakdown, materially changed the course of political events in Japan and was one more element in making her political isolation of the 19th century finally come to its end.

To arrive at a satisfactory understanding of the problem of peasant uprisings in Japan with the various social and economic forces behind them, to grasp adequately this phase of feudal society, and also to understand more fully the problems confronting rural Japan to-day, it is necessary to survey the feudal regime of the Tokugawa Period. With some conception of the political organization, the methods and amount of taxation, the village with its peculiar form of government and the position of the farmers in Japanese society

---

1. Cf. Ono, Takeo, *Hyakushō Ikki Sōdan,* 2 Vol.; Tōkyō, 1927, Vol. 1, p. 5.

after 1600, it will be possible to study various uprisings in their relation to that society. They will be found to be of varying types, some mere appeals, others the concentration into a mob of thousands of farmers, determined to have their grievances rectified through collective bargaining of unarmed communities. The causes of these uprisings, whether economic, political or administrative, were closely connected with the unseen yet real currents of change permeating the whole feudal structure. The warrior, supreme in power at the beginning of the period, was to be overthrown by the penetration of money into society, the rise of a powerful merchant class, the demands of foreign powers from without that Japan take her place among the nations of the world, and the movement within that the real power and control of the land revert to the Emperor and the Shōgun relinquish the authority usurped by himself and his ancestors. Erupting in such a society were the peasant uprisings, outbursts, on the most part, of peasants who were unwilling to endure oppression any longer and willing to die for their cause, if necessary.

Although there is necessity for detailed studies in such fields as the change in the standard of living of the peasant, the influence of the peasant uprisings at the time of the Meiji Restoration of 1868, and the modern agricultural problems facing Japan, a country whose majority of the population is still rural, the following survey may help clarify one part of the Tokugawa Period. If an understanding of the problems facing modern Japan is to be attained, if the West is to gain from a wider and more profound study of the East, it is not only necessary but essential that special studies throughout the various phases of Japanese history be made, and through them be attained a true and adequate picture of that intricate yet fascinating life of which they are a part. With that in view, the following work was undertaken.

CHAPTER II

CHARACTERISTICS OF THE TOKUGAWA FEUDAL REGIME

For the purposes of historical background, it should be noted that at the beginning of the 17th century, Japan became united under the control of the Tokugawa family. Tokugawa Ieyasu (1542–1616), profiting from the process of unification already started by Oda Nobunaga (1534–1582), and further continued by Toyotomi Hideyoshi (1536–1598), became master of the greater part of Japan after the victory of Sekigahara in 1600. After becoming Shōgun in 1603 and exterminating Toyotomi Hideyori (1593–1615), son and heir of Hideyoshi, at the seige of the Ōsaka Castle in 1614–1615, he established, until 1868, the control of his family throughout Japan by means of the Tokugawa *Bakufu*.[1] The power and administration of this new government were centered around Edo, present Tōkyō, and society was feudalistic in nature. Ieyasu's policy of unification included the establishment and sharp demarcation of the social classes, the centralization of power, an elaborate system of censors and secret spies to prevent political intrigues, the unification of currency, the monopolization of industry, and a careful isolation of all lords who were either real or potential enemies of the Tokugawa government.

With this centralization of political power came the an-

1. Tokugawa *Bakufu* 徳川幕府, is the term applied to the military dictatorship of the Tokugawa family over Japan after 1603. *Bakufu* literally means "tent government". It is also termed the Edo *Bakufu*, 江戸幕府.

nihilation of the peculiarly loose and complex *shōen*[2] or private domains and their conversion into veritable fiefs. Prior to this time there was a sharp distinction between the peasantry and warriors, stimulated by the development of wars, the use of gunpowder after 1542, and the professionalization of the warrior class. But following the arbitrary distribution of land by Tokugawa Ieyasu, the separation became irretrievable. For the *bushi* (warriors), this meant an increase in their landless stipends and for the peasants an increase in their self-government and the treatment of their land as definite unitary possessions. From this peculiar regime, Japan emerged with "*experience both of feudal life and a species of centralization, both of self-government in the village and of organized discipline in larger areas, with the warriors loyal and the peasants docile, and provided with remarkably even shares of landed wealth.*"[3]

Before taking up specific examples of uprisings when the peasants were decidedly not docile, it would be well to sketch, for purposes of background, the distribution of public and private domains, their income, taxation, the government of the villages,[4] and finally the position of the peasant in Tokugawa

---

2. The *Shōen*, 莊園, were the huge private domains which had developed in medieval Japan. They were under the patronage of a *ryōke*, 領家, or seignior, with a separate right or profit derivable from the land, a right invested in a person termed *shiki*, 職. The proprietors of these private domains were termed *Jishu*, 地主, or landholders who developed into the *bushi*, 武士, or warrior class. The cultivators, *sakunin*, 作人, thus developed into the peasant class. Cf. Asakawa, K., "Some aspects of Japanese fuedal institutions", T.A.S.J., Vol. 46, pt. I, 1918, pp. 83 *et seq.* Also an excellent account of the development of Japanese feudal institutions will be grasped from a study of materials by the same author in *Documents of Iriki*, 1 Vol.; New Haven, 1929.

3. Cf. Asakawa, "Feudal institutions", *op. cit.* p. 102.

4. For a complete account of this problem, Cf. Asakawa, K., "Notes on village life in Japan after 1600," J.A.O.S., Vol. 30 & 31, 1910–1911.

This is an excellent work with copious notes and references to primary Japanese sources. Other works relating to this are: Takizawa, M., *The penetration of money economy in Japan and its effect upon social and political institutions,* 1 Vol.; New York, 1927; Murdoch, James, *A history of Japan,* 3 Vol.; London, 1926 especially Vol. III, pp. 27 *et seq.* And

society. The official productive capacity of Japan was estimated at 18.5 million *koku*[5] in 1600 with an increase in double the area under cultivation by 1730 and a yield of over 25 million *koku*. Of a total of 26.4 million *koku* actually harvested, the public, or *Bakufu* domain, equalled 3.28 million *koku* plus 900,000 *koku* from the large cities, and was controlled by forty *daikan* or intendants,[6] with special salaries and with the control of the collection and forwarding of taxes, the reporting of the census, and the carrying out of the special government orders in the various *Bakufu* fiefs in the Kwanto, Hida, Mino and Kyushu. The private fiefs amounted to over four times this amount while the Imperial Household was given a mere 100,000 *koku* domain.[7]

For taxation purposes, the land was graded, the first grade estimated to produce 15 *koku* per *chōbu*,[8] and the poorest about eight to nine *koku*. Just prior to the Tokugawa Period, taxation had been 40% of the crop for the lord and 60% for the cultivator. This was universally increased to a 5:5 ratio as taxation laws of 1684–1687 clearly show.[9] However, as will become apparent from a further study of the peasant uprisings, the most objectionable forms of taxation were the extra taxes levied by the various officials both for

---

Smith, N.S., *A Tokugawa miscellany*, a work to be published shortly in London.

In Japanese Cf. Honjo, Eijiro, *Kinsei Nōson Mondai Shiron*, 1 Vol.; Tōkyō, 1925.

5. A *koku*, 石, of rice, the unit used in estimating not only the size of a fief but one's income, equals approximately 4.96 bushels. It was composed of 2½ bales(*hyō* 俵).

6. A *daikan*, 代官, a supervisor, was an official corresponding largely to an intendant.

7. Takizawa has noted the income of the *Bakufu* as 8 million *koku*, but this would include the income of their retainers amounting to about 4 million. The above figures are quoted from the the *Sui Jin Roku*, 吹塵錄, a collection of materials on Tokugawa finances. Cf. Sawada, Shō, (translated by Hugh Borton), "Financial Difficulties of the Edo Bakufu", H.J.A.S.,Vol. 1, No. 3, pp. 316 *et seq*.

8. A *chōbu*, 町歩, equals 2.45 acres.

9. *Jōkyō Denbata Sohō* (Tax laws of 1684–1687) as quoted in Abe, M., "Nōgyō Keizai", in *Sekai Rekishi Taikei*, Vol. 13B, pp. 24 *et seq*.

their own and for their lord's profit. Among these should be noted the *komononari*,[10] or additional miscellaneous tax, the *fuyaku*,[11] or labor required by the *daikan*, later being changed to a payment in money; the *kammai*,[12] or supplementary rice necessary to pay the loss sustained in transport; the *kayaku*,[13] or service for repairs on dykes, roads and bridges and finally the *sukegō*,[14] a tax levied on villages near the stations along the main highways for transporting goods or furnishing horses and men for the trips to Edo or official excursions to the mausoleums at Nikko.

Taxes were determined by two methods, the *jōmenhō*,[15] the settling of the tax rates on the total crop and the fixing a flat rate for several years or more regardless of the crop; and the *kemmihō*,[16] or yearly examination of the standing grain, taking the crop of one *tsubo* (3.95 sq. yd.) as a sample from each class of land.[17] The local administrative unit through which these taxes were collected was the village, of which there were over 63,000. The peasants in the villages, many of whom owned land and employed hired men, were divided into *gonin kumi*[18] or five-men-groups which took joint responsibility for the collection of taxes, assisted its members in time of need, and sealed documents regarding the transference of land and

10. *Komononari*, 小物成, were the various additional taxes as opposed to the regular taxes. They were levied in the form of service in the mountains, on rivers or fields, or other services. They differed in the various fiefs and were usually collected in money. For this term as well as others concerning agricultural problems see: Ono, Takeo, *Nihon Nōminshi Goi*, 1 Vol.; Tōkyō, 1926.

11. *Fuyaku*, 夫役. Labour requisitioned for various public works.

12. *Kammai*, 缺米. This supplementary rice often amounted to 3–4% of the total to make up the deficiency resulting from loss on long voyages when rice would rot or spoil from the moisture. It was also called *sashimai*. Cf. *infra*, p. 175 note 106.

13. *Kayaku*, 課役.

14. *Sukegō*, 助鄉, which was first levied in 1684.

15. *Jōmenhō*, 定免法.

16. *Kemmihō*, 檢見法, also read *Kemiho*, 毛見法.

17. Cf. Honjo, *op. cit.*, p. 20

18. *Gonin Kumi*, 五人組, punchayets.

the movements of its members. Officials of the village included the *nanushi* or *shōya*,[19] the heads of the village usually appointed by the *daikan*, or selected by the fief officials. He was assisted by a *kumigashira*,[20] or head of a small group of the farmers. The *hyakushōdai*,[21] representative of the farmers, was usually an elder who oversaw the actions of the other officials, examined their conduct, or gave advice.[22]

Such then, in briefest form, is the background for the administration of the agricultural community. Attention must next be directed to this group of some 24,000,000 farmers who were the economic foundation of not only the warriors, but all of Japan. Technically they were placed in the classification of Tokugawa society above the *chōnin*[23] or townsmen, but with the rise in power of these town merchants, the farmers fell far below them in power.[24] They were constantly referred to as the essence of the country, for Ogiu Sōrai relates that, "the farmers cultivating the fields nourish the world; and merchants, having no object, help no one; while the soldier governs it all, and sees that there are no dis-

---

19. The terms *nanushi,* and *shōya,* 名主, and 庄屋, were inter-changeable. The former was commonly used in eastern Japan. Professor Asakawa states that *kimori,* 肝煎, and *kendan,* 檢斷, are synonymous terms, and confined to the northern regions of Dewa and Mutsu. However, I have found the former used in Kaga and the latter in a MS. from Shinano in 1761. This same MS. also contains the terms *warimoto,* 割元, and *ōshōya,* 大庄屋, with a similar meaning although Professor Asakawa states these offices were abolished in 1713. Cf. *Ueda Ryōnai Sōdō,* a MS. in Tōkyō Imperial University, p. 11, and Asakawa, *op. cit.* Vol. 31, p. 165 and 169.

20. *Kumikashira,* 組頭, also called *osabyakushō,* 長百姓, who may originally have been the head of the *gonin kumi.* He was one of the leading peasants of his group, *kumi,* chosen for one or more years.

21. *Hyakushōdai.* 百姓代.

22. Cf. Asakawa, *op. cit.*, Vol. 31, p. 168. Professor Ono adds there were two or three *hyakushōdai* in each village, they being the wealthiest of the farmers and acting as the intermediary for the farmers and the other officials. Cf. Ono, *op. cit.*, p. 367.

23. *Chōnin,* 町人.

24. Cf. Kurita, Genji, *Sōgō Nihonshi Taikei, Edo Jidai,* Vol. IX, Tōkyō, 1927, p. 650 *et seq.*

turbances."[25] Still another writer, Yamakata Banto, writing in Ōsaka in the early 19th century says: "The farmers cannot be dispensed with, though we can do without merchants and artisans. It is the prerequisite of statesmanship to advance the interests of the farming population by encouraging agriculture at the expense of the townspeople."[26] While finally a saying has it: "First the farmer, next the *samurai*, third the beggars and finally the townsmen."[27]

It became the policy of the Tokugawa government to encourage agriculture and keep the peasant as content as possible. The intendants were told to consider the people as the foundation of the state, to study their hardships and to see that they did not suffer from hunger and cold. On the other hand, in 1649, the farmers were requested to respect the officials' orders, consider their superiors with real friendliness and above all, work industriously, neither evading the taxes nor taking part in temporal pleasures. In the morning they were to awaken early and cut the grass, till the fields during the day and at night make ropes, and bales, never remaining idle. They should buy neither wines nor tea and should save their rice for the fall. All must help in the fall harvest and must grow the five cereals. They were to think of the farmers who eat the leaves of the shrubs during famine and therefore not throw them away. They should refrain from smoking for it not only cost money but required their leisure time.[28]

As the period progressed, money began to penetrate into society and the *chōnin* consequently became more powerful. The extravagances which became the order of the day in Ōsaka and Edo at the end of the seventeenth century were soon reflected among the life of the peasants. Thus they

---

25. Ogiu Sorai, 荻生徂來, (1666-1728) was a celebrated Confucian scholar of Edo. Cf. Kurita, *op. cit.*, p. 719. For a translation of other writings of Ogiu see Smith, N.S., editor, "An introduction to some Japanese Economic writings", T.A.S.J., Vol. XI, 1934, p. 60 *et seq.*

26. Honjō, E., Economic and social history, p. 230 *et seq.*

27. Kurita, *op. cit.*, p. 705.

28. *Ibid*, p. 707. *et seq.*

were admonished to remain as farmers and not to imitate the townsmen who quickly made money only to lose it.[29] Again it is reported that the "farmers who live near the cities try to imitate its extravagances and search for wealth. If they are in the country they should make agriculture their main task; their children and grandchildren all grasping the hoe. If a weak child is apprenticed in the capital and makes money, then he should not be allowed to return to the village with his bad customs and habits."[30] Later in the century is related the fact that "the farmers formerly tied their hair with straw, while now they not only use cord from Edo, but also hair oils. They were not content with cotton clothing but wore various kinds of silk. Their food had improved and *tatami* (straw flooring) replaced the thin straw mats in their homes, while rain hats and umbrellas had even come into use. Pawnshops, baths, and barber shops had all been established and were credited with bringing about the downfall of the country."[31]

Against these descriptions of the development of the extravagant tastes of the peasants should be noted a specific example of the situation in Sendai in 1753. There it is reported that when the yearly tax and other charges were reduced from the peasant's income there remained 15 *kamme*, 210 *momme*.[32] The expenses of the family were approximately 4 *kamme* 210 *momme* per person, so taking five as an average size family, there remained a deficit of about 6 *kamme*. Thus the farmers were forced to supplement their food by eating roots and chestnuts, or receive what fees they could from travelers for service rendered them. Another example shows a deficit of from 2 to 3 *shō*[33] of rice per section

---

29. Honjō, *Nōson mondai, op. cit.*, p. 69.
30. *Ibid*, p. 70, quoted from *Kashoku Yōdō*, 家職 要道, a contemporary work by *Shōji Kōki*, 正司 考祺,
31. Ibid., p. 80.
32. One *kamme*, 貫目, of silver equals 1000 *momme*, 匁目. At that date 1 *koku* of rice cost 83 *momme*. Cf. *infra*, Appendix III.
33. One hundred *shō*, 升, equal one *koku*, and 1 *shō*, equals 3.18 pints.

of upper grade land, but an example in the district of Mito in 1830 shows a balance of 6 *ryō*[34] per *chōbu.*[35]

Most illuminating, however, are the conditions of the farmers as described in the early 19th century in the *Seji Kemmon Roku.*[36] "The farmers," it is stated, "till the soil with the labour of their bodies. . . . In summer they are scorched by the sun, suffering together with the horses and cattle; while in winter they endure the hardships of cold. The produce of their labours is heavily taxed . . . and producing the cereals and necessities of the country they are in truth, those who have contracted for the work of all. They are the foundation of the state, the treasures of the world.[73] Unfortunately, however, the wealthy farmers have forgotten their rank, have been given the right to have names, wear swords or even have yearly allowances. They are addicted to wearing beautiful clothes, practise military arts, study Chinese books and poetry, and even call courtesans from the prosperous centres to their homes. Frequently they are found gambling or patronizing brothels without paying, or leaving only promissory notes for their meals. Many being unable to labour, have left the country and formed homeless gangs which commit thefts, larceny and murder. The expenses of these "wealthy farmers" and the various groups of profligates,

---

34. The *ryō*, 兩, the gold unit of weight, equalled 60 *momme*.

35. Cf. Honjo, *op. cit.*, p. 98 *et seq.* In a study on Japanese money the following table for the Tokugawa period is of interest:

Expenses of farmer per *tan* (.245 acres) with 3 *koku* income included:

Seed	.06 *koku*
Work of 24 people	.72 *koku*
Five horses	.30 *koku*
Daimyō-tax	.50 *koku*
Kuchimai	.15 *koku*
Depreciation	.28 *koku*
Total	2.01

Cf. Miyashita, Koichi, *Beitrage zur Japanischen Geldgeschichte*, 1 Vol.; Wien, 1931, p. 124.

36. *Seji Kemmon Roku*, 世事見聞錄. This work was written in 1816 by an unknown author. The introduction is signed by one whose pen name was Buyō Inshi, 武陽隱士. Part two deals especially with farmers. The text is found in *Kinsei Shakai Keizai Sōsho*, Vol. 1.

37. *Ibid*, p. 47 *et seq.*

merchants and all others, all come from the poor peasants who stay in the village. Thus from among a hundred people, half are the poor farmers who stay in the villages breaking their backs and supplying the food for all. To their regular taxes are added others and to their loss further loss is mounted upon them. Families whose land is confiscated are forced to become tenants, so the prosperous increase in their fortunes and the poor are forced to sell even their homes. Peasant uprisings and riots are an outgrowth of this extreme situation, or the farmers are forced to it by the insufficient food. Though they may receive cash or products from their hand industries, yet they must borrow in advance for cash to buy their machinery and sell their products at low prices at the mercy of the purchaser. If they are in distant countries there is no hope for them. In winter they heat themselves by the mere glow of a burnt out fire. Thus finding it difficult to raise a family they resort to infanticide and abortion, and are so poor they drink only water and are called "water drinkers."[38] Naturally they default in paying their taxes and sell all they have, apprentice their children eight or nine years old to distant provinces,[39] or leave home themselves to seek a livelihood.[40]

Some intimation that social conditions were in a critical state can be inferred from the foregoing. However, a more

---

38. *Mizunomi*, 水呑. Professor Asakawa mentions this term as synonymous with "hired man," *op. cit.*, Vol. 31, p. 164.

39. Sixty years earlier it was not a question of apprenticeship but one of becoming an indentured servant, *shichimonotsu*, 質物, if we can believe a document from Shirakawa in 1741 to one Kanuemon of Yamashita village, from the parent of two children of Odakawa Village. It read: This will verify the report tendered that a girl Matsu, shall be indentured for 4 *ryō*, 2 *bu*, 歩, [4 *bu*, equal 1 *ryō*,] of gold from the end of the present year. The time of service shall be for two years from the end of 1741 to the end of 1743. If this person shall run away, the money must be returned immediately. Likewise the money shall be returned in case of illicit intercourse, drowning, sudden death or illness, protracted illness or failure to meet her master's wishes.........She must work diligently and her master shall have all rights regarding her chastisement." Cf. Abe, M. *op. cit.*, p. 38.

40. Cf. *Seiji Kemmon Roku*, *op. cit.*, p. 70 *et seq.*

detailed mention should be made of those forces, causing the distress of the farmers on the one hand, and leading to the inevitable downfall of feudalism on the other. As Japan of the Tokugawa Period was primarily based upon the supremacy of the Tokugawa family over the warrior class, and they in turn over all other groups, it was essential their power remain absolute and the stratification of society remain intact. Financially the Shōguns were dependent upon two sources of income: gold and silver from their mines in Sado, Izu and Kai,[41] and income from their domains of 4,000,000 *koku.* Thus it was that in 1605 when Ieyasu retired and transferred the office of Shōgun to his son, Hidetada (1579–1632), money in the Edo Treasury amounted to 150,000 *ōban* and *koban* pieces of gold,[42] and 13,000 *kamme* of silver. Moreover, Ieyasu hoarded a vast amount during the period of his retirement until his death in 1616 when his storehouses were found to contain some 49,530 *kamme* of silver and 940,000 *ryō* of gold, not to mention such imported articles as aloes wood, woolen cloth, velvet, embroidered cloth, silk damask, satin and silk thread. Nevertheless, this surplus of wealth was soon to vanish through various expenditures such as the construction of the Nikko mausoleums from 1624–1643 at a cost of 568,000 *ryō* of gold, and the subjugation of the Shimabara Revolt of 1637–1638, amounting to 398,000 *ryō.* Following the great Edo conflagration of 1657, 160,000 *ryō* was given the sufferers while it became necessary to reconstruct the Edo castle as well as rebuild the Imperial Palace in Kyōtō.[43]

---

41. It is reported that "Sado was a treasure island, composed of gold and silver only. Its products were shipped in boxes of 12 *kamme* each, one hundred of such boxes containing a shipload for uniform vessels. Each year five or ten vessels left Sado." Cf. Takekoshi, *op. cit.,* Vol. 1, p. 545 *et seq.* and Vol. II, p. 38. For accounts of uprisings in Sado Cf. *infra,* p. 137.

42. This *ōban,* 大判, was equal to seven *ryō* two *bu* at this time. The *koban,* 小判, equalled approximately 1/10 the *ōban.*

43. Cf. Sawada, *op. cit.,* p. 312 *et seq.* The revolt of Shimabara, 島原, in the province of Hizen though called a Christian revolt by many Japanese historians was also the result of tyranny of the local lords. Of the 37,000 who revolted, all were annihilated. Cf. Papinot, *Dictionnaire d' histoire et de geographie du Japon,* 1 Vol.; Tōkyō, 1906, p. 664.

Although the latter part of the 17th century is famous in Japanese history for its luxuries and extravagance, the lavish expenditures of the fifth Shōgun, Tsunayoshi (1646–1709), in the construction of numerous Buddhist temples and monasteries, together with a noted decrease in the production of the gold and silver mines, led directly to a total deficit of 1,800,000 *ryō* in 1709. Drastic economies were inaugurated by Arai Hakuseki[44] and later a policy of inflation was begun.[45] This seems to have relieved the situation, at least on paper, for there is reported an average yearly surplus from 1742–1751 of 75,594 *koku* of rice and 415,562 *ryō* of gold.[46]

Such drastic financial changes were necessarily accompanied by equally important social ones. Although strict social distinctions had originally been made in Tokugawa society between the *samurai* or warriors, the farmers, the merchants (*chōnin*) and finally the artisans, yet with the penetration of money and a consequent change from a rice to a money economy,[47] and with the general increase in financial strain, it was inevitable these social barriers would break down. Thus it was that:

> The *samurai* were regarded as the ruling class, the farmers as the productive class, and the *chōnin* as an unnecessary class; but after the middle of the Tokugawa Period their class characteristics underwent changes. The *samurai* class became so impotent, the farmer im-

44. Arai Hakuseki, 新井白石, (1656–1725), was a celebrated historian and writer largely at the service of Tokugawa Ienobu after 1693 and followed him to Edo in 1709 when the former became 6th Shōgun. Hakuseki pointed out one more financial stress of the finances of the government; namely, the outflow of gold and silver coin through foreign traders. He estimated 7,192,800 *ryō* of gold and 1,122,627 *kamme* of silver left the country between 1601 and 1707. Cf. Kurita, *Edo Jidai, op. cit.*, p. 414.

45. Cf. Sawada, *op. cit.*, p. 315 *et seq.*

46. Takekoshi, *Economic history, op. cit.*, Vol. II, p. 330 *et seq.*

47. For a detailed account of this process and its effects on Japanese social institutions, see Takizawa, *Money economy, op. cit.*,

poverished, and the *chōnin* class rose to social ascendancy.[48]

As the money power of the *chōnin* increased in direct proportion to the speed with which the various *samurai* became their debtors, they were able to buy themselves into more favorable conditions. The rulers, if they were to rule, were forced to rely more and more on taxation and levies, ineffectually assessed on these *chōnin*, but with more encouraging results on the helpless peasants. Any effectual settlement of the agrarian problem thus created entailed a drastic change in the whole political and social organization in which the *samurai* class was supposed to be the predominant and the farmers and *chōnin* subservient. An important and interesting outcome of this untenable situation was the increasingly large number of peasant uprisings to which we must now direct our attention.

48. Cf. Honjō, E., *Economic history*, op. cit., p. 202.

CHAPTER III.

PEASANT UPRISINGS AND FEUDALISM

A. Introduction

Turning from the general characteristics of society in which peasant uprisings in Japan were to develop and flourish, an analysis must be made of the types of uprisings peculiar to the Tokugawa Period, their causes, whether underlying or motivating, political, economic or administrative. A brief resume will then follow of the laws concerning these uprisings and the attempts to check their appearance. Before this can be attempted, however, it is necessary to mention the derivation and meaning of the Japanese term signifying "peasant uprisings," namely, *hyakushō ikki*,[1] or simply, *ikki*. The derivation of *ikki* has had a long history, the term first appearing in Japanese literature in 1185 with the significance of "a unit of an army", and was used again in 1346 as "a band" or "unit" into which soldiers formed under various banners; while in 1443 a text reports an "uprising of the soil," at which time the buildings of Buddhist temples were destroyed.[2] Thus throughout the Muromachi Period (1392–1490) this term "uprising of the Soil" (*tsuchi ikki*) was used to denote the efforts

---

1. *Hyakushō ikki*, 百姓一揆, or *ikki*,一揆.

2. Cf. *Koji Ruien*, *Heiji Hen*, p. 421 *et seq.* The character *ki*, 揆, Chinese, *k'uei*, has the meaning of "to consider, calculate, judge (of opposites)." It appears in the *Yi Ching* in the phrase: *Ch'u shuai ch'i tz'u erh k'uei ch'i fang*,初率其辭而揆其方, which Couvreur translates as: "D' abord suivez-en la lettre et etudiez-en la doctrine." In the *Shih Ching* in the *Yung Feng* it is used in the phrase, "After having determined the cardinal points." Mencius uses the character with the meaning "to examine" and later "principle" in the phrase: "The sages of all times have had the same principle, 其揆一也, *ch'i k'uei i yeh*. Thus those who adhere to the same principle belong to the same group. It is used in the *Hou Han Shu* meaning a military group. C. Couvreur, F. S., *Dictionnaire classique de la langue Chinoise*, Ho Kien Fou, 1911, p. 471 and *Mencius*, Book IV, pt. 1, Ch. 1 and pt. 2 Ch. 1.

of discontented elements in society to force the government to issue moratoriums on loans, mortgages, or pawned articles. These "Edicts of virtuous government" (*tokusei rei*)[3], had become particularly prevalent during the end of the period, thirteen having been ordered between 1443 and 1474. To persuade the government to promulgate these edicts, rebellious peasants banded together with robber gangs, dissatisfied roaming noble warriors and armed monks of new Buddhist sects, plundering, destroying or burning down store houses of the wealthy or pawn shops, temples and shrines.[4] Thirty-six such disputes have been recorded between 1426 and 1526, mostly centering around Kyōto and four appeared during the next seventy-five years, bringing us to the Tokugawa Period at which time they definitely took the shape of "peasant uprisings", or ***hyakushō ikki.***

The cycle through which most of the peasant uprisings of the Tokugawa Period passed were as follows. As a direct result of some grievance, natural disaster, or displeasure on the part of the peasants, they would assemble into a party or "mob" (*totō*) for the purpose of presenting an appeal (*esso*) to the authorities concerned, against the prevailing grievance. If the appeal was presented by the mob as a whole in the form of a "mob-appeal", (*gōso*), before the castle of their lord,[5] it was usually accompanied by destruction of property

---

3. *Tsuchi ikki,* 土一揆, an uprising of the soil. For a treatment of *tsuchi-ikki* and *tokusei,* 德政, see Nakamura, Kichiji, (abstracted by E. O. Reischauer) "Popular Uprisings and *tokusei* during the Onin and Bummei Periods (1467–1486)" *Abstracts of articles appearing in current Japanese periodicals,* Washington, 1935, pp. 63–68.

4. Cf. Rahder, "Kurume Uprising", *op. cit.,* p. 85 and Honjō, *Social and Economic history, op. cit.,* pp. 44–51.

5. The above terms, largely technical and frequently appearing in the Japanese texts are; *Totō,* 徒黨, any kind of a rebellious league, band or mob. The distinction in meaning between *esso,* 越訴, "to make an appeal," and *gōso,* 强訴, "a mob-appeal", is difficult to determine. *Gōso,* mob-appeal, carries with it the meaning of forming a mob and forcefully presenting an appeal before the authorities, while *esso,* "to make an appeal", may apply to a small group complaining to the local authorities in a peaceful manner. In the cases of Echigo and Sado, however, the term *esso* is applied to "appeals" made during uprisings with little distinction in meaning between the terms. Cf. *infra* p. 139 note 30 and p. 139 *et seq.*

of the wealthy or the officials representing the fief, as the mob approached the castle town. After the appointment of an intermediary, the demands were then presented to the proper authorities for their consideration. If the uprising was successful, and the demands were granted, the peasants would return to their villages. If unsuccessful, they were often dispersed by the soldiers. In either case, an investigation of the affair followed and the leaders were usually severely punished, either crucified, decapitated or banished. Though several of the uprisings studied below did not pass through all these stages, though some of them were dismal failures, yet it will appear that as the central government became weaker, as the conditions of the farmers became more pitiable, and as the foundation of the whole feudal structure became unsteady, many of the demands of the farmers were accepted.

B. Types of Uprisings

The thousand or more uprisings during the Tokugawa Period fall into two general types, those having no direct relationship with the warrior class as a whole who controlled the peasants, and those being directly connected with the governing class arising from this relationship. Among those in the first category should be placed those uprisings which were the result of regional or boundary disputes, struggles over water rights, mountain lands or the settlement of boundaries between villages or fiefs.[6] Such were among the causes of the uprising in the province of Kii in 1823, starting as a result of drought and a dispute over water rights and soon turning against the maladministration of the fief by the officials.[7] Likewise, in Sanuki in 1856 the peasants rebelled over the failure of the authorities to reach a satisfactory agreement concerning the boundaries of the villages and timber rights attached thereto.[8]

---

6. Cf. Kokushō, *Ikki no Kenkyū*, *op. cit.*, p. 8.
7. Cf. *infra* p. 80.
8. Cf. *infra* p. 124.

Another type of uprising, having no direct relationship with the authorities in control, was that resulting from occupational reasons. Uprisings of this type were directed against the townsmen who because of their money, scorned the farmers. Although often only one of many causes in various uprisings, this resulted in numerous house-wreckings and destruction of property by the farmers during their uprising. Thus directing their wrath not against the lord of their domain but the wealthy townsmen who had plotted against them, a mob of 70,000 peasants in Miyazu in the province of Tango began a ruthless destruction of the property of those whom they considered to be directly responsible for their misery. In this case, their demands for a more just administration were granted and the officials who had been accomplices of the merchants were dismissed from office.[9]

One more type of uprisings, those developing from religious reasons, has little direct connection with the governing warrior class as a whole. These were comparatively few in number, the most important being that in the realm of the Kōyasan Temple in Kii. The immediate causes of this uprising were exorbitant taxes levied upon the farmers by the priests, but the uprising was directed, not against the warrior class as such, but the priests who proved to be even harsher rulers than the most unscrupulous *daimyō*, inflicting taxes of 80% to even 93%, causing 12,000 farmers to march upon the temples and to demand a reduction in these taxes.[10] Another uprising connected with Buddhism was that in Owari in 1832, occurring when the people, thinking they were cutting timber for the reconstruction of Higashi Hongwanji in Kyoto, found the manager of the temple and local *daikan* had sold the material for their own profit.[11]

By far the majority of uprisings of the Tokugawa Period, however, are of a type having direct relationship between the peasants and the governing class that controlled them. From

---

9. Cf. *infra*, p. 78.
10. Cf. *infra* p. 54.
11. Cf. *infra*, p. 86.

an economic standpoint, they were against the land owners and their policies, similar to modern tenancy disputes. They became localized in many cases due to the fact that taxation was a joint responsibility of each village, and often arose from the demands of the authorities to open new lands which brought with them increased taxation, for it was by this process that the warriors could most easily increase their income and they were officially encouraged by the *Bakufu* itself. In situations where wealthy merchants had become land owners due to their appropriation of land which they had acquired in exchange for money and goods borrowed by the peasants, it was easy for the discontented peasant, especially if he were impelled by crop failures and famine as in 1783–1787, to direct his wrath against these merchants.[12] From a social standpoint, the uprisings were directed against the village officials, who, as the attorneys and representatives of the controlling class, collected the taxes, spied upon the plans of the farmers for insurrection, and added special taxes for their own profit. These uprisings were concentrated in the western provinces "where village officials were frequently wealthy, where they cleverly oppressed the farmers economically to their own advantage, having power equal to the warriors, and as their representatives, usurping their social position."[13] This factor, in a large degree at least, led to the series of uprisings in Kyūshū in 1811 and 1812 when a succession of disturbances broke out against the severe government imposed upon the peasants by unscrupulous officials, who planned with the local merchants, methods for their mutual aggrandizement.[14]

Although this is not the place for a discussion of social or economic theories and thought, nevertheless, as there exists among Japanese scholars of peasant uprisings a divergence of opinion concerning the fundamental characteristics of them, this controversy should not be overlooked. Briefly, Professor Ono and others of his school of thought feel that the farmers'

---

12. Cf. Kokushō, *Ikki no Kenkyū, op. cit.*, p. 16 *et seq.*
13. Cf. ibid, p. 27.
14. Cf. *infra*, p. 74 *et seq.*

insurrections of the Tokugawa Period, and especially those towards the latter part of the era, were the vanguard of the fighting which brought about the overthrow of the Tokugawa *Bakufu*; while Professor Kokushō believes that, "though they stimulated the downfall of feudalism, though they arose from the crumbling and contradictions of this feudalistic society, yet they did not have the motive to transform society, nor were they consequently of a revolutionary nature."[15] As the latter points out, one of the inherent characteristics of Tokugawa feudalism was the fact that it contained elements for its inevitable collapse. The establishment of a firm centralized government by Tokugawa Ieyasu, the formation of a stern social stratification of society, the sealing of the country from outside contacts, and the foundation of the whole economic structure on a rice economy, allowed no room for flexibility nor the new social classes developing simultaneously with the penetration of money economy. The uprisings became inevitable phenomena in the changing process of society, they were not so much a revolutionary movement as a continual protest against the economic distress in which the peasants found themselves.[16] As will be clarified by a study of the following material, with the exception of the rice riots in Ōsaka and uprisings connected with them in 1837,[17] most of the peasant uprisings were disconnected, having little concern for the overthrow of feudalism, as such, but caring more for a rectification of those minor injustices which were inherent in the feudalistic society of the times. True the whole movement among the peasantry aided in the overthrow of the feudal structure, but it is stretching a point to assume that the average peasant was conscious or desirous of taking part in a social revolutionary movement.

---

15. Cf. Kokushō, "Hyakushō Ikki" in *Nihon Keizai Jiten*, Vol, V., p. 2173.

16. For accounts of the respective viewpoints see: Kokushō, *Ikki no Kenkyū*, *op. cit.*, p. 32 *et seq.*, and Ono, *Nōson Shakaishi Ronkō*, 1 Vol.; Tōkyō, revised ed., 1935, 432 pp., especially pp. 78 *et seq.*, and Ono, T., "Hyakushō Ikki ya, Kinnō Gun ya," *Shakai Keizaishi Gaku*, Vol. 6, No. 4, 1936, pp. 387 *et seq.*

17. Cf. *infra*, p. 93 *et seq.*

C. Causes of the Uprisings

Although no single uprising throughout the Tokugawa Period was the result of any one particular cause, whether underlying or motivating, nevertheless an analysis of these various causes will be of value. The regional disposition and temperament of the people, influencing both their economic and social life, can be considered as an underlying cause. Uprisings were numerous, therefore, in districts where many stragglers settled after the incessant civil wars (1467–1600) as in Iyo, or where the people were naturally of a belligerent disposition as in Mimasaka.[18] Another primary cause was the changing of the lords of the domain by order of the *Bakufu*, either to protect itself against possible attack or intrigue, or to confer favours upon special friends through increasing their fiefs. As in Shōnai in northern Japan in the province of Uzen in 1840, the entire fief rose in revolt against the order for the transfer of the lord of the domain to another fief, resulting in the government having to change its orders and allow the lord to remain.[19] Jealousy of the various *daimyō* on the one hand and splitting of fiefs into small units and thus increasing the distress of the peasants on the other, played their part in bringing about disorder. Such was particularly true in the provinces of Mino and Iyo where small fiefs were numerous.[20]

A feature of Japanese feudalism, allowing officials to act arbitrarily, with an uprising of the farmers as an only check, was absentee ownership. Moreover, this situation was greatly aggravated by the system of "alternate attendance," *sankin kōtai*,[21] which required that every *daimyō* not only come to Edo at specified intervals and remain there, but also leave his wives and children there as a sort of hostages, to assure his

---

18. For a treatment of uprisings in Mimasaka where nineteen are recorded and for Iyo where there were fifty-one, Cf. *infra*, Ch. VII pp. 167 *et seq*.

19. Cf. *infra* p. 100 *et seq*.

20. Cf. *infra*, p. 165 *et seq*. and p. 172 *et seq*.

21. *Sankin kōtai*, 參勤交代.

good conduct when he returned home to his fief. This "alternate attendance" not only impoverished the *daimyō* and made them less formidable enemies of the Tokugawa *Bakufu*, but also persuaded many *daimyō* to remain in the capital and have their fiefs governed as their officials willed. An excellent example of uprisings resulting from this situation is that in the province of Echigo in the fief of the Makino family at Nagaoka. Here six different uprisings arose between 1828 and 1868, directly the result of the maladministration of the fief and the heavy taxes imposed upon the peasants by officials who administered with a free hand as their lord always remained in Edo.[22]

Additional underlying causes of uprisings, usually accompanied by other causes, included ignorance on the part of the peasant, the increasing difference in wealth between the rich and poor, the isolation of fiefs by distance and mountains as in the provinces of Echigo, Sado and Shinano, and a disproportion of the population, with men predominating, as in the case of Mimasaka.[23] On the economic side, there was an ever increasing demand on the part of the *Bakufu* and the officials of the various domains for the extension in the area of cultivated land. That their efforts were effective becomes obvious from the fact that in 1600 there were 5,000,000 acres under cultivation while in 1868 this figure was more than doubled to 11,500,000 acres.[24] Along with this fact, was a population which remained practically stationary,[25] which meant that the burden of labour of the peasant in the amount of land he was supposed to cultivate, had doubled; and since many of his former fellows had escaped to the towns, it made

---

22. Cf. *infra*, p. 137 *et seq.*
23. Cf. Kokushō, *Ikki no Kenkyū*, *op. cit.*, p. 65 *et seq.*
24. Cf. Asakawa, "Village Government", *op. cit.*, Vol. 30, p. 287.
25. Dr. Yanagisawa gives the following population statistics:

1721	Non-warriors	26,065,423
1852	Non-warriors	30,000,000.

Cf. Yanagisawa, "Histoire critique des travaux statistique au Japon depuis l'antiquite jusqu'a la restauration imperiale," *Bulletin de l'Institut International de Statistique*, Vol. 19, p. 301.

it practically impossible for those that remained on the land to carry the burden alone.[26]

With these primary causes as the underlying forces in many of the uprisings, although not specifically mentioned as such, the more immediate or motivating causes are easier to determine. In the first place, they readily fall into economic, financial or administrative causes, of which the first was of supreme importance. Among these economic motivating causes, first to be mentioned are the effects of natural calamities, whether volcanic eruptions, drought, floods, or frost, ruining the crops and directly affecting the farmers whose livelihood and very existence was dependent upon the rice crop. Thus there was a marked increase in the number of uprisings resulting from the famines of 1783-1787 from thirty-five during the decade 1773-1782 to one hundred and one during the decade 1783-1792, that of the Temmei Famines as they are called. Famine and distress extended in 1783 from Kozuke in the north where Mt. Asama had erupted and destroyed the crops, to Izumo on the west coast. The same situation was repeated during the period of famine of 1834-1835, culminating in 10,000 farmers in four districts of Kai marching on the town of Kofu demanding food, and the rice riots in Ōsaka under the leadership of Oshio Heihachirō.[27] Closely connected with crop failures and directly dependent upon it, was the increase in price not only of rice, but of other commodities as well. This was largely responsible for the rice riots in Edo and Ōsaka in 1787, rice riots again in 1837 and for a total of 101 uprisings due to high prices throughout the Tokugawa Period.[28]

---

26. For examples of uprisings resulting from this situation see that in Etchū in 1813 and Ōmi in 1842: *infra* p. 77 and p. 107 *et seq.*

27. For accounts of uprisings in Kōzuke and Izumo, cf. *infra* p. 60. For those during the next famine period in Kai and Ōsaka, cf. *infra*, pp. 88 and 94: for the results of bad crops in Echigo in 1814 cf. *infra*, p. 125.

28. This total of 101 uprisings resulting from the increase in prices, making 8.7% of all the uprisings of the Tokugawa Period, was distributed during the latter part of the period as follows: Thirty-one from 1783–1792; fifteen from 1793–1832; twenty-two from 1833–1842; nine from 1843–1862 and eleven from 1863–1867. Cf. Numazaki, *op. cit.*, Chart XIII. For a chart of the price of rice see *infra* Appendix III, Chart I.

Among the financial causes as a motive for peasant uprisings oppressive taxes must be mentioned first. Although the tax was generally 50% following the establishment of the *Bakufu*, with the villages taking joint responsibilitiy for its payment, not only the regular taxes gradually increased but special taxes were added. Uprisings resulting from this fact alone comprise over 25% of the total and amounted to 295 incidents, largely occurring after the middle of the 17th century.[29] In 1739, 84,000 peasants successfully revolted against their heavy taxes in Iwaki Daira, while in 1761, 18,000 appeared before the Ueda castle in Shinano demanding the abolition of the order that they pay advance taxes. When taxes were apparently raised from 69% to 80% and then to 93% by the priests of Kōyasan on the farmers of their domain in Kii, as already pointed out, they revolted in 1776; and five years later, in 1781, 10,000 farmers in the provinces of Kōzuke and Musashi, objecting strenuously to a new sales-tax on silk, demanded the withdrawal of the unfair tax. Their efforts won the cancellation of the obnoxious tax, though many of their numbers were imprisoned, and four of the ringleaders received death sentences. And so the list might be continued, but an examination of the various demands of the farmers related in detail below will reveal the constant request for the reduction of taxes.[30]

Another motivating financial cause for disorders and appeals on the part of the farmers, came as a by-product of the financial distress of the *Bakufu* itself. To overcome any deficit the central government might have acquired, or to aid in the reconstruction of the Imperial or Edo castle after fire or earthquake, it began the policy of ordering special "forced levies" (*goyōkin*),[31] not only upon the rich merchants in Ōsaka and Edo, but also upon the *daimyō* in proportion to their incomes. To pay for this extraordinary levy, the *daimyō* in

---

29. Cf. Numazaki, *op. cit.*, Chart X.
30. For references to the above incidents in order of their mention cf. *infra* p. 41, p. 158, p. 54, and p. 57.
31. *Goyōkin*, 御用金.

turn taxed the farmers which resulted in various uprisings. This was one of the chief causes of the uprisings in Shinano in 1761, it forced the fishermen of Zeze in Ōmi to make common cause with the farmers in 1781, and resulted in two distinct uprisings in Kaga in 1838 and 1858, both times the *Bakufu* having ordered the Maeda family to pay their share in the reconstruction of the burnt Edo castle.[32]

In addition to regular taxation on agricultural products, the special taxes as that on silk in Kōzuke in 1781, and the "forced levies" from the *Bakufu*, there were especially obnoxious taxes of labour or horses, the most objectionable being the *sukegō* tax. *Sukegō*, as already noted, was a special levy of horses and men on villages along the through highways to convey Korean delegates to and from Edo or officials enroute to the mausoleums at Nikkō. Beginning with a levy of 2 horses and 2 men per 100 *koku* income of each village in 1694, and increasing to 50 men in 1730 and from 300–400 men in 1790, it is little wonder to find three provinces and some 200,000 men beginning a march on Edo as a result of this type of taxation in 1764, one of the biggest uprisings of the whole period.[33] Approaching to the very outskirts of the city, hundreds of the insurgents were arrested and thrown into prison, but the *sukegō* was abolished.[34]

Still another motivating cause of uprisings was the planned interference on the part of the lords of the fiefs, and their representatives, with the farmers' financial interests. The warriors as a class, realizing the advantages to be derived from money, attempted to supplement their lack of funds by a control of the townsmen's industries within their domains and the prohibition of the free exchange or sale of goods by the farmers. This led to a monopolistic control of local industries, such as the paper and indigo in Awa after 1756; the paper industry in Iyo in 1792, Tosa in 1787, Suwō and

32. Cf. *infra*, p. 158, p. 69, p. 97, and p. 125.
33. Cf. *infra*, p. 47.
34. Cf. Honjō, *Nōmin Mondai*, *op. cit.*, p. 150 *et seq.*

Nagato in 1831; the purchase and shipment of salted fish in Hokkaidō at Matsumae in 1768; the control of the cotton market at Fukuyama in Bingo in 1786; the monopolistic control of all the markets in Bungo and Hyuga in 1811 and 1812; the purchase and sale of beans, raw silk, hemp, seaweed, bone powder used for fertilizer, and timber in Nambu in 1853. All these led to uprisings, many of which were successful in forcing the *daimyō* or their officials to abolish these monopolistic methods.[35]

And finally among the financial causes for peasant uprisings in Japan was that of financial disorder within the fief itself. This usually meant that the officials of the fief, in order to improve the domain's exchequer, had issued paper currency of a questionable value, to circulate at par. In 1754, in Kurume in Chikugo, 52,000 farmers rose in revolt as a result of this policy, while in Akita the farmers were accompanied by the townsmen the next year in protest to the new currency.[36] In Mito, the domain of one of the three chief branches of the Tokugawa family, special permission had been granted for the minting of iron coins which brought with it hardships on the people, who revolted in 1771 and again in 1774 until the mints were abolished.[37]

Closely connected with both the economic and financial causes for uprisings were the various administrative motives; the unlawfulness of the village officials, the corruption of the direct representatives or special envoys of the *Bakufu*, the arbitrary actions of the representatives of the government of the various domains, the failure of universal governmental administration, and finally changes in the relations of villages to the domains. In the first place, by far the most common

35. For accounts of the most interesting of these, see that in Iyo in 1793 and in Nambu in 1853; *infra*, p. 172 and p. 114. Numazaki lists a total of 39 uprisings resulting from monopolistic methods with the majority occurring in the west and south. Cf. Numazaki, *op. cit.*, Chart XI.

36. Cf. *infra*, p. 46, and p. 47.

37. Cf. *infra*, p. 54. Other uprisings resulting from poor finances within the fief were Kaga in 1756, Buzen in 1837, Harima in 1837, Aki in 1838, Awa in 1841, Chikuzen in 1842 and Bizen in 1854.

administrative cause for insurrection was the action of the local officials and representatives of the *daimyō*. This was an outcome, of course, of the whole situation created by absentee ownership, and a total of sixty-two uprisings are recorded throughout the entire Tokugawa Period as a result of the maladministration of the village officials alone.[38] It was a natural outcome of the fact that the *shōya* and other village officers came to hold hereditary posts and that the social and economic differences between themselves and the farmers had increased. Although it was often the homes and store houses of these village officials which were wrecked by the mobs as in the case of the Ueda uprising in Shinano in 1761,[39] nevertheless, by far the majority of uprisings from administrative causes were the result of the corruption and greed of the higher officials, the *Daikan*, the *Kōri bugyō*,[40] or those in similar posts. This was particularly true of the series of uprisings in the *Bakufu* domain in Hida beginning in 1771 when the peasants continuously rose in protests against the government's representative, taking their appeals to Edo where they presented them directly to the Elder Minister and Finance Minister as they passed in their palanquins.[41] In the domain of the Kii branch of the Tokugawa family, 100,000 farmers revolted in 1823 as a direct result of the corruption of the *bugyō* in alliance with the rice merchants,[42] and a similar number in Suwō could not endure the fact that their officials had prayed for a bad harvest and attempted to enrage the dragon-god that he might destroy the crops, thus allowing the same officials to profit from the increase in the local price of

38. Numazaki lists these as 5.9% of the grand total with twenty in the south. They were most frequent towards the end of the period. Cf. Numazaki, *op. cit.*, Chart XII.

39. Cf. *infra*, p. 158.

40. *Kōri bugyō*, 郡奉行, an official in charge of the administration of a district (*kōri*).

41. Cf. *infra*, p. 49 *et seq.*

42. Cf. *infra*, p. 80.

rice.[43] As for the special envoys of the *Bakufu*, an excellent and most interesting example is found in the case of the surveying party sent to the province of Ōmi in 1842. When the farmers once became aware of the corruption of the leader of the party, his willingness to receive bribes, and his false measuring stick, they retaliated by an uprising in the districts concerned, 42,000 strong. Their efforts not only caused the cessation of the survey and forced the *Bakufu* official to flee for his life, but also directly affected the resignation of the *Rōju* or Elder Minister of the *Bakufu* government, Mizuno Tadakuni, in 1843.[44]

It has already been shown that the system of changing the *daimyō* from one domain to another was among the underlying causes of uprisings, but closely connected with this were the disorders motivated by the change in relations of the domains, or villages within a single fief. One form of this was the confiscation of the domain by the *Bakufu*, due to maladministration of the *daimyō*, as in the case of Kanamori Yorikane in Mino in 1758, due to his inability to cope with the continual uprisings within his realm.[45] In Echigo two different groups of nine villages complained of their change of status and jurisdiction under a new domain in 1789 and again in 1866 six villages of the same province raised a similar objection;[46] while in other provinces, eighteen villages in Ōmi disliked their change of possession status in 1846, and villages with a total of 2,000 *koku* income in Kii raised the same objection in 1855.[47]

And lastly there remain those uprisings which arose from what might be called social causes. Although not the only motivating cause, they were a definite factor in several incidents. Before mentioning these however, a fuller explanation

43. Cf. *infra*, p. 84 *et seq.* A glance at the uprisings in Nambu, Echigo, and Sado will likewise show a large number of these to be the result of the maladministration of officials. Cf. *infra*, Chapter VII.
44. Cf. *infra*, Chapter VI, B.
45. Cf. *infra*, p. 165.
46. Cf. *infra*, p. 133 and p. 138.
47. Cf. *infra*, p. 123 *et seq.*

of these social conditions is necessary. There were throughout the Tokugawa Period an increasing number of *rōnin*, lordless warriors,[48] the result of the fief of their lord having been confiscated or the *daimyō* having been transferred or having died without issue. They formed a certain discontented element in society and their influence was definitely to be felt at the time of the Restoration of 1868, but the surprising thing to note is not the frequency with which they allied themselves with the farmers, leading them in revolt for their own ends, but the opposite. The reason for this doubtless lies in the disdain with which they considered the farmers as in a class of society far below them, and the lack of common grievances of the two groups. There were, however, uprisings in which *rōnin* took part. They seem to have formed a definite element in the uprising of 1786 in Fukuyama in Bingo against the heavy taxes and monopolistic control of the cotton market, while 150 are mentioned as having joined the large uprising in Kii in 1823.[49] They appear in two more cases, first in the province of Settsu in 1837 as the leaders of an uprising of 1,400 men who had allied themselves to the cause of Ōshio Heihachirō and his rioters in Ōsaka; secondly in 1847 in an uprising in Amakusa in Higo where "ruffians and *rōnin*" are reported as composing one of the main elements of the insurgents.[50]

Another element in society, which on the most part had little in common with the peasant, was the townsman or *chōnin*. Neither he nor his servants were inclined to make common cause with the peasant against the warrior that ruled them both. The townsman usually profited from the farmers and

---

48. *Rōnin*, 浪人. Professor J. Rahder points out that in some cases the instigators of uprisings were the *kyōkaku*, 俠客, chivalrous roaming warriors, who formed a distinct class and were always willing to take up the cause of the weak against the strong as in 1686. It will require further research to determine what role they may have played in the peasant uprisings, as the texts do not refer to them especially.

49. For reference to the *rōnin* in Fukuyama cf. *infra*, p. 65, note 118, and for Kii, *infra*, p. 80.

50. For Settsu cf. *infra*, p. 94 and for Higo p. 122, note 55.

it was to his economic advantage that they remain peaceful and productive. His servants, on the other hand, many of them having escaped from the farms and given up their old livelihood, were able to live a more luxurious life within the towns and were content with their new station in life. They did not wish to risk arrest or punishment by joining the actions of the peasant mobs.

As we have seen, the peasant very often directed his wrath and destruction against these very townsmen and merchants who were working in close cooperation with the officials of the domain against the peasants as a class. However, a few exceptions to this should be noted. The first of these was in Akita, in the province of Ugo in 1755 when the townsmen and farmers made common cause against the domain officials who had ordered the circulation of silver certificates worth 60 *momme* to be bought for 68 *momme* of silver.[51] Likewise in Izumo, at the time of the uprising in 1783 against the collection of taxes during a year of famine, the farmers were supported in their demands by the townsmen.[52] There was, however, to be no great movement of farmers and townsmen rising against the ruling class, either during the Tokugawa Period or after 1868.

D. Desertions and Tenancy Disputes

The foregoing reference to types and causes of uprisings has dealt largely with what are usually classed as positive forms of resistance of the peasants. There were, however, a sufficient number of disturbances which had primarily a negative form. Their causes were similar to those already mentioned but rather than following the usual procedure of forming a mob, destructive advance upon the castle town, and "mob-appeal", they developed into desertions. Originally, individuals would secretly desert into a neighbouring village or fief to avoid some specific grievance or hardship, but

---

51. Cf. *infra*, p. 46.
52. Cf. *infra*, p. 60.

gradually the habit developed into an organized group of one or more villages leaving en masse. If the villagers crossed into the neighbouring fief or province, they would petition the lord of that fief that they either be allowed to remain within his domain, or that he intervene on their behalf. A total of 106 desertions have been recorded, by far the majority occurring in Shikoku.[53] In the north in the Nambu fief at Morioka, one of the largest desertions of the Tokugawa Period occurred in 1853 when some peasants, goaded on by the general corruption among the fief officials and their monopolistic control of all transactions, deserted to the neighbouring fief of Sendai, asking they be allowed to live there and finally presenting their complaints to the Sendai officials.

There also developed after the middle of the Tokugawa Period, and increasing in intensity even up to most recent times, a series of farm tenancy disputes. As these are a special type of disturbance and concern more modern times, they will not be dealt with at length here.[55] However, in spite of a law against division of farms into sections less than one *chō* (2.45 acres), or the sale in perpetuity of cultivated fields, it was inevitable that the land fall into the hands of the propertied class, that the farmers become tenants, and that tenancy disputes resulted. There were two types of farm tenancy, that of a farm belonging to a landowner, called *myōden kosaku* and the tenancy of a mortgaged farm, *shi-*

53. For examples of these desertions in Shikoku see the description of Iyo and Tosa uprisings below in Chapter VII. Numazaki says desertions formed 9.2% of the uprisings in the Tokugawa Period, seventy-six coming after 1703. Of the total number of desertions, 40% were in Shikoku, 21.6% in Kyūshu and 11.6% in the north. Cf. Numazaki, *op. cit.*, Chart VIII.

54. For accounts of these uprisings cf. *infra*, p. 144 *et seq.*

55. For treatment of this subject see Honjō, *Social and economic history of Japan*, *op. cit.*, pp. 51 *et seq.* For Japanese sources see: Ono, T., *Nōson Shakaishi Ronkō*, *op. cit.*, pp. 113-225, and his more recent study of tenancy disputes in *Nōmin Keizaishi Kenkyū*, 1 Vol.; Tōkyō, 1924, 485 pp. Also for a survey of the question of land reform after 1868 with the new types of taxation and problems arising from these reforms, cf. Ramming, "Die Boden Reform der ersten Meiji Jahre," *Mitteilungen des Seminars fur Orientalische Sprache*, Vol. XXXVI, pp. 77-90.

chiji kosaku.[56] Cases of farmers working the land for a large landowner usually arose from the opening of new lands and after twenty years of tenancy, they became perpetual tenants. In reference to the agreement between landowner and tenant there is the following:

> In regard to cropping [tenancy], the law is that there should be a written instrument but usually there is only a private agreement by word of mouth; and as there is no fixing of the term, the landlord has the right to take back the estate at any time, even though the tenant may have been cultivating it for many tens of years.[57]

In cases of the tenancy of a mortgaged farm, two types developed; those of tenancy by the owner himself who had mortgaged his farm, and those of tenancy of land by a third party other than the owner or holder of the mortgage.[58]

It was among the tenants that the most deplorable conditions developed and their disputes with their landlord became prevalent after about 1730. They were directly related to peasant uprisings in cases where the tenants formed groups in their own village out of which an uprising might start. As examples of tenancy disputes, during the Kyōhō Era, (1716–1735), crops were poor and the tenant farmers abandoned their land. As a result of this the landowners consented to reduce the rent or give the farmers money for their fertilizer. Documents of 1768 and 1790 show that whenever trouble occurred only a makeshift solution was reached by the exchange of memorandums. Again in 1844–1853 the farmers of Musashi province demanded a reduction in rent, but the landowners decided that they as a group were to fix the rent and the tenants who objected were to be denied tenancy. This finally forced the tenants to give up their complaints.[59] But following the Restoration of 1868 and the increase in tenants,

---

56. *Myōden kosaku,* 名田小作, and *shichiji kosaku,* 質地小作.

57. Cf. Wigmore, "Materials for the study of private law in Japan," T.A.S.J., Vol. 20, supplement Pt. II, p. 54.

58. Cf. Honjō, *Economic and social history, op. cit.,* p. 52 *et seq.*

59. *Ibid,* pp. 54-55.

the problem became more acute. In 1886 there were 3,021, 000 farming families who tilled their own soil and 2,397,000 families of tenants. By 1930 the figures for the former show a decrease of 1,743,000 families and for the latter an increase in 3,857,000; while over two thousand disputes arose the same year.[60]

E. *Laws and Methods of Suppression of Peasant Uprisings*

Although there is no need for a detailed narration of the various laws of the Tokugawa Period,[61] a glance at the development of those laws directly affecting the peasants and their uprisings will show the reaction this agricultural movement had upon Tokugawa Legislature. It will also clarify some of the circumstances of the uprisings treated below.

In 1603, although the peasant was forbidden to appeal concerning questions of local taxation, nevertheless after two or three petitions concerning other matters, he could make a direct appeal against the intendant (daikan). In 1637, the intendant was ordered to examine all groups of peasants and especially those recently moved into his territory. The peasants were to report all their movements to the intendant and the whereabouts of any wicked men, and were to be prepared to assemble at the sound of the gong to help arrest any culprits.[62] Although rewards were offered in 1633 for secret information regarding the formation of any kind of subversive groups, it was not until 1638 that the term *totō*, a rebellious

---

60. Cf. *Hyakka Jiten*, Vol. 9, p. 477 *et seq.* where there is an article on the whole problem of tenants.

61. For accounts and translations of Tokugawa legislature compare the following: Asakawa, "Village Government," *op. cit.*, J.A.O.S., Vol. 30 and 31. Wigmore, J. H., "Materials for the study of private law in old Japan,' T.A.S.J., Vol. 20, supplement, 1892. Hall, J. C., "Japanese feudal laws,' T.A.S.J., Vol. 34, 36, 38, and 41. Gubbins, J. H., "The 100 Articles and the Tokugawa Government,"*Transactions and Proceedings of Japan Society of London*, Vol. 17, 1920, pp. 128 *et seq.* Professor Kokushō has collected those relating to peasant uprisings in his *Ikki no Kenkyū*, *op. cit.*, pp. 332 *et seq.*

62. Cf. Asakawa, "Village government", *op. cit.*, Vol. 31, p. 202.

league, band or mob, [conspirators] was actually used. At that time the following order was sent to the *daimyō* of the west:

> If there are conspirators [*totō*] you shall disperse them without reporting to Edo, getting reinforcements from neighbours if necessary.

There was, as yet, no special law against peasant uprisings, *hyakushō ikki*, as such, showing they were of little importance in this earlier period.[63]

Another law in 1644, important because of the complaints raised by the farmers later concerning its infraction, stated that the assessment of tax-rice was to be shown to the peasants in writing and such a document was to receive their seals. The record of the returns of the tax were to be certified by the officials and the latter were required to give receipts to the tax-paying peasants. Under edicts issued in 1666 to all the villages were the following: 1. The sale of land in perpetuity was forbidden. 2. It was forbidden to evict peasants and seize their lands. 3. When an official visited a village, he was not to be entertained with anything specially bought. He should pay for everything he needed and should receive no presents from the village head or a peasant. His case should be reported if he annoyed a peasant.[64] As will become apparent if the infringement of this law was a justification for an uprising, many of them were well grounded.

As late as 1670 there were laws concerning the process of petition of the peasants to Edo. One such read:

> A peasant's petition shall be presented to the intendant or bailiff. If he fails to give justice the peasant may bring his petition to Edo after notifying the intendant of his intention. If he has failed to give this notice, his case cannot be entertained.

However, sign boards declared in 1682 that all kinds of as-

---

63. Cf. Kokushō, *Ikki no Kenkyū*, *op. cit.*, p. 332 *et seq.*

64. Cf. Asakawa, "Village government," *op. cit.*, Vol. 31 p. 205, 208 and 209.

sembling of peasants under oath would be severely punished.[65] In laws to the warriors the next year it was made clear that, "in regards to quarrels and disputes, great caution must be evinced. Private disputes are absolutely forbidden and those with farmers must be settled with their headmen [*shōya* or other village officials] and the feudatory in charge."[66] To peasants in the *Bakufu* domains the following was issued in 1713:

> Recently at the examination of land by the intendant, villages have bribed the assistants to secure low values and the tax returns have decreased. . . The peasants shall, therefore, devote their energies to cultivation shall not be remiss in the returning of taxes and shall report an unjust assistant to the intendant. Village heads are also reported to be partial and corrupt, but henceforth both the giver and receiver of a bribe will be punished.[67]

But as will be seen, it was not the unjust assistants to which the peasants of Hida made objection as early as 1746, but the intendant himself.[68]

It was just at this period, however, that the frequency of peasant uprisings resulted in the following specific laws concerning them:

1721 All the farmers were ordered to form five men groups (*gonin kumi*), and take joint responsibility for aiding each other. They were forbidden, under pledge taken by them, to form mobs (*totō*.)

1734 A re-emphasis upon the above law.

1741 The punishments for appeal, forming a mob (*totō*) or desertion should be death for the leaders, banishment for the *nanushi*, confiscation of fields and banishment from the village for the

---

65. *Ibid*, p. 210.
66. Cf. Hall, "Japanese feudal law," *op. cit.*, T.A.S.J. Vol. 38, Part IV, p. 298.
67. Cf. Asakawa, "Village government," *op. cit.*, Vol. 31, p. 211.
68. Cf. *infra*, p. 49.

kumigashira, and an increase in taxation for the villages.[69]

1744 Awards and privilege of wearing a sword should be given the *nanushi* and *kumigashira* who seize farmers [during the time of an uprising] and who refuse to join them.

1750 The farmers were forbidden to form groups and to appeal to the garrisons of the *daikan*.

1767 The peasants of western Japan were forbidden to appeal to another domain and if they deserted, they must return to their village.[70]

1770 The offences of assembling of many peasants for evil purposes (*totō*), and the forcing a petition (*gōso*) and desertion of a village have all been forbidden and any such case discovered was to be reported at once.[71]

1777 Following the uprisings in Hida, heavier penalties were enacted for the leaders.

1797 Neighbouring *daimyō* were allowed to join together to suppress an uprising.

1836 Appeals, and the formation of mobs were again forbidden.

1839 The use of guns or swords was allowed to tranquillize the farmers.[72]

---

69. Cf. Kokushō, *Ikki no Kenkyū*, *op. cit.*, pp. 337, 338.

70. *Ibid*, p. 339.

71. In this connection it should be noticed that Professor Asakawa has translated *gōso*, referred to in this text as "mob-appeal", as "the forcing a petition." It has been brought to my attention that the general social phenomenum termed *gōso* is common throughout south-eastern Asia. It occurred in Java, Sumatra, British India and Madagascar. Desertions to a neighbouring fief were encouraged by the landowners in Java but prohibited by the Netherland's authorities. One form of appeal in Sumatra was to menace the lord with the threat of burning down his house if he did not grant the demands of the people. Other forms of complaint included a type of passive resistance and refusal to pay the taxes or to give the required manual labour. Individual oral complaints were also frequent, and are still made to the Netherlands officials. Cf. Haga, J. *Indonesische en Indische Democratie*, 1 Vol.; The Hague, 1924, p. 126 *et seq*.

72. Cf. Kokushō, *Ikki no Kenkyū*, *op. cit.*, p. 345 *et seq*.

Such were the main laws dealing with the uprisings but a brief analysis of the actual methods of suppression of the peasant uprisings is necessary. In the early cases, an offer on the part of the officials to accept the demands of the farmers usually resulted in their return home, but following the enactment of the law of 1741, tranquilization by intimidation became common. Death sentences were ruthlessly prescribed to the leaders of the uprisings in Kaminoyama in 1747 and in Aizu in 1749.[73] Furthermore, orders were issued in 1765 to shoot upon the mob of 70,000 from Musashi and Kōzuke if they approached nearer to Edo.[74] When the situation became uncontrollable in Hida in 1772, orders were sent to neighbouring lords to come to the assistance of the *Bakufu* representative, and the same was true in Kii in 1776 when the priests of Kōyasan were forced to rely on nearby *daimyō* to tranquillize the peasants in the Kōyasan realm.[75] In private domains, if the uprising became too violent, troops were called out from the castle. These methods were to continue down to the end of the Tokugawa Period.

In some cases, however, the policy of intimidation was changed for that of using priests as intermediaries. This was true both where they made the use of troops unnecessary and where the peasants had advanced regardless of the soldiers sent against them. These priests, acting as representatives of the governing class and at the same time demanding the respect of the farmers, were particularly effective in the settlement of a desertion of peasants in Tosa in 1787. Also the fief officials called upon the priests to protect other officials from the anger of the farmers in Shinano in 1761, but the priests agreed to do so only in return for a promise that the leaders of the farmers be spared.[76] In Shōnai, in 1840, however, they definitely sided with the farmers and did everything

73. Cf. *infra*, p. 42 and p. 44.
74. Cf. *infra*, p. 48.
75. For Hida cf. *infra*, p. 51 and for Kōyasan, p. 54.
76. For the role of the priests in the Tosa uprising, cf. *infra*, p. 181, and in Shinano p. 160.

in their power to make the uprisings successful in demanding a withdrawal of the *Bakufu's* order that the lord of the fief be transferred. Lastly their role as intermediaries in the desertion of the farmers from Nambu to the Sendai realm in 1853 was of extreme importance.[77]

One other method of tranquilization, although not authorized by the authorities, was for the domain official to take sole responsibility for the disorder upon himself. In so doing, he would appear before the peasants and confess his neglect of duties, admonish them to present their demands to their lord for acceptance and to retire peacefully. Then to verify this feeling of guilt, he would commit suicide. Such action before the mob on the part of the minister of the Yoshida domain in Iyo in 1793 resulted in the immediate withdrawal of 10,000 farmers and their peaceful return to their villages.[78]

Having dealt first with the general life and political structure of the village and communities of the Tokugawa Period out of which the peasant uprisings were to take place, having treated of the types of these uprisings, their political, economic or administrative causes, and lastly the legislation and methods of suppression this entailed, a detailed study of specific cases of these uprisings will follow. They will, as already intimated, be grouped chronologically to obtain some idea of the frequency and growth of their occurrences. They will then be treated geographically affording opportunity for study of their special characteristics in various isolated provinces, as well as giving an insight into the economic and social life of those fiefs in these special regions in which material has permitted a special study to have been made. Finally a glance at the appendices and charts will clarify questions concerning the frequency, geographical distribution and occurrences of these peasant uprisings.

---

77. Cf. *infra* p. 100 and p. 144 *et seq.* for references to the Shōnai and Nambu uprisings.
78. Cf. *infra*, p. 174.

CHAPTER IV

GROWTH AND DEVELOPMENT OF PEASANT UPRISINGS

A. Examples and Occurrences During Early Tokugawa Period

In studying the various peasant uprisings under the *Tokugawa Bakufu,* whether chronologically or geographically, it is difficult to determine the exact number of disturbances.[1] However, most recent calculations show a total of 1,153 cases having occurred between 1603 and 1867 with increasing frequency as the period progressed.[2] For the first hundred years there were only 157 cases distributed fairly evenly throughout the century, but for the next fifty years alone (1703–1753), 176 cases appear showing an increase of over 100%, with fifty-one of these uprisings falling between 1743 and 1753. For the last one hundred and fifteen years of this period there was an average of over six uprisings a year,[3] the period upon which this study will be concentrated.

Passing hurriedly over the first few years of the Tokugawa Period (1600–1868,) it should be noted that following floods, frost, famine and the consequent increase in price of rice in 1704,[4] the unprecedented maximum of six uprisings are recorded but this total was not reached again until 1710. It was just at this point, let it be remembered, that the extravagances of Tsunayoshi had produced such a marked deficit

---

1. Cf. *supra,* preface p. xii.
2. Cf. Numazaki, Hidenosuke, *Hyakushō Ikki Chōsa Hōkokusho,* Kyōto, 1935 Chart IV.
3. *Ibid.* To avoid the tediousness of a detailed explanation of all the various uprisings, I will hereafter present either those of most importance or affording interesting material for study. For a chronological list, Cf. Appendix II.
4. The price of rice reached 93 *momme* per *koku,* the highest it had ever been. Cf. *infra* Appendix III, Chart I.

in the *Bakufu* accounts;[5] so it is not surprising to discover that this fact, plus a drought and famine, produced seven uprisings. Again in 1717 there occurred another drought resulting in disturbances which were particularly strong in Fukuyama, in the Province of Bingo.[6] Fukuyama had originally been the domain of Mizuno Katsushige[7] under whom the farmers had been happy and content. After 1710, this domain came under the control of the Abe family,[8] the lord spending most of his time in Edo and consequently increasing the expenses of the domain. Finally in 1717 several thousand of the farmers of the fief rose up with bamboo spears and banners made of straw matting, pressed towards the Castle of Fukuyama, there presenting their complaints.[9] In this same district many farmers died or suffered intensely because of the floods in 1721, the heavy winds and rains of 1724, the great famine 1732 and 1733[10] and a fire at Fukuyama Castle the next year.[11] Again in 1753, during the time of Abe, Iyo no

---

5. Cf. *supra* p. 12.
6. Fukuyama, 福山.
7. In 1619, Mizuno Katsushige, 水野勝成, (1564–1651), became chief of the castle with a domain of 100,000 *koku*.
8. The Abe family, 阿部氏, moved to Fukuyama, a domain of 100,000 *koku* in 1710. Abe Masatomi, 阿部政福, received the fief in 1715; 5,000 *koku* going to his brother. He retired in 1748 and died 1769.
9. Cf. *Nuno Kuma Gunshi*, 1 Vol.; Matsue, 1923, pp. 809 *et seq.*
10. The loss and distress in 1732 was so great that little strength was left for insurrection except in the large towns. A total crop failure of over 70% is noted while those starving in the *Bakufu* domains amounted to 651,599, those in private domains to 974,059, with 12,172 deaths. Cf. Kimura, Seiji, *Nihon Nōmin Sōtō Shi*, 1 Vol., Tōkyō, 1930, p. 125. To relieve this situation the *Bakufu* sent over 3,000,000 *koku* of rice to the famine districts, but this did not prevent the prices from soaring and housewreckings in Edo. Cf. Honjō, *Tokugawa Beika Chōsetsu*, 1 Vol., Kyōto, 1924, p. 385.
11. *Nuno Kuma Gunshi*, *op. cit.*, p. 811. The fire brought with it the added hardship of having to pay for the castle being rebuilt. Three uprisings during this early period are mentioned in English studies. One in 1654 in Shimōsa as a result of a 60% tax to which 300 peasants complained in Edo, first to their lord, then to the Shōgun Ietsuna. The leader, his wife and child, were crucified and five others banished. Taxes were later

Kami, Masasuke,[12] there was a great drought in the summer and a ruthless frost killed all the crops in the fall. This forced the peasants to eat roots, trees and hides, while the taxes remained as before. Against these conditions, the farmers revolted, the movement extending into six districts and a petition similar to that of 1717 was again presented.[13]

Though there were uprisings in Mimasaka in 1739 and various disturbances in Iyo and Tosa during the next few years,[14] the most important disorders center around Iwaki Daira.[15] Here in 1739, some 84,000 farmers objected to a tax of 1 *ryō* 3 *bu* on every 100 *koku* of rice levied for seven years, wrecked the homes of officials, challenged the warriors of the castle to come out and presented such a solid front that all their demands had to be conceded.[16]

But of even more interest, however, is the uprising in

---

restored to normal. Other uprisings were in Suwō in 1719 against the inflationist policy of the Shōgun Yoshimune and in 1720 in Shirakawa against the oppression of local officials. For 1654 Cf. Asakawa, "Village Government", *op. cit.*, Vol. 31, p. 191. For the other two uprisings Cf. Takekoshi, *op. cit.*, Vol. III, pp. 134 *et seq.*

12. Abe, Iyo no Kami, Masasuke, 阿部伊豫守政右, (1724–1769) was son of Masatomi, mentioned above. Masasuke was named Iyo no Kami in 1738, appointed *Jisha Bugyō*, 寺社奉行, or supervisor of shrines and temples, 1756-1757, *Kyōto Shoshidai*, 京都所司代, or representative of the *Bakufu* in Kyōto in charge of supervision of the Imperial Palace, 1760-1764, and Rōjū, 老中, or councillor of state 1766-1769. Each *Shōgun* usually had five *Rōjū* who were chosen from the *daimyō* with fiefs above 25,000 *koku*. He is mistakenly given as *Rōjū* from 1766-1786 in *Dokushi Biyō*, *op. cit.*, p. 243.

13. Cf. *Nuno Kuma Gunshi*, *op. cit.*, p. 811 *et seq.*

14. Cf. *infra*, p. 167 *et seq.*

15. Iwaki Daira, 岩城平, was the domain of Naitō Tadaoki, 內藤忠興, (1592–1674) after 1623. Naitō, Bingo no Kami, Masaki (1703–1766) 內藤備後守政樹, received the fief in 1718 and in 1747 moved to Nobeoka in Hyūga.

16. Cf. Takekoshi, *op. cit.*, Vol. III, p. 135, *et seq.* Also Takimoto, S., *Nihon Hoken Keizai Shi*, 1 Vol.; Tōkyō, 1930, who mistakenly gives the date as 1738.

Dewa, at Kaminoyama in 1747.[17] Here conditions in the fief had been most appalling since 1745 when there had been a loss of crops due to floods, likewise no crop for the year 1746, and by the third month of 1747 all the rice in the storehouses had been exhausted.[18] When the sale and importation of rice was forbidden by the authorities, a revolt was planned in the fifth month. Directing their wrath upon the *gundai* and *bugyō*, officials of the lord of Kaminoyama,[19] the peasants from thirty-three villages presented the following fifteen demands:

1. If the taxation is to be made in money, the price of rice must be based on a fair price in comparison with that in the markets of neighboring fiefs.
2. All additional taxes, other than those registered, shall be reduced.
3. The question of closing the harbors must be settled. Previously the lord of the castle had ordered the closing of all communications with the outside as well as the exchange of rice from the 9th to the 3rd month. The present lord had ordered only

---

17. Kaminoyama, 上ノ山, in Dewa, was an old castle originally built in the 16th century. It was, at the time of this uprising, the domain of Matsudaira, Yamashiro no Kami, Nobumasa, 松平山城守信將, a fief of 30,000 *koku*. Nobumasa was a descendant of the Fujii, 藤井, Matsudaira family. His ancestor, Matsudaira Toshinaga, 松平利長, died 1560, was originally installed at Fujii in Mikawa from whence the family derived its name. His grand-son Nobuyoshi, 信吉, was at Sasayama in Tamba with a fief of 50,000 *koku*. Nobuyoshi's first son, Tadakuni, 忠國, (1597-1659) was transferred from Sasayama in 1649 to Akashi and in 1679 to Kōriyama in Yamato. In 1685 he was at Shimōsa and his son, Tadayuki, 忠之, became insane in 1693, was dispossessed, the fief going to Nobumichi, 信通. Nobumichi was then transferred to Kaminoyama in 1697. The third generation in Kaminoyama was called Yamashiro no Kami. Thus in 1723, Nobumasa received the fief and went there for the first time in 1737. Cf. *Kokushi Daijiten*, Vol. IV, p. 2199, also Tamura, Eitarō, *Hōken Seika no Nōmin Ikki*, 1 Vol., Tōkyō, 1933, p. 169. Also *infra*, p. 158 for the genealogy of the Ueda branch of the same family.

18. Material for the following incident is taken from Tamura, *Hōken Ikki*, *op. cit.*, p. 169-197.

19. The *gundai*, 郡代, was an official in charge of a district, or gun, 郡, with duties of collecting taxes and supervision of governmental affairs similar to the *bugyō*.

the 6th month left for travel and communication.

4. Abolition of mountain officials.[20]
5. Cessation of office of transportation which continually makes levies of horses for public use.
6. Abolition of the purchase of thatching reed by the "Manager of Public Works",[21] at a low price and priests buying it only to resell it.
7. The establishment of a satisfactory time for delivery of tax goods as timber, thatching reed and light stakes.
8. The abolition of unnecessary and unofficial visits of government officials to *shōya* of villages and forcing the villagers to pay for such expenses as well as their food and drink.
9. The abolition of the recent restrictions on collecting roots and pine cones—an order of the mountain officials.
10. Permission be granted to sell firewood in Yamagata, where a better price had been offered.
11. Townsmen in Kaminoyama [be freed from] taxes for horses.[22]
12. There be leniency and exactness in recording the registration of the population.
13. Service rendered in lieu of delinquency in paying yearly taxes was formerly worth 6 bales of rice in Kaminoyama and ten in Edo. As the present lord has halved this amount we ask to be allowed five bales in Kaminoyama and ten in Edo.
14. The size of bundles of thatching shall be 6 *shaku* 3 *sun* not 9 *shaku* and 3 *sun*.[23]
15. The prohibition of the purchase of rice at a cheap price.

As the lord was absent from the fief at the time of the

---

20. *Yama bugyō*, 山奉行.
21. *Sakujikata*, 作事方.
22. This as well as article five refers to *sukegō*. Cf. *supra*, p. 6.
23. A *shaku*, 尺, is .994 feet and equals 10 *sun*, 寸.

presentation of these demands, on official duty in Ōsaka, a conference was held among the elder ministers of the fief and other officials. The farmers' demands were not only granted but they were given 300 *ryō* of gold and 1,100 bales of rice. The farmers consequently dispersed and three men from each of the villages were sent to pay their respects to the castle. Investigation of the affair then took place and the leaders were called out and tortured,[24] finally confessing. By the 11th month most of those who had been arrested were released and orders as to punishments were awaited from the *Bakufu* and the lord in Ōsaka. Five of the leaders received a death sentence for having banded together during the past summer, having become disorderly, disregarding the orders of their superiors to cease, and having planned an appeal to their lord and causing disorder in the castle.[25] The officer responsible for the levies of horses was dismissed and banished. Four women relatives, a brother and a child of three of the five men sentenced to death were banished while seventeen men and four *kumigashira* were fined three *kamme* each. Thus though the untenable economic situation of the fief had caused the riot and the demands of the farmers were met, nevertheless the leaders were to pay for it with their lives.

During the same general period, there occurred in Aizu[26] in 1749, in the fief of Matsudaira Narisada,[27] an uprising which likewise was the result of increased economic pressure due to crop failure. It is interesting, not so much for its size nor for the promises made to the farmers that their taxes would be halved, but for the extreme penalties inflicted.

---

24. For an elaborate account of modes of punishments and tortures Cf. Hall, J. C., "The Tokugawa Legislation", T.A.S.J., Vol. XLI, Pt. V, 1913, pp. 683 *et seq.*

25. Cf. Tamura, *op. cit.*, p. 197.

26. Aizu Castle, 會津, with a fief of 230,000 *koku* was in 1644 the domain of Hoshina Masayuki, 保科正之, (1609-1672) the son of the second Shōgun, Hidetada, who was adopted by Hoshina Masamitsu, 保科正光, (1561-1631)

27. Matsudaira Narisada, 平松容貞, (1719-1750), a descendent of Hoshina Masayuki. He received the fief in 1731, the title of Higo no Kami in 1735.

Among the officials, the two *Kōri bugyō* were ordered confined to their homes for fifty and thirty days respectively, but among the farmers the penalties were ruthless. Three farmers were to be tied and exposed outside the limits of the town and then killed by crucifying; two others to be burnt at the stake; three men to be beheaded and a total of 229 men received any one of the following sentences: exposure for three days, imprisonment, permanent exile or the prohibition from entering the castle town.[28]

The above will serve as examples of some of the fifty uprisings recorded for the decade ending in 1753. Nearly the identical number appear the next decade,[29] developing over a large area, resulting from poor crops, unjust administration, poor finances, and special local conditions. This next decade witnessed, two calamities in 1755, a famine in the north and floods and storms in the west. Estimates that a loss in the north of 70% of crops in all old fields and 90% in new land have been made,[30] and the situation was further aggravated by the fact that it was repeated in 1757. In Izumo it is reported that a wind in the 8th month destroyed 68,000 *koku* of rice, 720 houses, and 320 trees. As a result of this, the farmers of eight villages went to their *shōya* to appeal,

28. Cf. Kimura, *Sōtō Shi*, *op. cit.*, pp. 202-204. A letter on the 16th of the 1st month, 1750, adds that two of the farmers who came to the castle were killed and their demand that five of the officials be turned over to them was refused but a promise was made that the officials would be punished. Cf. *Kyōhō Hōreki Kammonsho*, a MS. in the Tokyo Imperial University.

29. Cf. Numazaki, *op. cit.*, Chart IV. It gives 51 uprisings for 1743–1752 and forty-nine for 1753–1762. I have been able to study over twenty of these, among them several which occur in the local studies. Cf. Chapter VII.

30. Cf. Abe, *op. cit.*, p. 52.

then started toward the castle at Hirose,[31] only to be restrained by the officials who promised them a loan of 1,000 *koku* of rice, with five years time in which to pay it.[32]

Fortunately, accounts of two of the uprisings during this period have appeared in English so only brief mention will be made of them here. The first of these, that in Kurume in Kyūshū,[33] was the direct result of a head tax of 4 *momme* per month levied on all those between the ages of 8 and 80 to help meet the expenses of the lord going to Edo on his alternate attendance upon the Shōgun, and the issuance of silver notes which travelers found difficult to exchange as legal tender. Of a probable total of 52,000 who took part in the uprising, 18 were put to death, a hundred deported from their villages and fined, though they received a promise of the abolition of the obnoxious head-tax. The second, that in Hyūga, Kyūshū in 1759 where the peasants, revolting against an unjust *daikan* and exorbitant taxes, were only suppressed when troops were called from neighboring domains.[34]

But it was not alone in Kyūshū that trouble was to arise

31. In 1637, Izumo was first transferred to Matsudaira Naomasa, 松平直政, (1601-1666) the third son of Tokugawa Hideyasu, 徳川秀康, second son of Tokugawa Ieyasu. The fief was subsequently divided among the three sons of Naomasa: Tsunataka ,綱隆, who remained at Matsue with a fief of 186,000 *koku*; Takamasa, 隆政, who was stationed at Mori with 10,000 *koku* and Chikayoshi, 近榮, with 30,000 *koku* at Hirose. The Hirose domain was then handed on to his grandson, Chikatomo, 近朝, in 1728 to his brother, Chikaakira, 近明, (1702-1755) who retired as head of the domain in 1749. At the time of the present uprising, the fief was under the control of his eldest son, Chikateru, 近輝, (1730-1757) who received the domain in the 12th month, 1749. Cf. *Kokushi Daijiten*, Vol. I, p. 198; Vol.IV, p. 2201; *Matsudaira Kafu Izumo kuni Hirose Jōshu*, a MS. in Tokyo Imperial University. For a continuation of the Matsue branch of the family Cf. *infra*, p. 60.

32. Cf. *Iishi Gunshi*, 1 Vol.; 1917, pp. 596-597.

33. Cf. J. Rahder, "Kurume Uprising", *op. cit.*, p. 81 *et seq.* For an uncritical Japanese account of this uprising Cf. Takimoto, S., ***Hōken Shi***, *op. cit.*, p. 296 *et seq.*

34. Cf. Takekoshi, *Economic history, op. cit.*, Vol. III, p. 137 and Murdoch, *Japan, op. cit.*, Vol. III, pp. 374-375.

from the local issuance of paper money. In 1755, in Akita[35] in northern Japan, the officials of the domain had ordered paper currency of 68 *momme* to be exchanged for 60 *momme* in silver coins. The coins were collected but as the paper money rapidly fell in value trade was considerably hampered. The townsmen and the farmers making a joint front against the officials, attacked the official in charge of the exchange.[36] Similar trouble arose in Kaga[37] the following year. There during the absence of the lord in Edo, the majority of the councillors decided upon the circulation of silver certificates. In this case, however, it became not only a question of the people refusing to use the money, but also one of counterfeiting and a consequent rise of price in terms of silver certificates, of all commodities. Thus the farmers rose in revolt, smashed the homes of the wealthy men of their district and demanded relief money from Edo. To aid the general economic distress of the fief, it was finally ordered that all those with an income above 500 *koku* were to be reduced 10% in all income and those below that amount were to receive a proportionate reduction. Though the town magistrates and officials issuing the silver certificates were punished, additional taxes were added in the future.[38]

Of particular interest, also, is the general disturbance in the provinces to the north and west of Edo; Kōzuke, Musashi and Shimozuke, in 1764–1765. As early as the spring of 1764, a tax (sukegō) of 3 *ryō,* 1 *bu,* 2 *shu,* had been levied upon each 100 *koku* to help defray the expenses of the Korean envoys who had an audience with the Shōgun on the 27th of

---

35. Akita, 秋田, in the Province of Ugo, was the castle town of the Satake Family, 佐竹氏, a domain of 205,000 *koku.*

36. Cf. Kokushō, I, *Ikki Kenkyū, op. cit.,* p. 115 and for a primary source, *Akita Suginao Monogatari,* in *Rekko Shimpi Roku, op. cit.,* pp. 456–492.

37. Kaga, on the west coast of Japan, was the domain of Maeda Shigemichi, 前田重教,(1741–1786). He received the fief in 1754 and held it until 1771.

38. Cf. *Ishikawa Kenshi,* 3 Vol.; Kanazawa, 1927, especially Vol. II, p. 736.

the 2nd month. Again a levy of 45 *momme* plus six men and three horses per 100 *koku* was ordered for the Imperial and Shōgunal court messengers who were going to Nikkō in the 4th month to worship at the tomb of Ieyasu. When the officials arrived to collect the men and horses, over 70,000 farmers revolted, smashing the windows of the tax collectors.[39] Signs were placed in front of temples warning all those who did not follow them that their villages would be burned, so it is not surprising that by the time they reached the outskirts of Edo[40] their numbers totaled more than 200,000.[41] During the various skirmishes and final order from the *Bakufu* that the guards shoot if they approached nearer the city, there seem to have been many who lost their lives. Several hundred of the leaders were arrested and crowded into Shinagawa and Asakusa prisons,[42] where it is reported many died, to which the *Bakufu* paid little heed.[43] The affair was finally settled on the 10th of the 1st month, 1765, when the farmers

---

39. Cf. Tsuji, Zennosuke, *Tanuma Jidai,* 1 Vol.; Tokyo, 1915, especially p. 135 *et seq.*

In reference to the Korean Embassy, it had been the duty of the feud between Tsushima and Edo to entertain the ambassadors and their train, but in 1710 the custom was abolished. The *Bakufu* assumed all costs of their mission so in 1764 their domains were taxed accordingly, some of them being the districts mentioned above Cf. Murdoch, *op. cit.,* Vol. III, p. 252 *et seq.*

In contrast to this treatment of the Koreans, the Hollanders, it is reported by Von Siebald, had to pay 25,569 florins for themselves and 23,738 florins for the Japanese members of their party at the time of their trip to Edo in 1826. Cf. Von Siebald, Fr., *Nippon; Archiv zur Beschreibung van Japon,* Leyden, 1832, Vol. II, p. 6.

40. They advanced to Warabi, 蕨 and Ōmiya, 大宮, both stations of the present Tōkyō electric fast line.

41. Cf. *Tōbu Hyakushō Ikken* in *Kinsei Shakai Sōsho, op. cit.,* Vol. X, p. 2 and pp. 269–279 for an account of this affair especially in Musashi.

42. Shinagawa, 品川, and Asakusa, 淺草, were execution grounds as well as prisons. The latter is now famous for a recreation centre for the populace of Tōkyō.

43. Cf. *Atomi Gusa,* in *Shiseki Shūran,* 33 Vol.; Tōkyō, 1900, especially Vol. 17, p. 674 for a contemporary account.

were promised their demands of exemption from the additional tax (*sukegō*) would be granted.[44]

B. Period of Tanuma Nototsugu and the Temmei Famines 1781–1788

The maladministration of the Tokugawa *Bakufu* is nowhere better exemplified than during the period in which Tanuma Mototsugu[45] controlled the finances. This unscrupulous man was irreconcilably opposed to the three leading Tokugawa families, gave favours to any who bribed sufficiently, and attempted to fill the government coffers by additional taxes on the common people. By 1772 he was appointed *Rōjū,* or Councillor, so that his power was unquestionable. His rule, the injustice of which was to have direct effect upon peasant uprisings, lasted until 1786; when a series of natural calamities increased the misery of the peasantry, and when remedial measures became ineffectual.

A study of contemporary uprisings in Hida, a domain of the Tokugawa Shōgun, is therefore of special significance.[46] Corruption in Edo presupposed corruption among officials in charge of the public domain. As early as 1746, as a direct result of an increase in taxes, the farmers of the two districts petitioned that, "having found it difficult to pay our yearly taxes, we ask that the inspection officials who have recently come do not inspect our land. Ours is a mountainous country

---

44. Cf. Tsuji; *op. cit.,* p. 136; Takizawa, *op. cit.,* p. 79, and Murdoch, *op. cit.,* p. 392 *et seq.*

45. Tanuma Mototsugu (田沼意次) (1719–1788), first received a fief under the Shōgun Yoshimune. In 1758 he was given Tōtōmi with a 20,000 *koku* income and appointed *Sobayōnin*(側用人) in 1767. He was *Rōjū* from 1772–1786, having received "the rank of *Rōjū* in 1769. Cf. Sawada, *op. cit.,* p. 319 *et seq;* Murdoch, *Japan,* Vol. III, p. 380 *et seq;* Tsuji, *Tanuma Jidai* and *Dokushi Biyō,* 1 Vol.; Tōkyō, 1932, p. 243 and 244.

46. In passing note should be taken of the well organized and effective uprising in Hizen, Kyūshū, in 1771. There 23,000 farmers from 15 villages rose in opposition to the intendant's attempt to increase their assessment by 15,000 bales of rice, as well as his orders to plant 30,000 mulberry trees. Though the leader was beheaded, the peoples' demands were met after they dispersed. Cf. Takekoshi, *op. cit.,* Vol. III, pp. 138–140.

with frequent frosts, where the crops do not ripen and where cold is severe."[47] In the 12th month of 1771, the farmers revolted and decided not to pay their rice tax because of the illegal practices of the "assistant store-keeper".[48] They destroyed the home of one, Maruya Hihachi, whom they blamed for having asked for a collection of 3,000 *koku* of rice urgently needed in Edo when he was not a real official. A priest from a neighboring temple made fruitless attempts at intervention, and the farmers attacked the homes of two *toshiyori* or village officials.[49] When the head of the local temple finally gave the farmers a document saying it was obvious the *toshiyori* were responsible for the farmers' actions, they retired.[50] However, on the 16th of the 8th month, 1774, the *Bakufu* decided on the following punishments: one leader was to be killed, three were to receive banishment, thirty-seven were fined, and three *nanushi* were fined, while all the farmers were to be scolded. No blame was placed on Maruya.[51]

In the 10th month, 1772, ten *nanushi* asked the intendant if the taxes were to be collected as previously. When told such would be the case, and when they in turn reported this to the farmers, the latter objected strenuously. They also took exception to the fact that they had neither seen nor had read to them the official document stating the amount of the taxes they were assessed.[52] Thus four thousand of them met about five miles from Takayama, the main city of the domain. Encircling the town, they permitted no outsiders to enter. Orders were then sent to Toyama, Dewa no Kami, lord of Naeki Castle in Mino,[53] to help tranquillize the uprising. An

47. *Hida Kuni Ono Gunshi,* 3 Vol.; Takayama, 1925, especially Vol. II, p. 439. For a modern study of a village in Hida, interesting as a comparative study in folklore, Cf. Kawaguchi, Sonjirō, *Hida Shirakawa Mura,* 1 Vol.; 1934.

48. *Kuraban,* 藏番, an assistant store-keeper.

49. *Toshiyori,* 年寄, were village elders.

50. *Hida Ono Gunshi, op. cit.,* Vol. II, p. 490 *et seq.*

51. *Ibid.,* p. 565.

52. *Etchū Shiryō, op. cit.,* Vol. III, p. 126.

53. Tōyama, Dewa no Kami, Tomokiyo, 遠山出羽守友清,(1717–1781) lord of Naeki Castle, 苗木城主, a fief of 10,500 *koku* from 1753–1777.

expeditionary force of about 500 men was then organized, taking with them seven cannon and fifteen guns. They reached the border of the province, however, only to learn that all was tranquil in Hida.[54] Following an examination of this particular incident by the *daikan,* four of the leaders were imprisoned.[55] In 1773 the *daikan,* Ōhara, decided to examine the domain for the opening of new fields, and the *Bakufu* survey officials arrived in the 3rd month. At the news of this, the farmers decided to raise objections to Ōhara, asking that this survey be suspended as one had been made in the late 17th century. This was of no avail so they attempted to appeal to the neighboring fief which had previously carried out the survey, asking that only the new lands be surveyed. In the meantime, the surveying was under way and in the 5th month an examination was carried out of those who had formed a mob and appealed. The *nanushi* and farmers were called to Takayama where they were arrested and received heavy tortures in order to force them to confess either themselves or the names of the leaders.[56]

In spite of permission having been refused by the *daikan* for twenty farmers to make an appeal in Edo, they reached there by the 7th month. On the 26th they divided into two groups, one presenting their petition to the *Rōjū,* Matsudaira Terakata,[57] as he was passing in his palanquin; the other to the *Kanjō bugyō,* Matsudaira Tsushima no Kami,[58] at his home. This petition included the narration of matters and the complaints made heretofore, followed by a list of the following complaints:

1. Hida, being a mountainous country, there were endless difficulties in transportation; likewise mines had lost their value and timber was no longer cut.

---

54. *Etchū Shiryō, op. cit.,* Vol. III, p. 118.
55. Cf. *Etchū Shiryō, op. cit.,* Vol. II, p. 500.
56. *Ibid.,* Vol. II, p. 511 *et seq.*
57. Matsudaira Terataka, 松平輝高, was *Rōjū* from 1761–1781.
58. The *Kanjō bugyō,* 勘定奉行, was the finance minister of the Shōgun. Matsudaira Tadasato, 松平忠郷, is referred to here, having been finance minister from 1768 to 1773.

2. It was only possible to have one crop a year and only one good one every three years.
3. Taxes on the old fields had been increased from 30% to 50%.
4. Money had failed to circulate recently due to the impossibility of selling articles outside when the roads were impassable.
5. Since 1730 there had been nothing but increased taxes.
6. The collection date had previously been the 5th of the 10th month, but had recently been advanced to the 7th of the 8th month.[59]

By the ninth month, taxes for the current year were ordered collected, resulting in further insurrection on the part of 10,000 farmers. As Ōhara was unable to tranquillize them, he asked for a command from the *Bakufu* to order troops to be sent from the neighboring provinces.[60] In two months time, domains in Mino and Etchū had been ordered to send aid. Thus neighboring troops soon arrived and with their assistance, armed with spears and guns, the guard of Toyama attacked the peasants, killing three, wounding several with swords and capturing and imprisoning a hundred and fourteen.[61] By the middle of the 12th month the uprising was tranquillized though the farmers were to suffer severely for it. A special envoy to examine the whole affair was sent from Edo, but Ōhara still remained in office as *daikan*. Of the six men who appealed directly to the palanquin of the *Rōjū* in Edo, and who entered the house of the *Kanjō bugyō*, one died in prison and the other five men were decapitated, their

59. Cf. *Hida Ono Gunshi, op. cit.*, Vol. II, pp. 520 *et seq.*
60. *Ibid*, Vol. II, p. 538.
61. *Ibid*, Vol. II, p. 540. Professor Tsuji states that this was the first time to tranquilize an uprising with gunfire, but the *daikan* ordered an uprising in Harima settled by gunfire in 1749. This mistake probably comes from that in *Atomi Gusa, op. cit.*, p. 683 which reads: "The soldiers from Kōriyama met the mob first in the shelter of a woods and were ordered to blow them to bits with gunfire the first time they have been tranquilized through the use of gunfire." Cf. Tsuji, *Tanuma Jidai, op. cit.*, 1 p. 147 and Tamura, Eitaro, *Ikki Kumosuke Bakuto*, 1 Vol.; Tōkyō, especially p. 457.

heads being sent to Takayama to be exposed as a lesson to their fellow peasants. One farmer in Miya village, the center of the disturbance, was to be crucified as were two of the priests of the shrines where the farmers had met, together with a *nanushi.* Seven other farmers were sentenced to have their heads exposed; two received an ordinary death sentence, nineteen were banished. Two others received the death sentence though they had previously died in prison.[62] In accord with the law issued by the *Bakufu* in 1770 rewarding all informants who bring accusation or information about which they can swear against those connected with conspiracies, appeals or desertions,[63] the following awards were made: six men, mostly *nanushi* and *toshiyori,* were given a name and permission to wear a sword,[64] five men were given a name and silver coin; nine farmers were given an annual stipend of from three to ten *koku* yearly and silver was given to four men.[65]

The *daikan,* Ōhara finally died in 1778, only to be succeeded by another Ōhara, Kamigorō, probably his son whose excesses caused the farmers to complain again in 1789 which resulted in his dismissal and banishment to Hachijō Island, together with one of his assistants. Two of his assistants were decapitated; thirteen ordered exiled and two farmers killed. The various local officials were either banished, imprisoned or detained,[66] but this all occurred after the downfall of Tanuma. Such was the general disorder and corruption in Hida, one of the direct domains of the *Bakufu,* reflecting somewhat the situation in Edo and the central government itself.

Turning from the troubles in the public domain of Hida, to those in the domain of Mito, it is found that local uprisings developed there as a direct result of financial disorder within the fief. Mito was the center of one of the three main

---

62. *Hida Ono Gunshi,* Vol. II, pp. 580–584.
63. Kokushō, *op. cit.,* p. 342.
64. It should be noted in this connection that the farmers never had a family name, that privilege and that of wearing a sword being granted to warriors, who wore two swords, and later to distinguished townsmen, many of whom bought the privilege.
65. *Hida Ono Gunshi, op. cit.,* Vol. II, p. 596.

branches of the Tokugawa family, where Tokugawa Yorifusa,[67] ninth son of Ieyasu, was enfiefed in 1609 with 350,000 *koku* and where his descendants continued to live until the Meiji Restoration. As one of the three chief Tokugawa houses, Mito enjoyed special privileges, among them that of casting iron coin in place of issuing paper currency. Thus in 1771 permission was finally granted for the establishment of 97 mints, employing over 4,000 people. These workers were collected from among the farmers or waifs in the district and the new coins, with little real value were ordered circulated as legal tender, bringing hardships to the surrounding country. As a result, a thousand farmers rose up, set fire to the mint, burning two hundred people to death, after which the mints were reduced to a total of twenty-four and by 1772 abolished entirely.[68]

This suspension of operations was only temporary, for by the third month of 1774, recasting had begun, with a consequent rise of prices. This time five hundred farmers revolted, accompanied by others who planned an appeal before the castle in Mito, but still the casting continued. However, on the occasion of the burning of the "iron coin guild" in 1775, the mints were permanently discontinued, bringing therewith, desired relief for the peasants.[69]

One of the most interesting uprisings of this period is that in the realm of the famous Buddhist Temple of Kōyasan.[70]

---

66. *Ibid., op. cit.,* Vol. II, pp. 660–665.

67. Tokugawa Yorifusa, 徳川頼房, whose third son was the famous Mitsukuni, 光圀, (1628–1700) who is well known for undertaking the compilation of the *Dai Nihon Shi* in 1657. His descendant, Nariaki, 齊昭, (1800–1860) was a leader in the movement for the expulsion of the foreigner and the restoration of the Imperial Family. The lord of the fief of 350,000 *koku* in 1771 wasTokugawa Harumori, 徳川治保, (1751–1805). He became head of the fief in 1766 upon the death of his father, Munemoto, 宗翰. He was followed in 1805 by his son, Harutoshi, 治紀, (1773–1816).

68. Cf. Kokushō, *Ikki Kenkyū, op. cit.,* pp. 118–120.

69. *Ibid.,* pp. 120–121.

70. Kōyasan, 高野山, is a mountain in the province of Kii, famous for its temples. There a temple was first founded in 816 by the Buddhist priest Kūkai, 空海, (774–835) better known as Kōbō Daishi. It then became

Though it was the home of the Shingon Sect, the fief of 21,000 *koku* soon became a victim of bad administrative policies. Thus its farmers were oppressed as in any other domain and uprisings occurred in 1692, 1719 and 1776.[71] In 1719 in an uprising throughout the entire Kōyasan realm, demands were made for reductions in rent which were granted, though the fundamental faults of administration were left unchanged. Thus by 1776 the farmers were suffering hardships equally as bad as, if not worse than those in other districts, especially since the realm was largely mountainous. Taxes equal to 69% were collected, then from 80% to 92% or 93%;[72] while an additional levy was made for the support of the *Bakufu.* The priests, having lost much prestige through the uprising of 1719, as well as having had their finances become worse, exerted every effort to force the farmers to open new fields, only to have them abandon the old ones. Finally resorting to deceit, they offered an income of 30 *koku* and the privilege of a name, to one Okamoto if he would carry out a new survey, and by the use of false measurements, increase a 7,500 *koku* income to 8,500 *koku.* To this the farmers objected as early as the third month when the taxable crop of

---

the central temple of the Shingon Sect, 眞言宗. Its monastery soon flourished with over 723 buildings and was a place of refuge for many famous people, such as Hidetsugu, nephew of Toyotomi Hideyoshi, who because of political reverses, fled there and committed suicide in 1595. Cf. Papinot, *Dictionnaire Historique, op. cit.*, pp. 363, 369 and 672. For a translation of part and an outline of the remainder of the basic Shingon text, the *Dainichikyō,* 大日經, cf., Tajima, R., *Mahavairocana-Sūtra,* 1 Vol; Paris, 1936, 186 pp.

71. For a primary source on these uprisings see *Kōya Ryōmin Ikki Shimatsu* in *Kinsei Shakai Sōsho, op. cit.,* Vol. X, pp. 162–265. For a secondary source based on this material see Kokushō, *Hōken Shakai no Tōsei to Tōsō,* 1 Vol.; Tōkyō, especially pp. 403–429.

72. Cf. *Kōya Ryōmin Ikki, op. cit.,* Vol. X, p. 170. The text reads as follows: 此節高免成. 八ツより九ツ貳三歩に入り候. *Kono setsu takamen nari. Yatsu yori kokonotsu ni san bu ni hairi sōrō.* At first sight the phrase *takamen,* 高免, "high exemption", seems a contradiction to the above translation. Although *men* literally means to exempt or pardon, it came to be used for the "Tax one paid in order to be exempt", hence "the tax itself". Thus a farmer with a *yatsumen,* 八ツ免, meant a farmer's paying a tax of 80%. See also Ono, *Nōmin Goi, op. cit.,* p. 434.

one village was increased by 300 *koku* due to this new survey. Some 4,000 farmers rose up, attacked the home of Okamoto and wrecked it, as well as thirty-eight other places and store houses.[73] In the eighth month, ostensibly gathering to worship for the protection of themselves and their children against a raging epidemic of measles, over 12,000 farmers started towards the temple, the priests having to call upon troops of a neighboring fief for protection. Representatives sent to Kōyasan to negotiate for the cancellation of the order to open new fields and a reduction of taxes to 69%, were imprisoned, causing the farmers again to rebel in the tenth month. This time, however, they were successful in getting the release of the prisoners, as well as a reduction in taxes.

In order to save their own reputation, two priests were sent to Edo to explain the situation, but in the 3rd month, 1777, the Overseers of Shrines and Temples,[75] Makino, Etchū no Kami, Sadanaga, summoned six leaders of the farmers, seventeen student priests, nine travelers and fifteen novices to Edo to inquire concerning the uprising.[76] As a result of those investigations, four of the leaders among the farmers were sentenced to have their heads exposed: though as three of these had previously died in prison, only one was actually executed.[77] Throughout fifty-six villages, fifteen landowners were deprived of their names and the privilege of wearing a sword, about 250 *shōya* were fined ten *kamme* each, 3,000 farmers were fined 170 *kamme* per village; while the *shōya*, *toshiyori* and farmers who did not take part, were rewarded and highly praised. The blame for the uprising was thus placed entirely on the farmers, although the priests lost still more prestige by having become so weak they allowed a rebellion to drag on for nearly a year.[78]

---

73. Cf. Kokushō, *Hōken Tōsei, op. cit.*, p. 434.
74. *Ibid.* p. 413.
75. The *Jisha bugyō*, 寺社奉行, was Makino Sadanaga,牧野貞長, from 1764–1777. He was lord of Kasama in Hitachi, a fief of 80,000 *koku*.
76. Cf. *Kōya Ryōmin Ikki, op cit.*, Vol. X, p. 231 *et. seq.*
77. *Ibid.*, p. 234.
78. Kokushō, *Hōken Shakai no Tōsei, op. cit.*, p. 424 *et seq.*

Beginning with the year 1781, Japan was to face a series of famines which were to leave her devastated, decrease her population and only increase the hardships already begun by the policy of Tanuma. These facts, together with his policy of resorting to any scheme to increase the revenue of the treasury on the one hand, and persuading the Shogun Ieharu (1737–1786) to adopt the eldest son of the Hitotsubashi branch of the Tokugawa family as his successor,[79] on the other, made his downfall inevitable. Conditions were such that contemporary authors lamented:

> "During the present time when innumerable people band together and destroy the products and wealth of the country, send appeals to the government, when the peasants secretly form groups and perpetrate disorder, when the lords of the fiefs and the government representatives lose their power and it is usurped by the lower classes, then it seems that the end of the world must be near."[80]

Among the many wild schemes of Tanuma was his approval of the appeal made by three men of the province of Kōzuke, one of whom was a *nanushi* of the village of Kanai, the other two, a wholesaler (*tonya*)[81] and a *nanushi* of the public domain in Shimmachi Yado. These men, for the profit through bribery and squeezes which they saw in the plan for themselves, asked for the establishment of silk taxes in Kōzuke and Musashi. These two provinces were especially famous for their silk thread, the farmers bringing their silk to the markets in Takasaki. It was here that purchaces of 3,000 bolts (*hiki*)[82] were made by the *daimyō* of Mito and several thousand by the lord of Kaga. Thus money came to be used and cherished by the farmers, but they were never able to save.[83] Borrowing from the more wealthy, they would then

79. Cf. Murdoch, *op. cit.*, Vol. III, p. 402.
80. Cf. *Atomi Gusa, op. cit.*, p. 686.
81. A *tonya*, 問屋.
82. A *hiki*, 疋, was a bolt of cloth 30–35 feet in length.
83. Cf. Tamura, *Ikki Kumosuke, op. cit.*, p. 408 *et seq.* Also for a brief reference to this uprising see Murdoch, *op. cit.*, Vol. III, p. 393 and Takekoshi, *op. cit.*, Vol. III, p. 140, and Sawada *op. cit.*, p. 230.

be unable to pay their interest and be forced to remit in silk worms or hemp.[84]

Finally by the 7th month, 1781, the tax bureaus were established with orders to collect 2 *bu* 5 *rin* for one roll of silk fabric and 5 *bu* for 100 *momme* of silk thread, from all buyers, and silk without the official seal was to be confiscated. The farmers appeared as usual at market, but the usual purchasers from Edo, Kyōto, Ōsaka and Nagoya, did not come, thus causing the market to be closed.[85] The *gundai* then ordered the markets to carry on business with the local people, but the farmers were still unable to sell their produce. Complaining in vain to the *Kanjō bugyō*, they began a series of most devastating housewreckings.[86] Apparently over fifty places in all were smashed by the enraged farmers, including those of two of the men who had originally asked that the silk exchanges be established, as well as a *daikan* of the *Bakufu*. Their places were destroyed, all their food eaten, the household articles burnt or thrown into the wells, and the record books pillaged.[87] Dissatisfied peasants from fifty or sixty villages numbering 10,000 are reported to have taken part in the plundering on the night of the 11th and 12th and 2,000 more to have advanced towards Takasaki Castle the next night.[88]

A letter written the following year gives a picture of the effectiveness of the destruction of the mob. The auther states that:

> "At this time I was living in my home with sixteen members of my household. I am a holder of 20 *chō* (nearly 50 acres) of land which we cultivate, and a keeper of a pawn shop for the surrounding neighborhood. From the 13th day of the 8th month, (1781) about ten

---

84 Cf. Tamura, *op. cit.*, p. 404 *et seq.*
85. *Ibid*, p. 412.
86. Commonly called *uchi kowashi*, 打毀, but also pronounced *bukkowashi*.
87. Tamura, *op. cit.*, p. 422 *et seq.*
88. These figures are quoted from Tamura, *op. cit.*, but Takekoshi says 3,000 invested the castle. Cf. Takekoshi, *op. cit.*, Vol. III, pp. 429–430.

men came every day for their pawned goods. Hearing that I was considered among those in charge of the silk tax and that my house would be attacked, I become extremely anxious. At 2 A.M. on the 15th, we were surprised by the innumerable shouts of the people coming from all directions. They left nothing within our house or the seven godowns, smashing and burning all our utensils, the *tatami* (straw mat flooring) cutting up all the bales of rice and distributing the gold and money."[89]

In the meantime, a strict guard had been kept over the castle at Takasaki and the leader of the garrison at Maebashi finally called out his soldiers who advanced to within about half a mile of the peasants only to have them suddenly disappear. It was on this same day, the 16th, that an order was sent from the *Bakufu* stopping all tax bureaus and silk taxes in all the villages of the private and public domains. Shortly all the villages learned of this command, and having won their cause, were quiet again. Investigation and inquiry into the leaders of the insurrection naturally followed, together with a death sentence for four of the leaders, three of whom died in prison and an order to scold all the heads of the villages and heads of the groups who took part in the trouble. However, by the continued opposition of the peasants, this new source of revenue became closed to Tanuma.

But this was to be merely the beginning of the troubles of Temmei (1781–1788). In 1783 a universal famine spread over the north, to be increased in severity by the eruption of the volcano, Mt. Asama,[91] "when burning rocks causing fires in the neighborhood, were followed by a dust storm which either buried or demolished the grasses and animals within a radius of a hundred miles."[92] Tales of half the population starving

89. A letter by Wanosuke, written 4th month, 1782, and quoted in Tamura, *op. cit.*, pp. 429–430.

90. *Ibid*, p. 446.

91. Mt. Asama, 淺間山, is the volcano still active near modern Karuizawa, whose ashes sometimes drift as far as Tokyo.

92. Cf. *Atomi Gusa*, *op. cit.*, p. 688.

give some idea of the conditions[93] so it is natural to find twenty-seven uprisings noted for that year alone.[94]

Likewise as there had been no harvest in the Province of Izumo in 1783, on the southwestern coast of Japan,[95] a severe disturbance developed there in the fief of Matsudaira Harusato, lord of the Castle of Matsue,[96] an uprising breaking out in the villages of Ōzu, Mitoya and Takuwa, in Kando and Iishi Districts.[97] Since the previous year, a new tax of 3 *koku* on each ten *chō* of rice fields and 5 *koku* on each ten *chō* of dry lands had been ordered; as well as a *fumai* tax or duty of

---

93. Cf. Takekoshi, *op. cit.*, Vol. III, p. 138 *et seq.*: Murdoch, *op. cit.*, Vol. III, p. 394; and Titsingh, M., *Memoires et anecdotes sur la dynastie regnante des Djogouns, souverains du Japon,* 1 Vol.; Paris, 1820. 301 pp. Especially pp. 180–186.

94. Numazaki, *op. cit.*, Chart IV: In defense of Japanese statistics it is interesting to note that an entirely independent source and unpublished MS. states that: "Reports have it that in *twenty-seven* provinces in Japan in 1783 there were peasant uprisings." The same MS. mentions an uprising in Awaji about 1783, where only three of the thirteen demands of the farmers were accepted, so that two of the leaders, a father and a son, feeling remorseful over the failure of their project, committed suicide. Another reported to have been worse than that in Izumo mentioned below is stated to have occurred in Iwami in 1783. Cf. *Hyakushō Sōdō Ikken,* pp. 11 and 12, a MS. written on the 6th day of the third month of 1783. The original is in the collection of Morihiro Sakusuke of Ōzu village, Kando District, Izumo, a copy in the *Shiryō Hensanjo,* of Tōkyō Imperial University. Thanks to their generosity, free access was given the author to this document.

Uprisings in Kōzuke where the loss from the eruption of Mt. Asama was the worst, spread to Shinano. Cf. Kobayashi, H., *Ina Nōmin Sōdōshi,* 1 Vol.; Tōkyō, 1933. 291 pp., especially p. 7.

95. Cf. *Temmei Sankyōsaku Ichizu,* a contemporary MS. in the library of the *Shiryō Hensanjo* of Tōkyō Imperial University.

96. As has been noted previously, Matsudaira Tsunataka, 松平網隆, inherited the fief of 186,000 *koku* of Matsue from his father, Matsudaira Naomasa. Cf. *supra*, p. 46.

Matsudaira Harusato, 治郷, (b. 1751) , lord of the castle of Matsue, succeeded to the fief in 1767 from his father, Matsudaira Munenobu, 宗衍, (1729–1782), descendant of the 6th generation of Tsunatake. Known as Dewa no Kami, he was famous for having founded a military school, practising economy in his fief, and received the posthumous name of Daienan-大圓庵. Cf. *Kokushi Daijiten,* Vol. IV, p. 2201; *Matsudaira Kafu Izumo, kuni, Matsue Jōshu,* a MS. in the *Shiryō Hensanjo* library in Tōkyō.

97. Ōzu, 大津, Mitoya, 三刀屋, and Takuwa, 多久和, in Kando, 神門, and Iishi, 飯石, districts.

villagers to provide money for the work to be done in the lord's mansion in the city. There had also been levied a *sunshimai*, or special rice tax to be collected in the 4th instead of the 6th month.[98] One of the elders of the fief, therefore, appealed several times for relief, but the lord merely complained of the increase in expenses. In Kando District, the price of rice had risen since the first of the year,[99] and the people were wandering about demanding rice gruel. A strange person appeared and ordered everyone to appear the next day at Ōzu Machi to make a mob-appeal, the doctors, townsmen, acupuncture doctors and heads of the shrines coming to the support of the peasants.[100] On the night of the 19th of the 1st month, several thousand men,[101] beating on the doors with split bamboo sticks and calling out with loud voices demanding the people to come out and join them, came from the west of Ōzu, dressed in sandals and with towels wrapped around their heads for the occassion. They then broke into the home of Morihiroya Gampei, breaking down the walls of his home, entering his garden and pulling down the out-buildings, tearing off and destroying the storm doors and entering the house in muddy feet. Taking out all of his furniture and moveable goods, they broke them into bits; and opening his godown, they distributed some 533 bales of rice. The rioters then demanded that Morihiro Ikuta be their mediator and present their appeal to the officials, leaving him the alternative of having his own place ruined, and thus precipitating his quick departure for

98. Cf. Shimane Gakubu, editors, *Shimane Kenshi*, 10 Vol.; 1931· especially Vol. 9, p. 495. *Fumai* is written, 夫米, and *sunshimai*, 寸志米, The latter was a special rice tax levied in Izumo and Bingo. Deriving its name from "a trifling token in appreciation of one's gratitude", (*sunshi*), this tax was first levied in Izumo in 1723, amounting to 4,000 *koku*, approximately 5% of the crop. Professor Ono gives this tax as exclusively used in Izumo. Cf. Ono, T. *Nōmin Goi*, *op. cit.*, p. 229 and *infra* p. 64.

99. *Hyakushō Sōdō*, *op. cit.*, p. 1. Unfortunately no unit of measurement is given. Honjō gives the rise in price of rice as 56 *momme* per *koku* in 1781 to 98 *momme* in 1783. Cf. *infra*, appendix III, Chart I.

100. *Shimane Kenshi*, *op. cit.*, Vol. 9, p. 499.

101. This number is given as 10,000 in *Shimane Kenshi*, Vol. 9, p. 499 and 2,000 in *Temmei Sankyōsaku Ichizu*.

Matsue on their behalf.[102] The demands of the farmers, to which they added the terse comment: "If you do not listen to our appeal, all the farmers in the district will rise up and attack the castle. This is important!" included the following:

1. They be freed from an increase in taxes.
2. They be allowed five years in which to pay back any borrowed money.
3. They be allowed a loan of 10 *koku* on every 100 for food to be paid in five years.
4. The abuses of the villages be changed and help be given the starving.
5. The sale and manufacture of *sake* (Japanese rice wine) cease.
6. They be lent money for the purchase of livestock.
7. There be restrictions on payment of *yōmai*, or rice paid in lieu of wages.

Meanwhile a similar uprising had broken out in Iishi District, being joined by farmers from Nita District, making a total of at least 7,000 participants. This group ruthlessly destroyed the property of a rich merchant in Mitoya village, who had profiteered on the change in the prices of rice. Bursting open some 1000 wine kegs in his store-houses, they drank profusely and left a pool of *sake* as deep as one's knees.[104] Officials were soon dispatched from Matsue to begin investigation of the uprising and sixteen prisoners were taken from Ōzu, including a tile maker, named Rinzo.[105] After having been tortured unmercifully with boiling water baths, beating and being forced to drink water, Rinzo confessed, possibly falsely, that Morihito Ikuta had come to consult with him and that the farmers, being delighted with the idea of appeal, had then sent Ikuta as their intermediary to Matsue.[106] Ikuta was then ordered to Matsue, deprived of the privilege of wearing

---

102. *Hyakushō Sōdō, op. cit.*, pp. *2 et seq.*
103. *Yōmai*, 用米. Cf. *Shimane Kenshi, op. cit.*, Vol. 9, pp. 500 *et seq.*
104. *Ibid*, p. 497 and *Hyakushō Sodo*, p. 9.
105. *Hyakushō Sōdō*, pp. 4–6.
106. *Shimane Kenshi, op. cit.*, Vol. 9, p. 504.

a sword, and imprisoned, together with a *toshiyori*. Seven men in Ōzu village and fourteen in Musashi village were confined to their homes in the district in the west.[107] In Iishi District, four men were arrested as leaders, eighteen banished to another district, one of whom committed suicide. Configcation was also ordered of Ikuta's property, but there arose some question as to his sole responsibility for the uprisins. Thus some of his household effects were given to his wife and children, his real property being bought by members of his family. The same policy was likewise followed for the personal property of twelve others who had been banished. On the 6th of the 3rd month, all of Ikuta's confiscated property: fields, mountain lands and remaining household effects, were returned to his wife and children.[108] Because of illness, he was released from prison on the 1st of the 5th month, and transferred to a hot spring, and by the 17th of the 2nd month, 1784, all were pardoned from connection with the uprising.[109]

As a final result of the uprising and the evident distress of the peasants, they received the following:

25,000 *kamme* of silver to the most needy in various villages.

Rice for those starving.

Special decrease in taxation and in the circulation of silver certificates in the province.

Friendly gift money.[110]

The situation of general distress throughout the country was considerably alleviated the next year when there were reports of better crops and the price of rice fell about 35%.[111] Thus with the return to normal conditions, uprising diminished noticeably.[112] Having already mentioned the trouble in the

107. *Hyakushō Sōdō*, p. 13 *et seq.*

108. *Ibid*, p. 16 *et seq.* The text is slightly ambiguous.

109. *Shimane Kenshi*, p. 504. In a MS. entitled *Izumo Shishi* it is stated that Ikuta was killed.

110. *Shimane Kenshi, op. cit.*, Vol. 9, p. 507.

111. Cf. *infra*, Appendix III.

112. Cf. Numazaki, *op. cit.*, Chart IV in which seven are noted for 1784, three for 1785.

Abe domain in Fukuyama, Bingo, uprisings again appear there during this period of famine.[113] A succession of bad crops from 1782–1786 forced several tens of thousands of the farmers to present thirty-three demands in the winter of 1786.[114] However, other causes seem to have played important roles. Among the most important demands of the farmers was that their crop might be examined for purposes of taxation as most of it had failed to ripen, and also that the monopolistic control of the cotton market, forcing the farmers to sell at low prices, be abolished. Likewise, as the farmers preferred the paper currency of neighbouring fiefs to that of their own, it had become necessary to establish "silver certificate censors",[115] to assure circulation of the Fukuyama certificates and to arrest any who had money from outside.[116]

The immediate object of the wrath of the peasants was, however, the harsh and unjust action of Endo Nenzo, the Finance Minister and Assistant Manager. In spite of a bad crop, he had levied the usual tax, plus a special tax of 5,000 *koku* of rice (*sunshimai*). When the peasants learned in the middle of the first month that their demands would not be met, 20,000 went to the castle, and when threatened with being shot upon they retorted: "Better than the farmers' heads is the head of the *daikan* which we will cut off."[117] Naturally being unable to penetrate into the castle, they contented themselves with breaking up the houses of various *shōya*, the officials responsible for carrying out Endo's commands. At the report that orders had come from Edo that Endo would be

---

113. Cf. *supra*, p. 40.
114. Cf. *Nuno Kuma Gunshi, op. cit.*, p. 811.
115. *Ginsatsu Metsuke*, 銀札目付.
116. Cf. Kokushō, *Ikki Kenkyū, op. cit.*, p. 98 and p. 123.
117. Cf. *Nuno Kuma Gunshi, op. cit.*, pp. 812–813.

confined to his home and all avaricious *shōya* would receive the same treatment, the disturbances ceased.[118]

Around Kyōto there had been a drought in 1785, in 1786 there were heavy rains and frosts; so that when the crops failed throughout the greater part of Japan in 1787, the repercussion of the steadily rising price of rice from 61 *momme* to 187 *momme* over the same three years were felt even in the cities.[119] In spite of attempts of the government to control the situation through the prohibition of the manufacture of *sake*, forbidding the purchase of rice at a low price in Ōsaka to be shipped to Edo, and stopping of storing for sale elsewhere, rice riots broke out in the 5th month both in Ōsaka and Edo and spread to other cities. In Ōsaka the mob was quieted when special guards were stationed throughout the city and small shops were erected where rice was sold through chinks in the temporary fences erected to protect them. In Edo, after three days of lawlessness, those in need were granted 5 *gō* of rice and 3 *zeni*,[120] but the riots were quelled only after the importance of the Shogunate had been clearly shown.[121]

But it was not only in the cities that the power of the government had been questioned. The farmers had successfully challenged the new tax of the government on silk in Kōzuke and Musashi in 1781; desertions from their home

---

118. *Ibid*, p. 813. Professor Kokushō adds: "It was reported that thirty or forty men of large stature and pale countenance were seen among the crowd of farmers who carried spears concealed in bamboo poles. These were *rōnin*, lordless knights, who had come to lead the mob." Cf. *Ikki Kenkyū, op. cit.*, p. 237.

Though the names and dates differ from the above, this uprising is referred to in *Abeno Dōjimon* in *Kinsei Shakai Sōsho, op. cit.*, Vol., XI, p. 187 *et seq.*

119. Cf. *infra*, Appendix III, Chart I.

120. Cf. *Ibid*. A *gō* equals .318 pints. A *Zeni*, 錢, was a "cash" or copper coin.

121. For accounts of this famine and the accompanying riots, especially in the cities, cf. Takekoshi, *op. cit.*, Vol. III, p. 129 *et seq.*; Honjō, *Economic and social history, op. cit., p. 55 et seq.;* Murdoch, *op. cit.*, Vol. III, p. 398.

villages had been occurring not only in the north in Morioka and other districts, but also in Iyo in Shikoku.[122] Rebellious farmers in Izumo had not only been pardoned but sent relief; while in Fukuyama the officials, not the farmers, were to suffer as a result of their actions. Obvious it was that both the conditions in the country as well as unrest in the cities, necessitated a drastic change in policy on the part of the central government. This was to be attempted by Matsudaira Sadanobu for the next few years, but little could be expected from mere superficial changes. The farmers still remained the chief productive class in Japanese society, the *Bakufu* and *daimyo* still insisted on heavy taxes. Thus in spite of the downfall of Tanuma and the recovery from the natural calamities of Temmei (1781–1787), the conflicts which continued between the producing-peasant class, on the one hand, and the consuming-governing-warrior class on the other, were only one more proof of the real weakness of the Tokugawa administration.

---

122. Cf. *infra*, Chapter VII.

CHAPTER V.

FURTHER UPRISINGS REVEAL THE REAL WEAKNESS OF THE CENTRAL GOVERNMENT—EARLY BAKUMATSU

A. Attempts at reform of Matsudaira Sadanobu.

The situation facing the new President of the Councillors, Matsudaira Sadanobu[1], in 1786, was far from encouraging. It is estimated that during the widespread famines just covered, the non-warrior population had decreased about a million and a quarter out of a total 25,000,000[2], that land sufficient to produce several million *koku* of rice had been abandoned after 1787[3], while a contemporary account reports:

> "The farmers have recently abandoned their fundamental occupation and have been searching for luxuries. Many of them have entrusted the cultivation of their crops to boys and girls, themselves enjoying amusements and wearing beautiful clothes. Even the small farmers neglect their farms and come to Edo to earn wages"[4]

Furthermore, in spite of various debasements of the currency during the past few decades, the Treasury of the Shogunate

---

1. The term "Bakumatsu", 幕末, used in the title of this chapter, literally means "the end of the *Bakufu*" and is a common expression among Japanese historians for the period beginning with the breakdown of the Tokugawa government, together with the repeated attempts of foreign nations, such as Russia under Laxman in 1792, to open Japan's closed ports. Professor Inobe, one of Japan's best authorities on this period, begins his study of the "Bakumatsu Period" with Matsudaira Sadanobu, 松平定信, (1758–1829). Cf. Inobe Shigeo, *Bakumatsushi no Kenkyū*, 1 Vol.; Tōkyō, 1935.

2. Cf. Murdoch, *Japan*, Vol. III, p. 399. Dropper, G., "The population of Japan in the Tokugawa Period", *T.A.S.J.*, Vol. XXII, Pt. 2, 1894, and Yanagisawa, *op. cit.*

3. Cf. Takizawa, *Penetration of Money, op. cit.*, p. 80.

4. Quoted from a report in 1787 in Honjō, E., *Nōmin Mondai, op. cit.*, p. 135.

was showing a regular deficit.[5] Thus a drastic reform was in order.

Tanuma, having had his son assigned a seat to the Junior Council in 1783, saw his hopes of continuing in office vanish when this same son was assassinated in 1784. He himself, being implicated in the death of the Shōgun Ieharu in 1786, was replaced by Matsudaira Sadanobu, who immediately stripped Tanuma and one of his associates of half their fiefs.[6] Luxuries were ordered restricted, and education was encouraged as a substitute. Instructions were issued in 1788 to the rich in the north to encourage the cultivation of waste land by taking in their service any farmers who contemplated leaving, while in Yonezawa, Uesugi Harunori had established a fund for the encouragement of agriculture which was used to promote the cultivation of land within his fief, and as a remittance to new farmers, those reclaiming old lands were to be free from taxation.[7] In 1790, all feudatories were ordered to store 100 *koku* for every 100,000 *koku* of fief, and in Edo rice store houses were established. All debts of the *hatamoto* (direct retainers of the *Bakufu*) dated prior to 1782 were to be cancelled and any acquired after 1785 were to be redeemed at 3 *ryō* per 100 bales of income regardless of the debt accumulated.[8] These reforms, destined to fall in 1793 when the Shōgun Ienari took direct control, had little effect upon the eventual solution of the problem of peasant uprisings, although their occurrences are recorded on an average of about only four a year until 1811.[9]

---

5. Cf. Takekoshi, *op. cit.*, Vol. II, p. 331, where figures show an average yearly deficit of 21,764 *koku* of rice and surplus of 43,124 *ryō* of gold for the period 1762–1771 and a surplus of 12,636 *koku* of rice but deficit of 40,665 *ryō* of gold for the period 1802–1811. Cf. also Vol. III p. 143 *et seq.* for various currency reforms and Sawada, *op. cit.*, especially p. 322 for a list of new coins. For a general study of coins cf. Munro, G. *Coins of Japan*, 1 Vol., Yokohama, 1904.

6. Murdoch, *op. cit.*, Vol. III, p. 403 *et seq.*

7. Honjō, E. *Economic and social history*, *op. cit.*, p. 248 *et seq.*

8. Cf. Murdoch, *op. cit.*, Vol. III, p. 406 and Takekoshi, *op. cit.*, Vol. III, p. 161 *et seq.* *Hatamoto*, 旗下.

9. Cf. Numazaki, *op. cit.*, Chart IV. Among several of these which I have been able to study, I have found them to be mostly small uprisings, twenty-two of which occur in the regional studies.

A group of disturbances, though not strictly those of peasants, were those of the fishermen. With the exception of trouble in 1769 in an island off the Province of Sanuki over fishing rights with a neighbouring fief, that in Zeze in Omi in 1781 arising from taxes doubled on the fishermen and generally increased on the farmers,[10] and that in Etchu in 1789 where the fief monopolized the sale of fish and two officials took full responsibility by committing suicide, the uprisings of fishermen centered around Fukuyama in Hokkaidō in the north.[11] As early as 1768 they had revolted against monopolization by the fief of purchasing and sending their salted fish to Ōsaka and Nagasaki. By 1790 the situation became more serious, the people having been agitated, perhaps, by a revolt of the Ainu in Hokkaidō the previous summer. The supply of fish, upon which the people were solely dependent, had become exceedingly scarce. This fact the fishermen blamed upon the contractors who had been hauling fish with nets and extracting oil from their catch. Consequently over 2,000 fishermen rose in revolt, demanding the prohibition of the use of the nets and their own exemption from taxation. Matsumae Michihiro, lord of Fukuyama, wanted to admonish the fishermen personally, but priests were prevailed upon to act as intermediaries. The demands of the fishermen were accepted so they quickly withdrew. The next month, after the usual examination by the authorities, seventeen of the fishermen were either imprisoned or "restricted in their movements and placed on parole".[12]

---

10. Cf. Kokushō, Iwao, "Gyomin Sōdō", *Keizai Ronso,* Vol. 26, No. 2, pp. 140–141.

Zeze, 膳所, in Ōmi, on the southern shore of Lake Biwa, was a fief of 60,000 *koku* of Honda Yasusada, 本多康匡, (1757–1781), who held the fief from 1771–1781. He was followed by Honda Yasutada, Cf. *infra* p. 108, note 19.

11. Fukuyama, 福山, not to be confused with that in Bingo, was called Matsumae, 松前, and the castle town of the family of that name. Lord of the castle in 1790 was Matsumae Michihiro, 松前道廣.

12. Cf. Kokushō, "Gyomin Sōdō", *op. cit.,* p. 141 and *Hokkaido Shi, op. cit.,* Vol. I, p. 303–305.

Machi Azuke, 町預, is a term meaning not only being restricted within the *machi,* but also implies being on parole.

An interesting example of another uprising from exorbitant taxes was to break out in one of the outlying fiefs of the lords of Takada Castle in Echigo. This *daimyō*, Sakakibara Masaatsu,[13] had a total fief of 150,000 *koku*, 83,000 *koku* of which was in the four domains in the two neighbouring provinces of Iwaki and Iwashiro. In the villages within the domain at Asakawa in Iwashiro,[14] taxes for villages of a 1000 *koku* of income included:

200 *kamme* (bronze coin) for expenses of every *ōshōya*.[15]
6 *ryo* 2 *bu* of gold for each horse abandoned by the peasants.
3 *ryo* 2 *bu* each two servants.
3 *ryo* 2 *bu* for the stipend of each scribe.
High prices of lodgings in the inns all of which was collected from the farmers.
Taxes on farmers' clothes.[16]

Repeated requests that inspection be made of the standing crop for taxation purposes having been ignored, the farmers appealed anew when the official of the fief was changed. This time, however, the *ōshōya* informed the farmers that they must not, under any circumstances, appeal during the year in which a new official had been installed. However, having had one of their popular festivals stopped and their villages endangered by packs of wild dogs, the peasants sent out the following circular on the 22nd of the 1st month, 1798:

> "As there will be a general discussion on the night of the 24th, each village is requested to send a *nanushi*, armed with a hoe and a hatchet. Any village not represented will be wiped out by fire."[17]

This acted as the signal for all the farmers to assemble and to begin their usual house-wrecking of residences of officials

---

13. Sakakibara Masaatsu, 榊原政敦, (1754–1810) was the son of Masanaga, 政永, (1717–1789) who gave up the fief at his death.
14. Asakawa, 淺川, in Iwashiro Province is to the east of Echigo.
15. *Ōshōya*, 大庄屋, was a village officer in charge of several *shōya* or *nanushi*, usually having ten villages under his jurisdiction.
16. Cf. *Asakawa Sōdō Kembun Roku, op. cit.*, p. 177.
17. *Ibid.*, p. 178.

and *sake* shops, so that it was not until the priests intervened and took their appeals to Asakawa, that they became tranquil.[18]

B. *A Series of Successful Uprisings After 1811.*

The next important period for the study of peasant uprisings is that following 1811, and the district that of Bungo, Kyūshū.[19] The account of the various uprisings in or near Bungo from the 12th month, 1811 to the 3rd month, 1812, is somewhat complicated,[20] shifting from one fief, then another. To avoid unnecessary detailed narration of proper names, the following report will concentrate upon the disturbances in Takeda in the 12th month, 1811; in Usuki in the same month; and in Nobeoka in Hyūga in the 1st month of 1812, the other uprisings being derivatives of these larger ones. The fief centering around Takeda[21] was divided into sixty-six groups or *kumi* for administrative purposes. Recently the domain had been under the control of an extremely severe supervisor, Yokoyama Jinnosuke,[22] so that when the people appealed for a decrease in taxes in the fall of 1811, they were doubled instead. Thus by the 11th month, over 2,000 men, armed with guns and swords, rose up in insurrection, started towards Takeda, and presented their demands. The village officials hastened to report this fact to Takeda, while the women and children fled to the temples for refuge.[23] Their demands included the following:

18. *Ibid.*, p. 180 *et seq.*
19. Bungo, it is interesting to note, is the birthplace of Professor Takeo Ono, one of the leading Japanese scholars on peasant uprisings.
20. The source material for these uprisings is entitled: *Tōmin Ryūsetsu*, written by someone living in a neighbouring fief during the the troubles, a person probably without any official position. It is printed in Ono, T.; *Tokugawa Jidai Hyakushō Ikki Sōdan*, 2 Vol.; Tōkyō, 1927; Vol. II, p. 8–14 and pp. 359–458.
21. Takeda, 竹田, also called Oka, 岡, was a *Bakufu* domain of 70,400 *koku*.
22. Yokoyama Jinnosuke, 横山甚助, is given the title of Sōbugyō, 總奉行, an officer in charge of the various offices and duties of the *Bugyō*, hence a supervisor.
23. *Tōmin Ryūsetsu*, *op. cit.*, p. 365 *et. seq.*

1. The suspension of monopolistic purchasing agencies for the various cereals, tobacco and other goods.
2. The suspension of monopolistic purchasing agencies for timber, firewood, charcoal.
3. The suspension of the salt shops; the special markets, for purchasing salt.
4. Posting the name of one of the elder ministers.
5. Yokoyama Jinnosuke [be turned over to them]. He was a man in charge of the finances as well as supervisor.[24]
6. The official in charge of the priests and the pages[25] [be turned over to them].
7. An accomplice of Yokoyama, who had profited by Yokoyama's misuse of his official capacities [be turned over to them].
8. There be exemption from additional taxation on newly opened land, there having been an increase since last year.
9. The suspension of [the construction of] the river dam: This was the new dam to bring water to Takeda by a shorter route and also for the use of newly opened lands. It had been reported that a special levy would be made of two men per *koku* of income for this work or a total of 140,000 men.
10. There be no collection of rice for the store-houses, as this new custom had been extremely severe.
11. The suspension of a special tax of 1 *shō* of rye, 5 *gō* of wheat, and 1 *tō* of rice per *koku* of crop for each person.
12. The suspension of the tax on grass and reeds.[26]

---

24. The text reads: "Kore wa jōchū no hitonari": 是は常廚之人也, I have been unable to find the term *jōchū*, 常廚. However, *Chū*, 廚, is a common term for kitchen, read *Kuriya*. As the term *daidokoro*, 臺所, synonymous with *Kuriya* is often used during this period as meaning "finances", I have translated it as above.

25. The priests, *bōzu*, 坊主, and *chūkōshō*, 中小姓, a special class of pages of the castle.

26. *Tōmin Ryūsetsu*, *op. cit.*, p. 368–369.

To appease the crowd, the leaders of the fief passed new laws and forbade the purchase of goods at special markets as mentioned by the farmers. However, as a result of the circulation of the above articles of complaint, a group of 6,000 in another district wrecked a considerable number of places and presented their demands which were similar to the above with the following additions:

1. The suspension of the office of "Heads of the Shōya,"[27] as in sixty-six groups there already existed sixty-six *ōshōya* and three or four *koshōya* for every group and one *ōshōya* and one *koshōya* were sufficient.[28]
2. The reduction in number of other less important officials such as the village censors, and the head of the storekeepers,[29] of which there should be only one instead of two or three in each village.
3. The suspension of the collection of the bean taxes in summer and that they be collected in the ninth month. One *koku* 4 *tō* of beans had been collected as being equivalent to one *koku* of rice but as the Takeda beans were of a superior quality, they should be equal in price to rice.
4. The suspension of having to make up for the shrinkage in beans; exemption from payment of a special New Year's tax, taxes on water-wheels, blacksmiths, and dyers.
5. The suspension of a sales-tax of 1 *bu* per cow and 2 *bu* per horse.[30]

This mob, to make their demands more effective, wrecked the place of one of the village censors against whom they were complaining. In spite of threats of being fired upon, they entered Takeda. "Thus there remained no other course for

---

27. *Shōya tōdori*, 庄屋頭取.
28. Koshōya, 小庄屋, as the name implies, were under the the *Ōshōya*, and consequently in charge of either one or only a few villages.
29. The village censors or police were the *mura yokome*, 村横目, and the "heads of the store-keepers", the *Kurakata Kumigashira*, 藏方組頭.
30. *Tōmin Ryūsetsu*, *op. cit.*, p. 374–375.

the Elder Minister, who had received their requests, than to commit suicide, but the farmers seeing that he had made all preparation for such an eventuality, bowed respectfully before him and retired."[31]

An announcement was made by the Elder Minister to the following effect:

1. It is our intention to suspend the new laws concerning the establishment of market places [which have led to a monopolization] as stated by the villagers.
2. A representative has been sent to Edo to inquire concerning the reform of the laws.
3. As the expenses of the fief have increased, and after having inspected the losses recently sustained, you shall diligently collect the agricultural taxes.[32]

One representative from each of the various village officials was then summoned by the authorities and they were told that a loan would be made for those in distress.

The uprising in Takeda finally ended in the 3rd month of the next year when the group leaders were branded, whipped and banished, while several scores of others were imprisoned. From among the domain officials, Yokoyama, the supervisor, was made a commoner and imprisoned in Takeda, while his wife was banished from Edo. Other officials, including the Elder Minister who was ordered confined indoors, were punished, so many of the farmers' demands were finally met.[33]

In the 12th month, the farmers in Usuki,[34] "shamelessly

31. *Ibid*, p. 382. Suicide is considered an honorable death by the Japanese, and in this particular case the Elder Minister was ready to show his responsibility for the disorder among the peasants and also clear his own name from any shame by committing suicide. Cf. *infra* p. 97 note 110 and p. 174.

32. *Tomin Ryūsetsu, op. cit.*, p. 382–383. Although this last item was not favourable to the farmers a reason was given for necessity of collecting the taxes.

33. *Ibid*, p. 436–437.

34. Usuki, 臼杵, a realm of 56,000 *koku*, that of Inaba Chikamichi, 稻葉雍通, (b. 1774) who inherited the fief in 1792. Chikamichi was a

taking advantage of the victory of the Takeda farmers rose up, lit fires, burnt shops, robbed graves, and exposed corpses".[35] Some ten thousand of them, giving as their reason for insurrection their dislike of the officials and the rich whom they believed to be the cause of their hardships, refused to listen to official admonitions. Finally the Elder Minister of the Usuki domain appeared with 150 followers, having made his preparation to commit sucide. Seeing that they would be responsible for his death if they continued their lawlessness, the peasants then presented their demands of forty articles. Although these were similar in many respects to those made at Takeda, they included the following interesting items:

1. The abolition of a head tax of one *zeni* per day for forty years levied on every male and female.
2. The abolition of the sale of local products at special prices at government controlled market places.
3. The abolition of guards at all passes.
4. The abolition of the establishment of wholesale houses (*tonya*) in Usuki and the tax on purchase and sale of all goods.
5. The abolition of the selling of all types of manufactured paper at the newly established government controlled paper-market places.[36]

The people became tranquil when they received a written pledge from the Elder Minister that the new laws would be suspended, although some 5,000 revolted in another group at the same time in opposition to the head-tax. The punishments in Ushiku included the imprisonment of several score of the people, as well as the order that the officer in charge of the group which had caused the trouble be decapitated and his head exposed.[37]

---

descendant of Inaba Sadamichi, 稻葉貞通, (1551–1606). who had been transferred to Usuki in 1600. The fief was divided for administrative purposes, into fifty-three groups (*Kumi*) over each of which a *shōya* and *benshi*, 辨指, had control.

35. Cf. *Tōmin Ryūsetsu, op. cit.*, p. 388.
36. *Ibid*, p. 390 *et seq.*
37. *Ibid*, p. 436. This officer was a *benshi.*

The next and last important uprising near Bungo was that within the Naitō fief at Nobeoka.[38] Here disorder ruled from the 2nd to the 6th of the 1st month, 1812, while 67,000 farmers wrecked officials' homes and presented their demands, essentially the same as those already mentioned. Among their special demands were that the wages might be paid directly to labourers and that a rebate be allowed on the interest on borrowed money. They further asked to see the register books of the district, of the groups and the books of the village expenses. They asked that the use of palanquins be abolished for all those below the office of *daikan* and that 50 *kamme* of silver be loaned each person in the district. Although ten of the leaders of this group were sentenced to imprisonment, there appears to have been some delay in carrying out the sentence.[39]

Arising directly from these three larger disturbances, were ten others in the same general part of the country. These were of a much smaller nature and were more easily tranquilized, some of them getting no further than a proposal to make an appeal. Punishments were none the less severe; in one locality fifty-eight people were whipped twenty to fifty lashes; in others, there were death sentences for at least fifteen people, together with imprisonment, banishment, branding, and one peculiar case, a family was forced into the class of the outcasts.[40]

The Bungo uprisings, from an examination of the various

---

38. The Nobeoka, 延岡, domain in Hyūga, was 70,000 *koku* and had been that of the Naitō family since 1747, when they had been transferred there from Iwaki Daira in mutsu. Naitō Masayori, 内藤政順, son of Masatsugu, 政韶 (1773–1802), inherited the fief in 1806. He held it until his death in 1834. Thus he, *not* Masanobu, 政修, (b. 1751—retired from head of fief in 1790), was head of the fief at the time of this uprising and also in 1813, as mistakenly given in *Dokushi Biyō* 1 Vol.; Tōkyō; 1932, p. 494. Cf. *Denki Dainihon Shi, Daimyō Hen, op. cit.*, p. 457–458.

39. Cf. *Tōmin Ryūsetsu, op. cit.*, p. 397–402 & p. 437.

40. *Ibid*, pp. 403–433, and pp. 450–453. For an interesting treatment of the "outcasts" cf: Ninomiya, S., "An inquiry concerning the Origin, Development and Present Situation of the Eta in Japan", *T.A.S.J.*; Vol. X, 1933.

demands made by the farmers, show the precarious situation of the various fiefs concerned if it were necessary to levy so many special taxes on everything from the population itself to water-wheels. In spite of penalties and punishments, the people were successful on the whole in challenging the right of the authorities to continue to tax and oppress them. They show that the farmers were finally successfully revolting against carrying the entire burden of support of the contemporary social structure.

Turning to the north to the Province of Etchū, one of the three vast domains of the Maeda family,[41] an uprising broke out in 1813. Having found it difficult in the past to obtain sufficient irrigation water for their fields, the farmers had been forced to supplement their income by selling tea, wine, tobacco and sandals to travelers. In 1800 an order for the opening of new lands was promulgated and plans were made for the carrying of water across the mountain. The expenses for this project were to come from an additional levy of 10,000 bales of salt to be collected by the farmers and sold in the neighbouring province of Hida. The pressure to open new lands continued throughout the years until 1807 when everyone was commanded to plant wax trees as it had been reported they were profitable in the west. This order was again repeated in 1813, trees being transplanted and new fields opened. Finally the peasants rose against this, attacking those in charge of the opening of the new lands or the officers who examined the

41. The Maeda family, 前田氏, was one of the strongest of the "outside *daimyo*". In 1615 Maeda Toshinaga, 前田利長, (1562–1614), built a castle at Kanazawa in Kaga and his revenue amounted to 1,250,000 *koku*. His descendants continued to hold large fiefs in Kaga, Noto and Etchū. Lord of the Castle of Toyama, 富山, with 100,000 *koku* in Etchū, was Maeda Toshitsune, 前田利幹, successor to Toshinori, 利謙, (b. 1767) Toshitsune was called Awaji no Kami and held the fief until 1835. A word here in reference to the pronunciation of Japanese given names is in order. It is difficult to give their exact readings unless the family genealogy gives the pronunciation. Toshitsune, above, is a case in point. In the Japanese Historical Dictionary it is given as Toshitsune, in *Denki Dainihon Shi* as Toshitsugo. Cf. *Kokushi Daijiten*, Vol. IV, p. 2207 and *Denki Dainihon Shi, Daimyō Hen*, p. 503. I have followed that of the Historical Dictionary wherever possible.

wax-tree lands for taxation purposes. The people's demands that their taxes be paid in unhulled rice and that there be a suspension of opening new fields were finally granted in spite of the uprising having been unusually destructive.[42] Two years later it was announced that the three of the leaders "of the disturbances in 1813, having caused a rebellion, have been sentenced to death in accord with the preservation of governmental authority. However, in connection with the Buddhist memorial service of the late lord of Toyama, their death sentence has been pardoned and they are sentenced to life imprisonment; while nine men are to be banished".[43]

Passing over several years, there occurred in Miyazu, in the Province of Tango;[44] an uprising in 1822 of extreme interest. In this domain of Honjō Muneakira,[45] the wealthy merchants and rich farmers realized that the only way for them to receive back loans they had made to the *daimyō* would be to encourage drastic action on the part of the Elder Ministers and *Kōri bugyō*. Thus they persuaded the officials not only to levy a head tax of 2 *mon* per day on all between the ages of seven and seventy;[46] but also to order the collection of taxes two years in advance, the farmers already having recently paid 15,000 bales of rice in advance taxes. As unusual phenomena

---

42. Cf. *Etchū Shiryō,* 4 Vol.; Toyama, 1918 especially Vol. III, p. 324 *et seq.*

43. *Ibid.,* p. 338 & 339.

44. Miyazu, 宮津.

45. Honjō Muneakira, 本庄宗發, was a direct descendant of Honjō Munesuke, 本庄宗資, (1629–1699), who was the brother of the mother of the Shōgun Tsunayoshi. Munesuke was given a domain of 50,000 *koku* in Hitachi in 1692 by the Shōgun and his descendants, after various moves, finally came to Miyazu in 1758 with a domain of 70,000 *koku.* In 1705 the family had been permitted to use the name of Matsudaira.

46. Cf. *Ukiyo no Arisama,* 6 Vol., in *Kokushi Sōsho,* Vol. 37–42, especially Vol. I p. 31 *et seq.* This work, probably that of an Ōsaka physician, records the various calamities, local happenings and affairs from 1806–1840. As the author states in his preface: "He has been recording events for the benefit of his family and by reading it they could tell the good and bad conditions of the world at that time." Another text, *Tango no Hyakushō Ikki* in Ono, *Ikki Sōdan, op. cit.,* Vol. II, p. 27, gives the head tax as 3 *mon,* 文, (a farthing or cheap coin).

were seen in three places on the 13th of the 12th month, the farmers believed these to be signals for them to actively resist the extraordinary demands made upon them. Realizing that their plight was the result of the policy of the wealthy merchants, and not that of their lord, a mob of 70,000 rose against them.[47] Armed with spades, hoes, bamboo spears and throwing stones and snow balls, fighting with the guards at the south gate where several were wounded on both sides, they forced their way into Miyazu and on towards the establishment of one of the richest merchants.[48] Destroying the tea shops and rice store houses as they went, throwing everything including blankets, mattressess, refined and unrefined wine into the river, they finally reached the cloth merchant, only to find that he had anticipated their approach and had hidden his record-book, silks and cloth at the ancestral temple. The farmers, after distributing what gold and silver they could find, advanced on the temple, there demanding of the priests the hidden goods.[49] These, worth over 1500 *ryō*, they gladly burnt, pushing on to the houses of three other wealthy men where they again built fires of the goods: 120 bolts of silk damask, silk crepe, silk fabric and blankets. Dispensing with their pine torches, they used silk or the record-books[50] on the end of their poles for lights.[51] Finally an old man, Kurihara Umon, promised to appeal for the farmers if they would remain peaceful. The demands they forthwith presented were: 1. All advance taxes cease; 2. the bad officials of the fief, i.e. the elders, *daikan* and *Kōri bugyō* who had been accomplices with the wealthy merchants, be turned over to them, and 3. that no leaders of the uprising be accused of the crime of "having caused a re-

---

47. *Ukiyo no Arisama, op. cit.*, Vol. I, p. 32 *et seq.*
48. *Tango Ikki, op. cit.*, Vol. II, p. 34 *et seq.*
49. *Ibid*, p. 36 *et seq.*
50. These books would be an irretrievable loss for the merchants as they contained not only all outstanding accounts but lists of customers or names of any to whom they might have made loans. Witness to-day the care which all merchants take of their account books or *Go kayoi*, 御通.
51. *Ukiyo no Arisama op. cit.*, Vol. I, p. 33 and *Tango Ikki op. cit.*, Vol. II, p. 37–39.

bellion".[52] To these demands, the son of Kurihara, standing before the crowd, made the following answer:

> "I hereby appear before you in the place of my father. How is it that you thus defiantly appear in front of the castle in revolt? However, you shall be exempt from the head tax henceforth. Secondly, you shall receive recompense for the 15,000 bales of rice you have paid in advance taxes. As for not blaming the seven men recently arrested as leaders, you must first return peacefully to your homes".[53]

Thus was the disturbance settled within five days, although the garrison placed large cannon before the castle gate when rumors circulated that there was to be another petition.

Two of the leaders preferring death to betraying their fellow-farmers, refused to confess in spite of tortures. Following their death the evils of the government of the fief were removed and it is reported the officials were changed.[54] Conflicting rumors developed concerning Kurihara and his son. Both were probably arrested not only for having acted as the representatives of the farmers, but also because of accusations made against them by a revengeful prisoner. Young Kurihara is reported to have escaped, and attempted an appeal in Edo on behalf of his father, but to have had to hide in a temple enroute. There, after having given his appeal to the head abbott, he committed sucide rather than be caught by his followers; the abbott then had his request taken to Edo.[55]

Although not so drastic in the treatment rendered the intermediaries, the uprising in the Province of Kii, in 1823, in the domain of Tokugawa Harutaka,[56] was surprising not only

---

52. *Ukiyo no Arisama, op. cit.,* Vol. I, p. 37.
53. *Tango Ikki, op. cit.,* Vol., II, p. 43.
54. *Ibid,* p. 62 *et seq.*
55. *Ukiyo no Arisama, op. cit.,* Vol. I. p. 40. This same rumor is verified in *Tango Ikki, op.cit.,* Vol. II, p. 90. The same text also states that the farmer was forgiven eighteen years later when the fief changed to Munehide,宗秀, who took him to Edo. Cf. *op. cit.,* 82 *et seq.*
56. Tokugawa Harutaka, 德川治寶, (1771–1853) was lord of the Kii domain with its castle at Wakayama, 和歌山. He received the fief in 1789

for its size and destructiveness, but also for its success This was the first time for the peasants to rebel within the realm of the Kii branch of the Tokugawa family, as the direct result of a severe draught, water disputes, and maladministration of the officials of the domain, all of which was unknown to Harutaka in Edo. Plotting with two of their fellow officials, two of the *bugyō* decided to store goods for their own profit. Rice exchanges were established throughout the realm, the price of *sake* was forced up, the importation of rice from outside was prohibited, and tickets were required on all rice bags, *sake* tubs and similar articles to prove that they had not come from the neighbouring domain of Kōyasan. Added to this, the taxation of the land was increased, while taxes were ordered collected not only on new lands, but also on all waste land.[57] To these basic causes were added climatic conditions making an uprising inevitable. Although heavy rains had fallen in the 4th month, thereafter there had been nothing but drought so the people were unable to plant the rice, and by the 5th month the trouble began. Twenty-two thousand farmers would have destroyed a temple towards the end of the month had they not been repulsed by troops of the fief. On the 4th of the 6th month, a group who are reported to have been accompanied by 150 *rōnin* and robbers, tampered with the dams, attacked the local prison and captured the warden, causing the outcasts also to become agitated.[58] It was not until the 8th of the 6th month that the uprising was to reach its height. Affecting the farmers of the three districts, reaching to those living on the border of the province and causing them to cross the Kōyasan domain to accompany the others on their march towards

---

and held it until 1824. He was the direct descendant of Tokugawa Yorinobu, 德川頼宣, (1602–1671), 8th son of Ieyasu and founder of the Kii branch of the Tokugawa Family. It was from this branch that the 8th Shōgun, Yoshimune, (1677–1751) was chosen. Harutaka, son of Harusada, 治貞, (d. 1789) was a descendant of Yoshimune of the 5th generation.

57. Cf. *Wakayama Kenshi*, 2 Vol., 1924, especially Vol. I., p. 246 *et seq*. For further references Cf. *Kishū Ikki Oboegaki*, an account of the uprising by officials of the realm in *Shiseki Shūran*, Vol. 16, pp. 457–459; also *Ukiyo no Arisama*, *op. cit.*, Vol. I, p. 50 *et seq*.

58. *Ukiyono Arisama*, *op. op. cit.*, Vol. I, p. 55.

Wakayama, and finally reaching a total number of over 100, 000,[59] they divided into three parties, destroying the *sake* and rice shops, pawn shops, and places of the *shōya* and men in charge of the rice exchanges.[60] Refusing to surrender to 300 soldiers sent against them on the 11th, a blockade guarded by 1,000 outcasts, armed with bamboo spears and fire hooks, guns and cannon, and under the command of the *Machi bugyō* and *Kanjō bugyō*, was sent against them. On the same evening their demands of the following seven articles were received by the authorities:

1. The fixed taxes be as during the time of Tokugawa Yorinobu [first lord of Kii in 1619].
2. The tax on wet lands [rice lands] be similar to that on dry lands.
3. There be exemption from opening up old waste land
4. There be omission of *maikuchi*.[61]
5. The storing of goods for profit cease.[62]
6. There be exemption from the repairs of water ditches for irrigation and drainage,[63] and the cutting of the boundary [line].
7. Inspection be made of the standing crop [to assure a fair tax].

On the following day, a written document was presented to the farmers promising them acceptance of all their demands save the fourth and sixth. To further relieve the situation,

---

59. *Wakayama Kenshi, op. cit.*, Vol. I, p. 248.

60. *Ibid*, p. 248. Figures as to the exact number of the farmers differ. The same text gives the number at 130,000; while the *Kishū Ikki Oboegaki* states on p. 457 that there were 120,000 and *Ukiyo no Arisama* gives 70,000. Cf. Vol. I, p. 53.

61. The meaning of this phrase is not clear. The text reads: 米口御明け被下候様. *Maikuchi goake kudasare sōrōyo.* It is possible that *maikuchi*, 米口, was mistakenly written for *kuchimai*, 口米, one of the many additional taxes levied on the farmers to cover the expenses of the officials. Cf. *Wakayama Kenshi, op. cit.*, p. 249.

62. Those in charge of "storing goods" were called *Goshiire yaku*, 御仕入役.

63. The text gives *bunsui*, 分水, "a water shed" or more likely used for *hōsui*, 放水, "to drain or cause water to flow away". *Ibid* p. 249.

rice was permitted into the domain from outside in the near future.[64] In comparison to the fact that they had destroyed one village completely, that eighty houses of the rich farmers had been demolished, and that their aggregate number was unprecedented,[65] the punishments were surprisingly light. One of the ten leaders captured was ordered decapitated while others were banished.[66] Thus once more the farmers had collectively been able to correct the maladministration of the domain in which they lived and worked. This time, however, they were accompanied by another dissatisfied class, the *rōnin*, while the outcasts also became agitated. Signs were adequate for those in authority, if they were able to read them, that greater and more devastating troubles would ensue.

Continued disturbances on such a large scale as those reported in Kii caused contemplative writers to lament:

> "The habit of people leaving the true way of their ancestors and in the name of religion begging for food and money from house to house..... is very regrettable. Uprisings have sprouted up all over the country like bamboo, occurring, up to the 7th month of 1823, in Tango, Kii, Yamato, Ise, Bitchū and Iyo. Even the people became agitated and many were killed.... A hail storm is reported in Chikugo and the wind in Edo was strong enough to make stones fly and to breakdown houses. Thus the world yearly becomes more agitated".[67]

The following year there is recorded a most unusual incident. It appears that in Shimo Niigawa District in Etchū,[68] at the time of Shinran Shōnin,[69] an old woman had received three dried persimmons as a gift from him and had planted

---

64. *Ibid* p. 250.
65. Cf. *Ukiyo no Arisama, op. cit.*, Vol. I, p. 62 and *Wakayama Kenshi, op. cit.*, Vol. I, p. 248. Because of the violent nature of the uprising it is called "Kobuchi Sodo" in Kii, a local pronunciation of *Kobotsu*, 毀, "to wreck".
66. *Wakayama Kenshi, op. cit.*, Vol. I, p. 250.
67. *Ukiyo no Arisama, op. cit.*, Vol. II, p. 83 & 84.
68. Shimo Niigawa, 下新河.
69. Shinran, 親鸞, (1174–1263), was a famous Buddhist priest and founder of the Jōdo-shin-shū sect of Japanese Buddhism.

them in front of her house. As the seeds grew into flourishing trees, a certain man built his house near them for the worshippers who came there, and claimed them as his property. Likewise, the temple of Tokuhō claimed that Shinran had given them the seeds and threatened to move them to their property. At word of this, the two hundred families who were members of the temple split into two oposing parties and caused continual disorder. The whole affair was finally settled by order of the *Kōri bugyō* in 1824 who declared that three men who were leaders of the trouble, were to be punished, along with one representative of the farmers. The man who built his house near the trees, apparently to profit from the pilgrims who came there to worship, was punished and the trees were taken up; only to be planted again and presented to all the people. No special blame was attached to the temple for having claimed the trees as their property.[70]

Prior to reference to another uprising centering around a Buddhist temple, this time that of Higashi Hongwanji in Kyōto, notice should be taken of uprisings starting near Mitajiri, in Suwō, in the domain of Mōri Narimoto.[71] This particular region was famous for its paper so it was natural that the officials of the fief attempted to monopolize the purchase and sale of these products. Extravagance developed throughout the fief among many who had become wealthy from this industry at the expense and hardship of the people. After the establishment of exchanges for all local products in 1831, everything was bought at extremely low prices and shipped to Ōsaka where these products sold at a huge profit for those concerned. Moreover the farmers had been further oppressed by heavy taxes, the establishment of lotteries and gambling even among the outcasts. However, everyone believe that thanks to the good auspices of the Shrine at Ise, the crop had been unusually good so the officials decided to pray for a poor

70. Cf. *Etchū Shiryō, op. cit.*, Vol. III, pp. 387–392.

71. Mori Narimoto, 毛利斉元, (1795–1836), became heir to the fief in 1824. Mitajiri, 三田尻, was in Suwō. For the following incident Cf. *Ukiyo no Arisama, op. cit.*, Vol. II, p. 293 *et seq.*

harvest in order that they might profit from any consequent increase in price of rice that might ensue. Planning to enrage the dragon-god so that he would cause heavy winds and storms and thus destroy the crops, the officials decided to defile him by painting snakes on matting and spreading hides over the roofs of his temple.[72]

Learning of these corrupt and selfish plans of the officials, the farmers became exceedingly angry in the summer of 1831, assembled at the signal of the huge drums being sounded at all the shrines and temples, and 30,000 strong they captured the officials and forced them to confess their proposed plans. They then wrote down the names of those who had charge of collecting the manufactured paper and rice, with the intention of wrecking their places. People in the towns fled before the mob and the wealthy protected themselves from violence by giving them food. The rioters, being questioned by one of the *bugyō*, retorted they would not retire until a written pledge had been given to them, promising the fulfilment of the following demands:

1. In spite of the pitiable condition [of the farmers] there had been officials who had prayed for poor crops. All rice markets should be abolished.
2. Likewise, the newly established exchanges for the purchase of all local products have resulted in everything being bought at low prices. As all agriculture has suffered greatly from this, they should be abolished.
3. Lotteries should be abolished.
4. The large markets which have been established should be prohibited.

---

72. This particular year corresponded with that of the *Okagemairi*, 御蔭参, or the special pilgrimage every sixty-one years to Ise to thank Amaterasu-Ō-Mikami for her guardianship over the people and their crops. Here the term *Okage* is used with a religious significance, derived from the original meaning of "shadow". In contemporary Japanese, *Okage sama de* means "Thanks to your shadow" or "thanks to you". For a special account of *Okagemairi* Cf. *Ukiyo no Arisama op. cit.*, Vol. I, p. 236 *et seq.* For an account of dragons, Cf. De Visser, M. W., *The Dragon in China & Japan*, Amsterdam, 1913; 242 pp.

5. Silver certificates have recently been issued. One hundred *kamme* of silver have been exchanged for one hundred sixty *kamme* of certificates, and we ask that they circulate on face value.[73]

In fact the uprising had been so devastating that travelers passing there on the way to Edo reported that no large buildings were left standing and it was necessary for them to look elsewhere for an inn. A bill collector from Ōsaka found it impossible to collect his money in either Suwō or the neighbouring province, while two peddlars of household utensils had to give up trying to sell their goods in that locality.[74] At the height of the disturbances, as many as 100,000 are reported as having taken part, a few of whom appear to have been killed. All the villages of the outcasts seem to have been destroyed and many of them killed by the mob. Finally, when they started towards Nagato, the neighbouring province, they were met by a *daikan* who quieted them by writing on a huge piece of paper which he posted in front of them, that he would act as their intermediary. A captain of a boat arriving in Ōsaka the end of the 8th month reported that the ministers of the fief were all deprived of their office. Three of the group who went to defile the dragon-god were arrested and sent to the castle, and the special exchanges for local products, lotteries and big markets were to be abolished, while the silver certificates should circulate at par. Thus all the demands of the farmers were met and no one is reported as having been punished.[75]

Just prior to another period of famine and bad crops, there developed an uprising in Owari, the result of the corruption of both the local officials and the manager of Higashi Hongwanji.[76] In 1832, the lord of Owari had been asked for

73. *Ukiyo no Arisama, op. cit.,* Vol. II, pp. 296–297.
74. *Ibid,* Vol. II, p. 300.
75. *Ibid, op. cit.,* Vol. II, pp. 299–301.
76. Owari, 尾張, was the third of the three main branches of the Tokugawa family, *Gosanke,* 御三家, Kii and Mito the other two, already having been mentioned. It was the descendants of Tokugawa Yoshinao, 徳川義直, 7th son of Ieyasu, which formed the Owari branch and which

timber to rebuild the temple which had recently burned down. As the people of Owari had always been members of that temple, the farmers and hunters worked diligently cutting and transporting the desired timber to Edo where it was sold for their own profit. When pious Owari worshippers found no timber in Kyōto while there on a pilgrimage, they made further inquiries and the scandalous action of the officials leaked out. The farmers, therefore, demanded the manager of the temple be turned over to them, but learning of their intention to kill him, he fled. They further threatened to transfer their allegiance to Nishi Hongwanji, which incidentally had already sent priests to Owari to help fan the flames of rebellion against their rival temple.[77]

In contrast to the successful uprisings in Bungo, Etchu, Tango, Kii and Suwō, during this period, the threats and efforts of the farmers in Owari met with little success. The officials fled and the farmers alone remained to be arrested. However, when some materials fell and killed two of the workers during the construction of the gate of Higashi Hongwanji, the people were quick to blame it upon the evil ways of the priests.[78]

C. Natural Calamities and consequent Serious Troubles after 1833.

As a result of the excessive luxuries desired in the

received the fief of 550,000 *koku* in 1607. Its centre was that of Nagoya Castle, one of the few remaining perfect examples of Japanese feudal architecture. The lord of the Nagoya Castle, 名古屋, during this period was Tokugawa Nariharu, 德川齊温, (1819–1839) who received the fief in 1827. He was succeeded by Naritaka, 齊莊 (1809–1845), who held the fief until his death when it went to his adopted son, Yoshitsuku, 慶藏, (1836–1849). Higashi Hongwanji, 東本願寺, was originally built in 1602 by Ieyasu for the eldest son of the head abbott of the older Hongwanji, which brought about the division of the two temples into Nishi, 西, and Higashi, 東, Hongwanji. This huge temple in Kyōto was destroyed by fire several times, the last being in 1874. The old temple, Nishi Hongwanji, was the central temple of the Jōdō-Shin-Shū sect.

77. Cf. *Ukiyo no Arisama op. cit.*, Vol. II, p. 311 *et seq.* and p. 332.
78. *Ibid.*, Vol. II, p. 332.

Shogun's court, the additional demands made upon the *daimyō* for defensive measures to meet the encroachments of Russia, and the indifference and callousness of the rich merchantile class which was offending the aristocrats and warriors, a debt of over 500,000 *ryō* was accumulated between 1814–1836.[79] Debasement of the currency again became the order of the day, from which the Bakufu was able to make a profit of over 9,000,000 *ryō*, thus balancing their accounts. To this situation was added a series of interminable famines and bad harvest following 1832 so that it is not surprising to find a marked increase in uprisings.[80] This was to be the period in which highwaymen were to harrass the country while the clan and Shogun's authorities were afraid to interfere.[81] It was to witness special sheds being erected in Nagoya to provide gruel for the sick and homeless; though this was important in preventing many from dying so that up to the spring of 1837 there were 1500 corpses left unburied in the city.[82] And finally, it was to see the samurai taking cause with the plebian population and rising in open revolt in Ōsaka in 1837 against the high cost of living.[83]

Perhaps the best idea of the type of uprising from these pitiable conditions will be grasped through the study of the uprising in the province of Kai, beginning in Tsuru district, spreading to three other districts, with its focal point the city of Kōfu.[84] The province of Kai is unusually mountainous and

---

79. Takekoshi, *op. cit.*, Vol. III, p. 174.

80. Following the figures of Numazaki, fifty-five uprisings appear between 1813–1822; seventy-nine between 1823–1832; ninety-nine between 1833–1842. Cf. Numazaki, *op. cit.*, Chart IV.

81. Takekoshi, *op. sit.*, Vol. III, p. 175.

82. *Nagoyashi Shi*, Seiji Hen, 10 Vol.; Nagoya, 1915, especially Vol. I, p. 186.

83. Cf. *Infra* p. 94.

84. Kōfu, 甲府, in the province of Kai, belonged to the Shogun after 1824 and was governed by his representatives. Tsuru, 都留 is the easternmost district of the province. For references to this uprising, usually referred to as the "Gunnai Sōdō", 郡内騒動, Cf.: *Ukiyo no Arisama*, Vol. III, pp. 93–110, *Higashi Yamanashi Gunshi*, 1 Vol.;1916, 1088 pp., especially pp. 774 *et seq. Gunnai Sōdō* in Ono, *Ihki Sōdan*, *op. cit.*, Vol. II, pp. 280–355.

the meagre 18,000 *koku* which it produced was insufficient for its population who spent much of their time in weaving, exchanging these goods for rice from neighbouring provinces. However, in the year 1836, the price of rice become so high that they were forbidden to import it.[85] By the 8th month it was so scarce it was impossible to buy it so complaints were made to village officials to no avail. Finally four leaders were selected from among the farmers, and their representatives decided upon the following articles to which all jointly affixed their blood-seals.

> "Because of the scarcity of rice and grains, and being faced with hunger from which there is no escape, we have decided to go to Kōfu. There to throw away our lives if necessary. The following instructions are to be followed carefully."
>
> 1. Each person shall wear one sword.
> 2. Bed clothing and night clothes must be taken.
> 3. Care must be taken to provide oneself with a food basket as it will be asked for enroute.
> 4. Each village must have two groups each for carrying drums and bells.
> 5. Bring spears three feet long, large axes, ordinary axes and broad bladed axes.
> 6. Bring a flag for each village upon which shall be written its name.
> 7. At night there shall be a special guard, and there shall be no advancing during the night.
> 8. Do not cross bridges together in large numbers, crossing only so that [the number on the bridge at the same time] shall not break it.
> 9. At ferries cross as the boatman directs, and if he will not ferry you across, then grasp hands [and ford in that way].

---

85. In local silver currency it was 1 *momme* 5 *bu* for 3 trays, *bon*, 盆, whose measurement is uncertain. Other figures show a general price of rice at 155.7 *momme* per *koku* in 1836, and 250 *momme* in 1837. Cf. *infra*, Appendix III, Chart I.

10. As for the fees, pay as demanded by the boatman.
11. Do not comply to the admonitions of the officials.
12. Do not, under any circumstances, rob either gold or silver.
13. At all times be careful of fire.[86]

Thus having made their prepartions for departure, they set out on the 21st of the 8th month, 1836. From a group of 3–4,000 men who started in the morning, they radually increased to 10,000 by the time they reached Kōfu a few days later. House wreckings and the destruction of *sake* shops accompanied their march, and though officers from the villages which they approached sent out orders that the guards were to stop them, their advance continued. As their band increased in size, they seem to have been accompanied by outcasts, beggars and robbers. Their leader, however, demanded that these undesirables form their own group.[87] On the 23rd it was reported that insurrections were also occurring in the north and south of the province and by nightfall arrests had been begun, following the killing of some of the officials. This same day a special courier was sent to Suwa Tadamichi, lord of Takashima Castle in Shinano,[88] asking him to send troops to Kii to help suppress the rebellion. A vanguard of some 360 men was then dispatched from Takashima which seems to have come in direct conflict with the farmers, for casualties amounted to about 100 killed and 180 wounded who were taken prisoners.[89] Also on the 25th, the day of arrival in Kōfu of the troops from Takashima, it was reported that twenty-five of the leaders of the mob were arrested, three were

86. *Gunnai Sōdō, op. cit.*, Vol. II, pp. 294 *et seq.*

87. *Higashi Yamanashi Gunshi, op. cit.*, p. 775.

88. Suwa Tadamichi, 諏訪忠恕, (1800–1840), son of Tadakata, 忠粛, (d. 1822), received the fief in 1816 to hold it until his death. He is known for the aid he gave those in distress during the Tempō Famines (1830–1843).

89. Cf. *Gunnai Sōdō, op. cit.*, Vol. II, p. 321 *et seq.* For the interest in the type of persons sent on such an expedition, a detailed list follows: In the first division the officials included: *monogashira*, 物頭, superin-

killed and forty-five wounded. Aid was likewise asked from Mizuno, Dewa no Kami, Tadayoshi, lord of the Castle of Numazu,[90] but these troops, amounting to about 400 men, did not arrive until the 27th, remaining in Kōfu until the 6th of the 9th month when they returned, as everything was reported tranquil after the 25th.

Unfortunately the farmers were to pay heavily for their disorderly conduct, for at least 500 were arrested or "placed on parole."[91] However, from the announcement of punishment in the 5th month, 1838, it is apparent the officials were to suffer for their misgovernment. One of the three *daikan* was to be deprived of his offiice and confined to his home 30–50 days. Two others were dismissed from their positions and ordered to become *hatamoto* of low rank. A public censor and his assistant were deprived of office and their stipend, while four of the assistants of the *daikan* received a similar sentence.[92]

As for the leaders of the uprising; the *daikan* of Kuronoda Station, Tsuru District, in Kai, received the following order, dated the 7th day of the 5th month, 1839;

Concerning the farmer, Jiuemon, aged 64, of Shimowada

---

tendents, *Kōri bugyō, ōmetsuke,* 大目付, two doctors, *metsuke,* censors, 20 helpers, 70 *dōshin* 同心, or constables, 11 pack carriers, plus 200 footmen. In the second division were the same officials with 60 *dōshin,* 14 priests from shrines and 11 *shaban,* 社番, or shrine employees. Cf. *Ukiyo no Arisama,* Vol. III, p. 99.

90. Mizuno, Dewa no Kami, Tadayoshi, 水野出羽守忠義, inherited the fief in 1834.

91. Cf. *Gunnai Sodo, op. cit.,* Vol. II, pp. 323 *et seq.* In *Ukiyo no Arisama* it is reported there were arrests of 2–300 men. Cf. *Ukiyo no Arisama op. cit.,* Vol. III, p. 108.

"Placed on parole" is *mura azuke,* 村預. The accused was allowed to go free within his own village but must report at fixed times to the authorities.

92. Cf. *Gunnai Sōdō, op. cit.,* Vol. II. pp. 33 *et seq.*

The text contains many technical terms. "To be deprived of office" is usually given as *Goyaku gomen,* 御役御免. "Confined to his home 30–50 days" is *hissoku,* 逼塞. An official paper seal closed the gates to the house of the warrior or priest so confined and a notice forbade "going in or coming out." which was carried on at night through the small door in the gate.

Village in Tsuru District, and a hostel official, Hyonosuke, aged 41, of Inume:

> Whereas these individuals were leaders in the uprising in Kai over the question of the difficulty of purchase of rice in Tsuru District, and having wrecked the cereal stores in Tanimura and elswhere . . . . and having threatened to burn down an official's residence if he did not open his gate, and causing the various villages in the three districts of Yamanashi, Yatsushiro, and Koma to become rebellious . . . .and being the leaders during the march and carrying banners: they shall be crucified.[93]

A similar death sentence awaited a *nanushi* of a nearby village as well as a non-resident who had been arrested seven years previously for gambling and who took part in the uprising. Two *rōnin* were to be imprisoned for having given the farmers food and for being found carrying swords. Similar instructions announced that six *nanushi,* and one representative of the farmers (*hyakushōdai*) were to be banished from their village because of either having fled, acted as guides, or having provided horses and food for the farmers.[94] About twenty-five peasants and *nanushi* died in prison, and a homeless man, because of his refusal to be arrested and his disregard for the authorities by drawing his sword against them, was to be killed.

For their part in giving *sake* to the farmers, and thus helping to increase their disorderly conduct, 5 *nanushi,* 2 representatives of the farmers (*hyakushōdai*), 6 elders of the village, (*toshiyori*), 2 farmers and twenty others were fined 5 kamme cach.[95] And finally, among the 481 villages of the domain, there was a fine of 4,883 *kamme* imposed. *Nanushi* of 476 villages were fined 3 *kamme* each, while 40 *machi* or blocks in Kōfu were fined 350 *kamme.*[96] Thus with the ex-

---

93. *Ibid,* p. 343.
94. *Ibid,* p. 347 *et seq.*
95. *Ibid,* p. 351 *et seq.*
96. *Higashi Yamanashi Guṇshi, op. cit.,* p. 777.

ception of the dismissal of some of the officials, the farmers of Kai only increased their hardships by revolting.

The later years of the rule of the Shogun Ienari are well known for their famines and hardships to the people on the one hand, and the consequent revolt in Ōsaka in 1837, on the other. It should be noted, that previous to this, the *Bakufu* had arrested over 213 rice merchants who had been dishonest, forbidding at the same time the spreading of false rumors, and restricting the manufacture of *sake* to one-third the usual production, while rice was to be sold under government regulations, in small district shops.[97] Uprisings had been occurring in the central part of Japan, and in the 1st month of 1837, the people burnt the castle of Kokura in Buzen,[98] in opposition to an unusually corrupt government and increased discomforts due to the circulation of silver certificates in the place of coins.

The Ōsaka *emeute*, taking place in 1837, was planned and instigated by Ōshio Heihachirō, (1792–1837) an ex-police inspector, who found the corruption of the Ōsaka officials intolerable and the price of rice unreasonable. He planned the destruction of those whom he considered to be responsible, and the distribution of the money of the wealthy to the poor. His revolt was to fail, not because of a lack of courage on the part of its leader, but through the treachery of one of his followers. Realizing their cause was lost, they began destruction of the city by fire, but their forces were finally overcome and Ōshio committed sucide. Although this was

---

97. Cf. Honjō, *Tokugawa Beika Chōsetsu, op cit.*, p. 393.

98. Cf. *Ukiyo no Arisama, op. cit.*, Vol. III, p. 112. Uprisings in Ōmi, Yamashiro, Settsu and within three different fiefs in Mikawa have been studied of the twenty-three recorded by Numazaki for 1836. He also mentions nineteen in 1837. Cf. *Ukiyo no Arisama, op. cit.*, Vol. III, p. 10; *Nagoya Shishi, op. cit.*, Vol I, p. 187, 574 *et seq.* Also Numazaki, *op. cit.*, Chart III.

not an uprising of the farmers, *per se*, nevertheless it definitely affected several others.[99]

When news reached the surrounding neighbourhood of Ōshio's attempts to overcome corruption in Ōsaka, five hundred farmers of Kawachi, led by their village officials, decided to join him. However, due to failure in their preparations, many were captured, five imprisoned and one hundred and fifty handcuffed. Another group of eight hundred started towards the castle of Hiroshima under the banner of Ōshio, but more than two hundred of them were arrested.[100] In the Province of Settsu, eight *rōnin* met together and sent five of their group to the village office and asked for aid for the people, but were only threatened with death. Thus collecting a group of 1400 farmers who objected to the existing evils in the government, they threatened to kill the wealthy people if they did not give them money, making the following complaint:

> "With both the high price of rice and the prevalence of epidemics, there have been many who have died. Since spring twenty out of every hundred have died of starvation and this fall during the last ninety days, half of the people have died. We ask that just government be applied towards us".

They were however, finally tranquilized by troops sent from Ōsaka under the command of the *Machi Bugyō*.[101]

But the influence of Ōshio was to be felt in an even more remote region. In Echigo, under the leadership of a scholar

---

99. Cf. Murdoch, *Japan op. cit.*, Vol. III, pp. 453–456 and Takekoshi, *op. cit.*, Vol. III, p. 175 *et seq.* for accounts of this incident. Ōshio Heihachiro, 大鹽平八郎, greatly influenced by the philosophy of Wang Yangming (1472–1528) was attempting to put his philosophical theories into practice. Likewise in 1710, Arai Hakuseki, 新井白石, (1656–1725), prompted by Confucian ethics, advised the Shogun Ienobu to grant the demands of the farmers who had revolted in the fief of Matsudaira Terasada Murakami, Echigo no Kami. Cf. Knox, "Arai Hakuseki", *T.A.S.J*,, 1902, Vol. XX, pt. II, pp. 160–170.

100. Cf. *Ukiyo no Arisama, op. cit.*, Vol. III, pp. 171 & 225.

101. *Ibid,* Vol.III , pp. 349–352.

of Japanese literature, Ikeda Ban,[102] in the realm of Matsudaira, Etchu no Kami, Sadanaga, at Kashiwazaki,[103] eight hundred men, by far the majority of the townsmen and *rōnin*, rose in revolt against the high price of rice and its being shipped away from Echigo. Their banners said they wished to "strike down the robbers of the country" and that, "they were disciples of Ōshio". Their leader was killed, six of the insurgents were captured and killed and several were wounded.[104] Thus the authorities had successfully overcome the first general outbreak of a movement whose leaders were of another type than mere peasants.[105] That such a movement was prevented from spreading further at a time when distress was universal, was not so much the excellent vigilance of the authorities in control at that particular moment, as the fact that communications were so poor and the isolation of the peasants as a class so complete that it was difficult for them to rebel simultaneously with the townsmen or intellectual leaders.

---

102. Ikeda Ban, 池田番, (1801–1837) was a scholar and student of Japanese Literature, *Wagakusha*, 和學者, a disciple of the famous scholar, Hirata Atsutane, 平田篤胤, (1776–1843). After Ikeda's death, his wife and child were ordered killed, but to save the name of her husband's family, his wife first killed her child and then committed suicide. Cf. *Ukiyo no Arisama, op. cit.*, Vol. III, p. 226 and *Echigo Sado Nōmin Sōdō*, 1 Vol.; Niigata, 1930, 629 pp., especially p. 384 *et seq.* For Hirata Atsutane, Cf. Hammitzsch, h., "Hirata Atsutane", *Mitteilungen der Deutschen Gesellschaft fur Natur und Volkerkunde Ostasiens*, Band XXVIII, Teil E., Tōkyō, 1936.

103. This is probably Matsudaira Sadanaga, 松平定永, son of Matsudaira Sadanobu, who was transferred to Kuwana, in Ise in 1823. Unfortunately I have been unable to find his dates. The control of the fief at Kashiwazaki, 柏崎, in Echigo, shows the complicated nature of control of fiefs during the Tokugawa Period. It was natural that it be the fief of the Hisamatsu family, 久松氏, later called Matsudaira, when they moved to Takata in Echigo in 1710. However, in spite of their moving to Shirakawa in 1741 in Mutsu, then to Ise in 1823, Kashiwazaki still remained their fief, where a garrison was established.

104. Cf. *Ukiyo no Arisama, op. cit.*, Vol. III, p. 226.

105. In connection with these uprisings, Murdoch states: "There was a similar outbreak in Echigo and in the following year [1838] in Mikawa." It is obvious, however, that this is a conservative statement, although the uprising in Mikawa does not seem to have direct connection with the Ōshio affair. Cf. Murdoch, *op. cit.*, Vol. III p. 455.

With a whole leisure warrior class whose only duty was to suppress rebellion, any nation-wide revolution on the part of the peasantry, especially when jealousy existed between the fiefs, became practically impossible.[106]

In the following year, in 1838, there occurred in another of the Maeda realms an uprising which was the direct result of the financial policy of the Tokugawa *Bakufu*. As was usual in the case of a fire in either the Edo Castle or the Imperial Castle in Kyōto, the variouse *daimyo* were assessed a special levy following the fire in the Edo Castle in the 3rd month 1838. A general rate of 15,000 *ryō* per 100,000 *koku* brought the Maeda portion to 153,750 *ryō*.[107] At the same time, the people had been suffering from unusually cold weather so poor crops resulted. Enraged at their plight, the farmers smashed a theatre that had been constructed on a river bank. In the 8th month, the village officials asked for exemption from annual tax, only to be refused. The *Kaizaku bugyō*, or officer in charge of the re-assessment of land in case of bad crops,[108] then inspected the damaged area but returned with the report that the loss was only slight so the farmer's demands were refused. The village officers were then arrested, fifteen were imprisoned, of whom five died, the others being released the next year only to have their household effects confiscated.

---

106. Although not directly influenced by the riots in Ōsaka and the movement of Ōshio Heihachirō, uprisings continued. One of these, directly the result of poor finances was in the 51,000 *koku* fief of Wakizaka, Awaji no Kami, Yasutada, 脇坂淡路守, 安董, who served as *Jisha bugyō* from 1791 to 1804. He was lord of Tatsuno Castle in Harima, 龍野城, born in 1765. This is of interest because of the attempt to buy wheat with silver certificates, after which all the certificates circulating in his fief were ordered destroyed. Likewise, in the Province of Aki, an uprising broke out due to the use of silver certificates which were of questionable value. On this latter incident a version of the famous play *Chūshingura* or *Forty-Seven Rōnin* is based. Cf. *Ukiyo no Arisama, op. cit.*, Vol. III, pp. 18–19, and Vol. IV, p. 141 and 161.

107. The lord of Kanazawa, 金澤, since 1822 was Maeda Kaga no Kami, Nariyasu, 前田加賀守, 齊泰, son of Narihiro, 齊廣, (d. 1822). Nariyasu retired from his inheritance in 1866.

108. *Kaizaku bugyō*, 改作奉行. This was first established in 1651 at the time of Maeda Toshitsune, 前田利常, (1593–1658).

These however, were returned to them six years later.[109] That the assessment of the Shogun necessitated the full collection of the taxes in spite of a poor harvest accounts for the rather liberal treatment given the farmers as well as the fact that plans for relief were made and three relief outposts were established during the winter.

Thus during the period of famine and crop failures following 1833, from the city of Kōfu to Ōsaka, from the Province of Echigo to Aki, the townsmen and farmers both were revolting against an unbearable economic load, only to find little relief from appeals. It is useless to speculate as to how far-reaching the revolt in Ōsaka of 1837 might have become had not Ōshio been betrayed, but it is certain the end of feudalism and the Tokugawa regime was near. The central government and the officials of the local *daimyō* still maintained enough prestige and power to keep in control a few more years, but during the next period this power became even weaker as will become clear from the study of the peasants had in forcing the *Bakufu* itself to change its orders.[110]

---

109. Cf. *Ishikawa Kenshi,* 3 Vol., Kanazawa, 1928, especially Vol. II, p. 933 *et seq.*

110. The following reference to an uprising in Karatsu, Hizen, is of interest: The father of the lord of Karatsu who visited Deshima in 1842, is reported to have committed suicide following an uprising in his domain in 1839. By his suicide, "his honour has been saved, for he would have been punished, if not by execution, by dismissal or banishment". Cf. De Wolff, A. J. J., *Herinneringen uit Japan*; 1 Vol.; Brussels, 1890, edited by L. J. E. F. Von Ende, a resident of Deshima from 1840--1842. The uprising is mentioned in Japanese works in *Ukiyo no Arisama,* Vol. IV. pp. 298, 337, and 349.

CHAPTER VI.

BREAKDOWN OF CENTRALIZED FEUDAL CONTROL LATE BAKUMATSU

A. *An Uprising in Shōnai in 1840, forces the Bakufu to Change its Decision*

Practically all of the uprisings mentioned thus far have been those that were the result of some grievance: economic, financial or political, which had caused the farmers to rebel. However, a most unique uprising occurred in the fall of 1840 at which time the farmers supported their lord in opposition to the order from Edo for him to transfer his fief. Little has been said of the complicated transfers, the result of diverse causes, of the *daimyō* from one fief to another. To understand the reason for the particular order of transfer issued in 1840, it will be necessary to recall a few facts. In the first place, the finances of the *Bakufu* were decidedly unhealthy due to the extravagances of the Shōgun Ienari. Finally in 1837, he retired from office and was succeeded by his son, Ieyoshi, the twelfth Shōgun. Following this, Mizuno, Echizen no Kami, Tadakuni,[1] whose power had gradually been increasing, became even more influential and soon instigated economies and reforms. It was he who had levied the extra tax on Maeda Nariyasu and the other *daimyō* for the reconstruction of the burnt palace in Edo in 1837, only to withdraw it when he realized it was ineffective.

To carry out his proposed reform it was necessary for Mizuno to have strong allies among the powerful *daimyō*. Therefore among his friends was Matsudaira, Yamato no Kami,

---

1. Mizuno, Echizen no Kami, Tadakuni, 水野越前守, 忠邦, (1794–1851) was lord of Hamamatsu in Tōtōmi. He was appointed *Jisha bugyō*, (1817–1825) Kyōto *Shoshidai*, 所司代, from 1826–1828, and given the title of Echizen no Kami. In 1834 he was first appointed *Rōjū*, attempting the Tempō Reforms in 1841–1842. In 1843 he resigned from office only to be recalled in 1844. Cf. Murdoch, *op. cit.*, Vol. III, p. 443 *et seq.*

Naritsune,[2] lord of the castle of Kawagoe in Musashi Province. His fief was a large one of 150,000 *koku* but his expenses had greatly increased. He had adopted the fifty-third child of Ienari, Kigorō, in 1827 and by 1830 was forced to furnish him 13,000 *ryō* yearly for his expenses. Thus it came about that in 1840 it was planned that Matsudaira Naritsune should be moved to Shōnai with an increase in his fief of 20,000 *koku*. To carry this out, a guard was dispatched from Edo to Shōnai with the following message:

> On the first day of the 11th month, 1840, during the time of the Shogun Ieyoshi, Sakai Tadakata, Lord of the castle of Shōnai,[3] has been ordered to move to Nagoya in the Province of Echigo, a fief of 70,000 *koku* of Makino, Bizen no Kami, Tadamasa.[4] The lord of the Castle of Kawagoe, in Musashi Province, Matsudaira, Yamato no Kami, Naritsune, has been ordered to take over the castle at Shōnai with 150,000 *koku*.[5]

---

2. Matsudaira, Yamato no Kami, Naritsune, 松平大和守, 齊典, (1797–1850), had acquired the fief of Kawagoe, 川越, in 1816. He was the son of Naotsune, 直典, (d. 1810). The family had been moved to various fiefs since the days of Matsudaira Naomoto, 松平直基, (died 1648) who had received a fief of 150,000 *koku* in Himeji. There the family protected Edo from attacks or intrigues from the two powerful enemy houses of Mōri and Shimazu. They moved to Kawagoe in 1767. Naritsune was a man of unusual abilities and a scholar well acquainted with both Japanese and Chinese classics. He attempted reforms within his realm and held the Imperial Family in high esteem. Cf. *Denki Dai Nihonshi, Daimyō Hen,* Vol. III, p. 496.

3. Shōnai, 庄内, commonly called Tsurugaoka, 鶴ケ岡, was the fief of Sakai, Saemon, Tadakata, 酒井左エ門忠器. He retired from control of the fief in 1842 in favour of his son, Tadaoki, 忠發, who held it until 1861. It had first been given to Sakai Tadakatsu, 酒井忠勝, (1587–1662), in 1622, a domain of 140,000 *koku* covering two districts.

4. Makino, Bizen no Kami, Tadamasa, 牧野, 越前守, 忠雅, had received the fief of Nagaoka, 長岡, in 1832, a domain of 74,000 *koku* He was the son of Tadakiyo, 忠精, (1760–) who had received the fief while still a child. Tadakiyo was given the title of Bizen no Kami in 1775 and appointed a *Jisha bugyō* in 1787–1792, Kyōto *Shoshidai* in 1798, *Rōjū* from 1801–1816. Tadamasa held the following offices: *Jisha bugyō* 1836–1840, *Shoshidai* 1840–1843, *Rōjū* 1843–1857. He died in 1858. For further accounts of the Makino family and uprisings in their fiefs Cf. *infra* p. 136.

5. Cf. *Tempō Kaikyō Roku*, in Ono, *Hyakushō Ikki Sōdan, op. cit.*, Vol. I, p. 43.

In this way, Sakai Tadakata became involved in the movement of Matsudaira Naritsune to a new fief, to which the farmers in Shōnai immediately raised strenuous objections. As the Sakai family had held the fief for the past two hundred years, during the time of recent calamities, Sakai Tadakata had been unstinting in giving rations from his store houses to those in need. When the farmers of the two districts of Akumi and Tagawa[6] heard of this order, they could not bear the thought of separation from their lord. With one accord, they held services of devotion and purification in the various temples and shrines and prayed that their lord might remain forever in his present domain. In this, as well as in their meeting together to plan their course of action, they were greatly assisted by the abbott of Gyokuryū Temple, Bunrin.[7] When he heard of the order of 1840, he immediately planned, together with his brother and others, to stop it. Prayers were ordered in all the temples and he sent appeals to two temples in Edo and one in Nagoya to assist the farmers. Moreover the heads of the groups (*ōkumigashira*), heads of the villages (*shōya*), and the village chiefs (*kumoiri*), from five different places, as well as the doctors and priests all cooperated with the farmers in their attempt to stop the transfer of their lord.

---

6. Akumi,飽海, and Tagawa, 田川, districts.

7. Bunrin, 文隣, was born in the fief of Shōnai in 1799. He entered Honkyo Temple in 1821 where he became famous for his wisdom. During his youth he studied painting under Tani Bunchō, 谷文晁, (1763–1841) in Edo. In 1831 he came to Akumi District where he became the head Abbott of Gyokuryū Temple. Following the successful outcome of his efforts and that of the farmers in reference to the cancellation of the *Bakufu's* command for lord Sakai to be transferred, he planned and built a temple to the God of the Harvest within the precincts of his own temple, for the spirits of the Sakai family. In 1852 a commemorative tablet to Sakai Tadakata was contemplated, but never finished. Bunrin retired in 1858, taking the name of Suibokuan, 水墨庵, having established a reputation not only as a priest but as an expert detailed landscape painter. He died in 1863. Cf. *Tempō Kaikyō Roku, op. cit.*, p. 47–49.

For accounts of the Shonai uprising Cf: *Tempo Kaikyō Roku, op. cit.*, p. 43 *et seq.* Kiyono, T., ed: *Shōnai Tempō Gimin,* 2 Vol.; Tsurugaoka, 1935. Tamura, *Hōken Ikki, op. cit.*, pp. 224–268. Kokushō: *Hōken Shakai Tōsei op. cit.*, pp. 430–448.

It was finally decided that the strong were to leave the country and appeal in Edo, while the weak remain and offer prayers for the success of their adventure. Lord Sakai was greatly disturbed when he heard of this and sent guards to watch the houses of the farmers day and night. The borders were carefully patrolled and as many leaders as possible were arrested.[8]

Twelve farmers of Saigo Kumi in Takawa District, sent a memorandum to two of the village officials, the *kimoiri*, stating that they hoped the transfer of their lord to another fief be delayed. They also mentioned the fact that they were going to Edo to consult with a man there from their district and that this, their letter, would inform the officials of their departure. They further asked that the officials, as their mediator, report to the lord after seven or eight days, that it was absolutely essential for them to go even against his will.[9] Enduring the hardships of winter, crossing through ice cold water when there were no boats, and passing over dangerous precipices, they arrived at Edo the end of the 11th month. Learning of their intention to make an appeal, Sakai had the men arrested and returned to Shōnai. The appeal which they had drawn up and intended to present to the *Bakufu*, read as follows:

> To the *Bakufu* from the farmers of the villages of Tagawa and Akumi Districts. Dated: 11th month, 1840.
>
> "Whereas: We the farmers of the two districts on Shōnai unite in the following appeal:
>
> When we heard of the order that Lord Sakai Saemon [Takeda] was to be transferred, we the farmers of Tagawa and Akumi, young and old, men and women, all together, could not contain our grief. We had received the mercies of our lord from generation to generation since his family came to live here two hundred years ago. At the time of the unprecedented famine eight years ago [1832], in the provinces outside of Shōnai, those who died of starvation were without number. And although

8. *Tempō Kaikyō Roku, op. cit.*, pp. 43–44.
9. *Ibid*, pp. 59–60.

beggars came from other provinces in great numbers, the lord of Shōnai gave large presents of rice and money to those in the towns, and also lent large sums. We are further grateful for the fact that there were neither beggars nor mendicants in our province and much money was paid out by the rich to help others in our districts, even people from other provinces coming to buy rice to save them from famine. Though the rich in other provinces came to borrow gold and silver, yet among the townsmen and farmers of our two districts there was not a single individual who pawned his goods or who died of starvation.

Everyone grieves at the thought that when such a critical time again arises, they will not have the lord [if he is transferred] who has given them money, who has lent them rice and who has helped them when they did not have enough at the time of the collection of taxes. Needless to say, all those who have received help and support in Shōnai will wish to move to Nagaoka if our lord is forced to move his fief. Furthermore, with the succession of poor harvests and the consequent heavy loans, if our lord is forced to move, all those who posses any money in our two districts will go with him and how can there be any left to do the farming. Wishing from the bottom of our hearts that no change be made, everyone in our two districts, even the children, have been holding services at the temples in Shōnai and have been worshipping the gods and Buddhas. We humbly plead that you will allow our lord to remain as before and that he will not be transferred. Thus we the farmers of the two districts of Shōnai humbly petition that our benevolent lord be permitted to remain in Shōnai forever. This we, all the farmers, humbly petition.

Signed: Farmers of the villages of
Tagawa and Akumi Districts."

---

10. *Ibid*, p. 57–58. The original document contains even more repetitions than those in the translation above.

Unsuccessful though this first attempt had been, twenty-one farmers from Akumi District secretly left their homes and arrived in Edo on the 20th of the 1st month, 1841. There they actually appealed to the *Tairō*, Ii Naoaki,[11] the *Rōjū*, Mizuno Echizen no Kami, Takakuni, and others as they were in their palanquins on the way to the Edo castle. This appeal was practically identical with that written in the 11th month except for the following:

> Having exerted ourselves at our farming, through our lord's graciousness we have been able to save 12 *mon* each........ On learning that our lord is to be transferred, it is as though torches had been extinguished on a dark night. We also fear for what we have borrowed to sustain us duriug the past ten years of drought and bad harvests. In spite of the largest snow in seventy years, piled to five or six feet along the road, we have travelled the four hundred and fifty miles and finally arrived here to petition.... If you will assist us in having our lord remain forever in his present domain, everyone of his subjects will remain tranquil and we will all be deeply grateful for your assistance.
>
> Signed, this 2nd month of the Year of the Ox,
> 1841: The representatives of Arase and Yusa villages of Tagawa and Akumi districts in the domain of Sakai Saemon.[12]

These appeals, likewise, were of no avail, but the farmers continued their efforts. In the 2nd month a letter was sent to the officials of Kawakita asking specifically that the time for Sakai going on his "alternate attendance", (*sankin kōtai*), to Edo be postponed as they feared he would never return.

---

11. Ii, Kamon no Kami, Naoaki, 井伊掃部頭, 直亮, (1794–1850). He was *Tairō* from 1835 to 5th month, 1841. He was the younger brother of Ii, Kamon no Kami, Naosuke, (1815–1860), who was *Tairō* after 1858 and is well known for having signed the treaties with the foreign powers. For an account of the life of Naosuke Cf. Akimoto, Shunkichi, *Lord Ii Naosuke and New Japan*, I Vol.; Tōkyō, 1909.

12. *Tempō Kaikyō Roku*, *op. cit.*, p. 62 *et seq.*

Following this letter, it is reported the farmers from both districts collected and closed the pass, cutting down bridges so that Sakai could not leave. Though four of the leaders were arrested, Sakai feigned illness and did not leave his castle so the farmers returned to their homes.[13] Taking their case to the lords of the neighbouring fiefs, the farmers sent twenty-nine of their representatives to Akita and there they presented the following:

> Presented to the Lord of Akita, 6th month, 1841. We regret that our appeals to the lord in his castle of Shōnai in the 11th month of 1840 have all been useless. Since the last part of last year and up to the 2nd month of the present year, we have made four appeals to Edo, all of which have been in vain. The 20—30,000 farmers of both districts have assembled and decided to send delegates to Edo, also without results. Our prayers to the gods have been futile......The lord of Mito refused to listen to us. Though we may be stupid farmers, as you are our neighbour it became inevitable to appeal, especially since five to seven of us from each village secretly and under cover of night crossed the mountains and appealed at Sendai, and at Aizu, asking that the lords there prevent Sakai's transfer.....but we were only advised to return home. Thus we humbly appeal to you and beg for assistance.[14]

At this time there was a resident of Masugawa village of Akumi District, Satō Tōsuke, who was living in Edo. He had become wealthy and influential so together with another man from the same province, they planned to help the farmers. Through the good offices of the Edo *Machi-bugyō*, Yabe,

---

13. *Ibid, op. cit.*, p. 71 *et seq.*

14. *Ibid*, pp. 64–66. The lord of Mito was Tokugawa Nariaki, 德川齊昭; that of Sendai Date Narikuni, 伊達齊邦 (1817–1841), (having received the fief in 1828); and that of Akita was Satake Yoshiatsu, 佐竹義厚, (born in 1812, receiving the fief in 1815, and retiring in 1846). In Sendai it is reported they worshipped at a famous shrine and prayed for the success of their appeals.

Suruga no Kami, Sadakane,[15] an appeal was reconsidered and an order issued from the *Bakufu* on the 12th of the 7th month, 1841, saying that Sakai should "disregard the previous order in reference to his removal to another fief and should continue to be enfiefed in Shōnai."[16]

The farmers hearing of this order, wined and dined in honour of the success of their efforts. Lord Sakai presented a thousand bales of rice to the poor, while ten thousand more were given outlying villages. From the inquiries which developed during the investigation following this general uprising, the following was reported:

> You, the farmers, who have put up with difficulties of living in the country, crossing the mountains, and the risk of a long journey, have made a "mob-appeal". Such a thing has greatly surprised the authorities and been harmful to your lord. Moreover, a large number of farmers have gone to Edo and concerned themselves with the affairs of the government. The Prince of Mito asks: 'How is it that the farmers can cause such disorder and make an appeal to Lord Sakai?"[17]

Thus the time had finally come when the power of the Shōgun to transfer a *daimyō* from one fief to another had been challenged by the inhabitants of the fief. They had not only caused disorder within their own fief, but had secretly appealed to Edo and to all the neighbouring fiefs. Their constant appeals had been continued for over six months so that their insistent demands forced the *Bakufu* to withdraw its order of transfer. The centralized control of the Tokugawa family was obviously crumbling.

---

15. Yabe, Suruga no Kami, Sadakane, 矢部, 駿河守, 定邦, Edo *Machi bugyō* (1841) was imprisoned by order of Mizuno Tadakuni in the 3rd month, 1842 for his protests against the Tempō Reform measures. He was imprisoned in the Kuwana fief where he died in the 7th month, refusing to take nourishment. He is referred to as Taiken by Takekoshi. Cf. Takekoshi, *op. cit.*, Vol. III, p. 231.

16. *Tempō Kaikyō Roku, op. cit.*, p. 45.

17. *Ibid*, pp. 77–78.

B. *An Uprising in Ōmi in 1842, forces Capitulation of Bakufu Officials*

Cursory mention has already been made of the reforms attempted by Mizuno Tadakuni, following the death of the Shōgun Ienari, in the 1st month of 1841. Thus beginning with the dismissal of various officials, and even more important, intriguing court ladies, he continued his work by the abolition of lotteries and wholesale houses monopolizing trade, and inaugurated restrictions on dress, not only on the citizens of Edo, but even the farmers who were forbidden to wear leather soled shoes.[18] Protests from officials such as Yabei Sadakane, Edo *Machi-bugyō*, led to his dismissal, imprisonment, and early death. In the 3rd month, 1842, the reform was made even more rigid, but a glance at conditions in the provinces, such as Ōmi, will not only throw light on the attitude of the villagers towards such a government, but also give an insight into how ineffectual the reform was to be, as well as reveal one of the reasons for Mizuno's resignation from office a year later.

The Province of Ōmi, in modern Shiga Prefecture, lying along the shores of Lake Biwa, is traversed by the two main arteries between old Kyōto and Edo. These, the Nakasendō and Tōkaidō, follow the same route out of Kyōto, pass the city of Ōtsu, the center of a *Bakufu* domain, and the castle town of Zeze and fief of the Honda family, both on the

18. For accounts of this, the Tempō Reform, cf. Murdoch, *op. cit.*, Vol. III, pp. 443 *et seq.*; Takekoshi, *op. cit.*, Vol. III, pp. 229 *et seq.* The following incident is treated in detail for the following reasons. The present study of peasant uprisings is primarily an historical treatment and as this particular incident directly concerned the resignation of the *Rōjū*, it seems justifiable to devote more space to it. It also seems well to have one complete incident, fairly elaborately explained, for those wishing to study only one incident.

southern end of Lake Biwa.[19] Crossing the Seta River into Kurita District, they divide at Kusatsu.[20] The Tōkaidō, or Eastern Seaboard Road, then follows the valley of the Yasu River eastward into Kōga District and eventually reaches the seacoast and follows it to Edo.[21] The Nakasendō, the Central Mountain Road, traversing Yasu District and crossing the Niho River, passes on into Gamō District and by the town of Hikone on the central eastern shore of Lake Biwa, thence turning eastward through the mountains to Edo.[22]

It is centering around these rivers, the Yasu and Nihō, and the four districts of Kurita, Kōga, Yasu and Gamō, that the uprising of 1842 centres. Ōmi, a province with over 840,000 *koku* income, except for the domain of Ii, Kamon no Kami, Naoaki, at Hikone with 240,000 *koku*, was divided among the public domains and those of various other *daimyō;* the portion being affected by this uprising amounting to about 200,000 *koku.* Various surveys had been made of the land in the province, but the river valleys with the ever-changing river beds, always afforded opportunity for new land to be opened.[23] Thus during the Bunsei Period, (1818-1829) a survey had been carried on by officials who were able to in-

---

19. Ōtsu, 大津, was the office of a *daikan,* Ishihara Kiyosaemon, in charge of a 35,000 *koku* domain of the *Bakufu,* Zeze, 膳所, was the castle town of Honda Yasutsugu, 本多康禎, a 60,000 *koku* fief. He held the fief from 1806–1847 and was called Shimōsa no Kami, 下總守, later Gohyōbu Daiyu, 御兵部大輔. His father Yasusada, 康完, (b. 1764) took over the domain in 1782 and had charge of the reconstruction of the Imperial Palace in 1790. Cf. *Deuki Dainihon Shi, Daimyo Hen, op. cit.*, p. 485–486.

20. Kusatsu, 草津, in Kurita District, 栗太.

21. The Yasugawa, 野洲川, is the southern boundary for Kōga District, 甲賀.

22. The Nihōgawa, 仁保川, flows through Yasu District into Lake Biwa. Gamō District, 蒲生, is to the north.

23. It is reported to have been included in 1810 in the survey of all Japan made by Inō Tadayoshi (chūkei), 伊能忠敬,)1745–1821), during the eighteen years of travel in compiling his great map of Japan. Cf. *Shiga Ken,* Gamōgun Yakusho, ed., *Ōmi Gamō Gunshi,* 4 Vol.; 1922, especially Vol. 4, p. 44.

The *Bakufu* domains totalled 45,000 *koku,* over which a *daikan* at Ōtsu and another in *Kōga* had supervision. Over 125 *daimyō, hatamoto* and *kuge* controlled the rest of the fiefs in Ōmi, Cf. *Tempō Gimin Rōku;* Ono, *Hyakushō Ikki Sōdan, op. cit.*, Vol. I, p. 271 *et seq.*

crease the taxable crop in some places by over a third. Again in 1837, an Edo resident asked for permission to open up waste land along the shores of the Yasu and Nihō Rivers. This was granted and the *Bakufu* sent officials to work with those of the *daikan* from Ōtsu. Maps were drawn of possible land that might be opened, but the villages immediately objected, saying no waste land actually existed. They complained that: "Even though there were vacant land between the villages and the river, this had been included previously in the domain and was not available for opening as new land."[24]

But these complaints were a mere prelude to the opposition of 40,000 farmers in 1842 against a *Bakufu* official, sent with the specific task of surveying the lands along the Yasu and Nihō Rivers, and being forced to cease his activities and flee.[25] The *Bakufu* ordered Ichino Mosaburō,[26] through the medium of the *Rōjū*, Mizuno, Echizen no Kami, Tadakuni, to perform this survey for the purpose of increasing the income of Ōmi. Thus the *shōya* of all villages along the rivers and lakes in Ōmi Province received the following order from the Kyōto *Machi-bugyō* in the 11th month, 1841:

"You are hereby ordered to make preperations for an inspection of all newly claimed land, delta lands, and the

24. *Ōmi Gamo Gunshi, op. cit.,* Vol. IV, p. 59. There had been an uprising in Ōmi, at Hachiman Machi, 八幡町, in 1822 of a peculiar nature. In that year, although Hachiman was not directly on the through route, the Tōkaidō, it had been levied a special tax, *sukegō,* of men and horses for the Korean envoys going to Edo. However the people maintained they had been given a special exemption from *sukegō* by a document from Ieyasu. When the officials asked to see this, the villagers refused saying it was too sacred. In reality, however, the document, if it ever existed, was lost and the people protected only an empty box from the approaching officials. Four of the village officials were, therefore, sent to Edo in custody where they were reprimanded for their disobedience. Cf. *Ōmi Gamō Gunshi, op. cit.,* Vol. IV, p. 101 *et seq.*

25. The following incident is based largely on the *Tempō Gimin Roku.* It was written and edited by Kawamura Yoshimitsu, (1852–1916), in 1893, a native of Ōmi who spent elaborate pains in collecting materials from the districts in which the uprising occurred. It is published in Ono, *Hyakushō Ikki Sōdan, op. cit.,* Vol I, pp. 265–383.

26. Ichino Mosaburō, 市野茂三郎. His life, except for this incident, remains a mystery.

> boundaries of all land of villages contiguous with the various rivers and lakes in Ōmi. Furthermore, as this is an official order, the examination shall be different from other years. You shall inspect it yourselves, and there shall be no complaints."[27]

In spite of their fear that the hardships which had resulted from other inspections would only be increased by this order, the *shōya* of the various villages replied that they had received the order of the Kyōto *Machi-bugyō* and that they would humbly endeavour to carry it out.[28]

By the middle of the 1st month, 1842, Ichino and his surveying party of some forty members arrived and began their inspection of land along the banks of the Nihō River with its one hundred or more villages. The party, including assistants, representatives of the two *daikan* in charge of the *Bakufu* domains, and the Ōmi surveying official,[29] brought with it added hardships to the villages in which it stopped. Wherever they moved, it was necessary to construct new baths, rest houses, new roofs on old buildings and make other changes for their accomodations. Ichino ordered everyone to be careful of fires during his sojourn in their villages as he possessed valuable papers and the seal of the *Bakufu*. This order the *shōya* reported to their villages, where the people soon felt as though they were sitting on matting with needles in it fearing their carelessness would start a fire and that they

---

27. Cf. *Tempō Gimin Roku, op. cit.*, Vol. I, p. 273.
28. Cf. *Ibid,* Vol. I, p. 274.
29. "Survey official" or officer in charge of the examination, inspection or survey of land to determine the total taxable crop was termed, *kenchi yaku,* 檢地役. Other officials in the party included Ichino, who is called, *Go kanjō kata,* 御勘定方, one who collects imposts and taxes; his manager or *Goyōnin'* 御用人, a term also used for chamberlins in the *daimyō's* court; two *fushin yaku,* 普新役, officers in charge of general repair work; two representatives of the *daikan, tedai,* 手代; representatives of the eastern and western *bugyō* of Kyōto through his assistant officers, *kumi shimo,* 組下; and *doshin,* 同心, lictors; two men from the office of the *jitō,* 知頭; one cartographer and one doctor. Cf. *Ōmi Gamo Gunshi, op. cit.*, Vol. IV, p. 70–71 and *Tempō Gimin Roku, op. cit.*, Vol. I, p. 276.

would be severely punished. Thus they put out their kitchen fires and ate only cold food.[30]

These hardships the farmers would doubtless have been able to endure without protest had not even more serious grievances been added to them. In the first place, Ichino and his officials were using a false measuring sick. It was, in reality, 11 *shaku*, 6 *sun* in length, but marked 12 *shaku*, 1/5 *sun*, which would have meant an increase in the taxable area of land by about 3.6%.[31] To this deceitfulness was added bribery and unnecessary luxurious demand on the part of the surveyors. In one village, while taking a bath, Ichino demanded a "rice-bran bag" for scrubbing himself. Therewith the mother of a *shōya* brought out her bag in which she placed two gold pieces instead of the usual rice-bran. The village officials hesitated to present this to Ichino for fear of being imprisoned by the *daikan*, but were finally persuaded to do so by the old lady. The following day, his oppressive measures in that particular village suddenly changed to charitable ones and it was obvious that bribes would alleviate the inspection. In the next village, the *shōya* presented him with over a thousand *ryō* which resulted in the immediate cessation of the inspection of land. His scouts sent ahead to arrange for suitable lodgings expected bribes of at least 10 *ryō* while one village paid at the rate of twenty-five *ryō* for each *tan* exempt from being classed as barren land. In some villages, the right of ownership of land which had been cultivated by the same person for ten years, was questioned. Bribes finally eliminated the inspection of all but about eight villages and the farmers dreaded the arrival of the party to their village, whether for inspection or demanding bribes.[32]

---

30. Cf. *Tempō Gimin Roku, op. cit.*, Vol I, p. 275 *et seq.*

31. A universal law had been passed in 1716 that the length of the measuring stick of one *ken*, 間, should be 6 *shaku*, 尺, 1 *bu*, 分, (ten *bu* equal one *sun*, 寸) in length. Thus Ichino's stick was marked two *ken* but nearly 4% less in length. Other measurements established the same year were that one square *ken* should equal 1 *bu*, 歩, 1 *se*, 畝; equal 30 *bu;* 10 *se* equal 1 *tan*, 段, 10 *tan* equal 1 *chō*, 町, or 2.45 Acres. Cf. *Tempō Gimin Roku, op. cit.*, Vol. I, p. 277 *et seq.*

32. *Tempō Gimin Roku, op. cit.*, Vol. I, p. 283 *et seq.*

With conditions having reached such a deplorable state, a *shōya* of Mikami Village, Tsuchikawa Hirabei by name, decided to visit a man, Kise Bunkichi, of a village in Koga District, further up the Yasu River. Upon their finally meeting and Bunkichi suggesting it had been a dangerous journey for Hirabei, the latter replied, "What are the dangers of coming to see you at night compared to the dangers of this life with such an unscrupulous official surveying our lands." Bunkichi then answerd: "I too am suffering. . . . I have heard of the unprecedented activities of the land inspection and though I have resigned from office, [of village official], I will do all I can to help you." The outcome of this first meeting was their deciding upon a further conference to be held with another man of the same region.[33] In the meantime, Ichino and his party had finished their surveying along the Nihō River and the domain of Honda Yasutsugu. Next they turned to the fief of Katō, Noto no Kami, Akikuni at Minaguchi.[34] However, as the people in opposition to open bribery and the use of false measuring sticks had already made complaints to Edo, as well as to the lords of their domain, Ichino, fearing lest the Minaguchi castle could not withstand a possible attack from the people, awaited an opportunity to make a quick move elsewhere.

At the next meeting of Bunkichi and Hirabei, they were joined by Tajima Kyūbei, an officer of a fief of a *hatamoto* in Kōga District, who expressed his willingness to die for the cause of the farmers but who was not sure that a mob-appeal and their consequent arrest and death would bring about their desired ends. The *Rōjū*, Mizuno Tadakuni, he pointed out, had inaugurated a harsh government throughout the entire country and had been influenced by others as bad as Ichino,

33. *Ibid*, p. 289 *et seq*.

34. Katō, Noto no Kami, Akikuni, 加藤能登守明邦, succeeded his father, Akimasa, 明允, to the inheritance of the 25,000 *koku* domain at Minaguchi, 水口. Akikuni retired from head of the fief in 1845.

and thus had received false reports concerning Ōmi.[35] It was decided, therefore, to call a meeting, ostensibly for the discussion on the reduction of the price of fertilizer, but really to plan an appeal. Thus two meetings, one for the *shōya* of Kōga Districts to meet at Minaguchi, the other for those of Yasu and Kurita Districts to assemble at Rikko Temple in Toda village, were set for daybreak, the 26th of the 9th month. In Minaguchi, under the leadership of Tajima, seventy two *shōya*, representing 137 villages, gathered. They were then told the real purpose of the meeting and approved of a plan for further appeal as they pointed out all former complaints to the Kyōto *Machi bugyō* had been useless. At the end of the meeting, Tajima concluded:

> "As some of you have already explained, it is too late to go to Edo. However, if we follow the rash advice of some to attack the inn where Ichino is staying and kill him, then the *Rōjū*, Mizuno, will become even more angry and our hardships will become unbearable. Let us appeal again to Kyōto. The people of the three districts shall meet at the appointed places and Hirabei and I will appeal to Ichino. If he will not listen to us, then we will attack him with the combined forces of the three districts. His next move will be to Mikami Village, under the control of Hirano Hachiuemon.[36] As Hirano

35. Tajima refers in the text to "Torii, Kai no Kami", 鳥井甲斐守, who is Torii Yōzō Tadaakira, 鳥井耀藏忠耀. He was appointed Edo *Machi bugyō* by Mizuno but turned out be a most unfortunate choice. He was extremely severe, anti-foreign and orthodox in his philosophical beliefs. In 1843 he was forced out of office along with Mizuno. He died in 1873. Cf. *Dainihon Jimei Jisho,* I Vol., Tōkyō, 1903, p. 1338.

36. Hirano Hachiuemon was a retainer of the Endō family, 遠藤氏, lords of the fief of Mikami, 三上, with 12,000 *koku*. They had received Mikami in 1698 with the same income which continued to remain in their family. It has been difficult to identify exactly the lord of the fief in 1842. In 1790 Endō Tanetomi, 遠藤胤富, (b. 1761), received the fief to transfer it to his adopted son, Endō, Tajima no Kami, Tanenori, 遠藤但島守胤統, in 1811. His successor was first an adopted son, Tanemasa, 胤冒, then his third son, Tajima no Kami, Taneki, 但島守胤城, who is known to have held the fief in 1866 and was made a Viscount in 1884. As the *Gimin Roku* refers to him only as "Tajima no Kami", the head of the fief in 1842 must either have been Tanenori or Taneki. Cf. *Denki Dainihonshi, Daimyo Hen, op. cit.*, p. 388–89.

likewise has suffered greatly from this survey we must await our opportunity and receive his aid".[37]

To this plan the *shōya* agreed as did the second group, meeting at Toda.

On the 6th of the 10th month, 1842, Ichino and his party again moved, this time to a fief divided between a *hatamoto* and the Lord of Sendai. In this particular fief, however, a careful survey was begun, but as the border between the two domains was "as ragged as dog's teeth", only five acres were inspected after three days work. On the 11th instant, Ichino abruptly moved to Mikami Village, and Hirabei ordered the people to meet together as planned on the 15th. However, on the night of the 14th, with the moon shining as bright as day and the bells of the shrines piercing one's ears, the sound of the blowing of conch horns, war cries and the beating of drums, resounding as if Mt. Mikami would crumble and the Yasu River be torn asunder, several thousand gathered together and decided to attack Ichiro.[38] Beginning with the home of a *shōya* they rifled his house and house of other officials en route to Mikami Village. Tajima then attempted to admonish them, stating an appeal would be far preferable to pillaging, but he was overruled by the younger active members of the mob. Increasing as they advanced westward along the Tōkaidō, they formed a group of about 20,000.[39] Reaching a village a few miles to the east and across the river from their goal, 170 soldiers were sent to stop them to no avail. Rich families gave them food as they advanced and soon they were met by the groups from Yasu and Kurita Districts, making a total of forty thousand. Soldiers, this time from the Katō fief in Minaguchi, again attempted to stop them, but they replied they were not people who wished to revolt but because of the inroads of hunger and starvation and

---

37. Cf. *Tempō Gimin Roku, op.* cit., Vol I, p. 299 *et seq.*
38. *Ibid,* Vol. I, p. 306 *et seq.*
39. The group in Kōga District, having first felt the hardships of the survey in Minaguchi to the east of Mikami Village, were among those first to start the uprising.

the hardships of the survey, they merely wished to appeal to Ichino. The soldiers then let them pass.

Ichino was in Mikami Village at the time and called out the troops of the Endō fief, who demanded that the mob state their desires. They replied they wished the head of Ichino and on hearing this Hirano Hachiuemon was appointed as intermediary. More specifically, the complaints of the farmers presented to Hirano stated that though they worked incessantly and supported their families only with difficulty, yet the three inspections on the land recently increased their hardships and that they had come with the one demand that the inspection be stopped. If this were agreed to, they would disperse quietly.[40] Hirano, the intermediary, was then instructed to act as he thought best and presented the people with a document saying: "The second [present] inspection of the banks of the Yasu River shall be postponed." but the people fearing it was not definite enough, and seeing it lacked a seal, refused to accept it. As this point, Ichino prepared for his escape and the mob attacked the castle in which he was staying, ransacked his baggage, out of which fell many of the gold coins he had received as bribes. All the record books and registers they threw into the moat, thus nullifying the work of the survey. In the meantime, Ichino, with one of his assistants, fled to the mountains, escorted by soldiers from the Endō fief, where he hid in caves while the farmers searched for him. Finally he reached the office of the *daikan* at Ōtsu, where he rested. Troops had been called out to quiet the mob of whom several were injured, but none were killed as all the guns used by the soldiers were empty. After further bickerings between Hirano and the mob, the following was presented:

"To all the farmers of the villages along the Yasu River:

In accord with your request concerning the in-

40. Cf. *Tempō Gimin Roku, op. cit.*, Vol I, p. 308 *et seq.*

spection of the villages along the banks of the Yasu River, be it hereby granted that said inspection shall be postponed for 100,000 days [indefinitely]."

Signed and sealed, this 10th month, 1842,
Ichino Mosaburō
Yamashita Goshirō,
(Representative of the *daikan* of the *Bakufu* Domain of 35,000 *koku* at Ōtsu.)
Shibayama Kimba,
(Representative of the same of 10,000 *koku.*)

This being posted before the mob and Hirano announcing it would take effect immediately, the people gave a final war-cry, realizing their cause had been won.[41]

Ichino, having escaped to the edge of the province, continued the rest of the way to Kyōto at night, and sent a messenger to Edo to report. Other repercussions of the uprising included the halting of all shipping on Lake Biwa and the dispatch of troops from Zeze and elsewhere to establish order. On the 17th of the 10th month, 1842, Hirano Hachiuemon sent a full report of the uprising, the attack upon Ichino in Mikami, and his final escape, to Endō, Tajima no Kami, his lord in Edo. Thus on the 23rd of the same month, Endō tendered his report to the Shōgun which summed up the previous events: the objection of the surveying along the Yasu River, the attack upon the baggage of Ichino, his flight and the permanent postponement of the surveying.[42] In the meantime the Kyōto *Machi bugyō* had ordered officials sent to Ōmi to arrest the leaders.[43]

---

41. *Ibid,* Vol. I, p. 313 *et seq.*
42. Cf. *Ibid,* Vol. I, p. 321 *et seq.*
43. The actual officers sent were the Kyōto eastern and western *yoriki,* 與力. The *yoriki,* a kind of *gens d'armes* was under the guards of the three Shogun castles in Edo, Ōsaka, and Kyōto or the Head of the Library, *Shoin Ōbangashira,* 書院大番頭. He had control of the *dōshin* and had an income of 60–80 *koku* of rice. Other officers included: two *dōshin metsuke,* 同心目付, lictors and censors; four *shinya shitayaku,* 新家下役, assistant officers in charge of new buildings; and one *zōshiki,* 雜色, a general "handy man" or errand boy.

Among the first organizers of the uprising, let it be recalled, was Kise Bunkichi, who had made his plans together with Tsuchikawa Kirabei. Realizing that they would be arrested and possibly killed, Bunkichi and seven other male members of his family assembled at his home for a final farewell banquet. Calling his wife and children to his side, and while remarking that that night would be the last time for him to be able to sleep with sheets and blankets, an official appeared at his home, asking politely: "There is something I must talk over with the master of the house. May I see him?" Bunkichi, upon hearing this, dressed with the greatest of composure, gave himself over to the official and was thus taken into custody.[44] Other arrests, including Tsuchikawa Hirabei and Tajima Kyūbei, amounted to about a hundred and twenty-five, all of whom were incarcerated in the Nijo Palace prison in Kyōto. The guards sent from Zeze, on the contrary, seem to have been quite sympathetic with the uprising, for the leader, after seeing the document of the postponement of the survey, ordered that duplicates be sent to all the villages.

In its turn, the *Bakufu* sent two special officers to the *daikan* at Ōtsu, together with the following command to the *daimyō* of Ōmi:

> "As we are sending officials to inspect the recent uprising, the people must not rebel again. On this account you must guard the roads closely, and if there is another insurrection you must order your troops to attack and repel the farmers with bullets. If you do not comply, your fiefs will be reduced.[45]

These officials arrived at Ōtsu the middle of the 12th month and established a court of investigation at the office of the

---

44. Cf. *Tempō Gimin Roku, op. cit.*, Vol I, p. 331. This complete composure and resignation to the inevitable fate awaiting him, is typical of the Japanese sense of honour. To have attempted escape or offered resistance at such a moment would have been cowardice on the part of Bunkichi. He had taken the responishlity for the uprising, they had won their cause, so he would willingly be a sacrifice to that to which he had pledged his loyalty.

45. Cf. *Tempō Gimin Roku, op. cit.*, Vol. I, p. 334.

daikan. Two "temporary judicial examiners",[46] were appointed and the perusal of the records of 330 villages began. The prisoners in Kyōto were ordered back to Ōtsu, but one of these, Kise Bunkichi, had already died in prison. Representatives were summoned to the trial from among the village officials and farmers, who reluctantly appeared, after drawing lots as to whose fate it would be, as they feared tortures awaited them. Their fears were well founded, for they were subjected to having heavy stones piled upon their legs, being hung up by their arms tied behind their backs, or roasted on a wooden horse over a fire, in attempts to make them confess.[47]

The *Bakufu* had had its own official forced to flee, its orders had been disregarded, and its prestige badly injured, so it was to retaliate through merciless examinations, tortures and punishments. Over half of the two thousand men who were summoned to the trial at Ōtsu were imprisoned, including some who were apprehended unjustly. In the actual trial itself, both Tsuchikawa Hirabei and Tajima were ruthlessly tortured. The former asked that he be permitted to state his cause before the court in Edo, while Tajima, nothing daunted, openly accused Ichino of having carried on an illegal survey making a meeting of the farmers to petition against it, inevitable. He asked that he receive the blame for the entire affair and be sent to Edo to face further trial there. When some twenty-five prisoners were released, they went to a Kyōto Shrine to offer their gratitude, but found upon their return to their village, that one of their number had hung himself because of his shame for having made confessions.[48]

The Zeze guard who had ordered duplicates of the docu-

---

46. *Shita-shirabe yaku,*下調役. There is also the term *chōeki,* 調役, *Chō* the tax and *eki* the labour, "a tax on houses and men" which could not apply in this case. The two men sent from Edo were called *kanjōkata rusuyaku,* 勘定方留役. *Ibid,* p. 336.

47. These tortures are called *soroban,,* 算盤, *tsuriage,* 釣上ゲ, and *mokuba,* 木馬. Cf. *Tempō Gimin Roku, op. cit.,* Vol. I, p. 336 *et seq.* and for the death of Bunkichi, Cf., p. 381. See also Ono: *Hyakushō Ikki Sōdan, op. cit.,* Vol. II, p. 673 *et seq.* and Hall: "Tokugawa Legislation" *op. cit., T.A.S.J.* Vol. XLI pt. V., for an illustrated account of tortures.

48. Cf. *Tempō Gimin Roku, op. cit.,* Vol. I, p. 340 *et seq.*

ment postponing the survey sent to the villages was likewise examined, as was Hirano of Mikami Village. The trial dragged on with thirty dying in prison during the proceedings, including relatives of Bunkichi. The shrine at Mikami Village became a popular refuge where the bereaved came to worship, while the Emperor Ninkō, (1817–1846) hearing of the people dying from chastisements, asked the priests of the temples of Mt. Hiei, overlooking Ōtsu, the crowded prisons and the court itself, to offer incense and prayers for those who were suffering; while sutras were recited and prayers given on behalf of those already dead. By the 3rd month, 1843, most of the prisoners had either returned to their villages or died, leaving twelve culprits to be transferred to Edo under military escort, one of whom died just before departure, and three others on the way. Little wonder they were not recognized by their families who came to see them depart.[49]

In Edo, Tsuchikawa Hirabei again stated the case of bribery and injustice against Ichino, together with the unfairness he saw in not inspecting the fiefs in Ōmi of influential *Bakufu* officials as Ii, Kamon no Kami, Naoaki, in Hikone. This unfairness, he maintained, necessitated rebellion on the part of the peasants.[50] His statements, therefore, clearly placed the blame on Ichino and other officials of the *Bakufu*, and was to have far-reaching effects. Three warriers of Kato's domain were imprisoned for one hundred days, twenty-eight assistant officers of the *daikan* were arrested or hand-cuffed, and Nakamura, the leader of the guards from Zeze who ordered the postponement circulated, just escaped being banished. Naturally enough Tsuchikawa and Tajima were condemned, but they had already died in prison.[51] Hirabei's family was finally arrested in the 11th month, 1843, his

49. *Ibid,* Vol. I, p. 353–361. The culprits included Tsuchikawa Hirabei and Tajima Kyūbei as leaders, five other leaders, their two accomplices, the man who wrote the postponement notice and two others.

50. *Ibid,* Vol. I, p. 364 *et seq.*

51. Hirabei died in the 4th month, 1843, but the exact date of Tajima's death is not recorded. Cf. *Tempō Gimin Roku, op. cit.,* Vol. I, pp. 373 & 379.

property confiscated, his wife, two sons and two daughters banished. As for those directly responsible for the uprising, Ichino was ordered back to Edo late in 1842, but he either committed sucide en route or was condemned to become a commoner.

But before all the sentences had been carried out, with the accusations in mismanagement and despotic laws piling up against him Mizuno Tadakuni, the *Rōjū*, instigator of the reforms in 1814 and 1842, and the official ordering Ichino to carry out the survey of Ōmi, was forced to resign in the 9th month, 1843.[52] It is impossible to say how much this incident was responsible for Mizuno's overthrow. Other factors such as his attempt to remove the *daimyō* from around Edo played a leading role, The real significance of the whole Ōmi uprising lies in the fact that the corrupt *Bakufu* official, sent out on a survey of land which meant an increase in the hardships of the already over taxed farmers, was challenged, and forced to flee. The orders of the *Bakufu* government had not only been defied, their representatives had capitulated and fled. With such obvious corruption of officials on the one hand, and their impotence to carry out their orders on the other, it is only surprising that the whole regime did not crumple sooner, especially when additional blows to its prestige were inflicted during the next decade by the demands of Perry and other westerners that harbours be opened to the outside world.

C. *Uprisings prior to the Restoration of 1868*

It is not the purpose of this study to trace the intricacies of the political events preceding the Restoration of 1868. Suffice it to say that in spite of the increasing tension within Japan over the question of the expulsion of the foreigner on the one hand, and the re-establishment of the power and prestige of the Emperor developing from the new thought movements and the inevitable collapse of the Tokugawa *Bakufu* on the other, there appears to be no marked difference in either the type or number of occurrences of peasant up-

52. *Ibid*, Vol. I, p. 366–371.

risings of this period. True it is that the number was increasing in frequency as the downfall of the Shogunate approached, but was to reach its peak only after, not before the Restoration. Thus the uprisings as they existed during these turbulent years were isolated from these great movements, many of them doubtless left unrecorded, due to their unimportance compared to the other troubles throughout the country. Their effect upon the downfall of the government had been accumulative during the whole period of Tokugawa Shoguns. The peasant as a class, did not rise simultaneously in revolt and demand reform, his continual localized appeals and uprisings had already warned the authorities that his burden had become unbearable and that the system must be changed. Thus the period from 1843 to 1868 was filled with various disturbances, varying little in their causes from those already mentioned: the rise in price of rice, the change of their lord's fief, poor administration of the domains. Little would be gained, therefore, from a detailed study of these but a few remain of singular interest.[53]

One of these is another example of an uprising in support of the lord of the fief and in opposition to a transfer to another domain, in Gamō District in Ōmi in 1846, less than three years after the final settlement of the troubles resulting from the unfair survey of Ichino Mosaburō. An order had been received in the 11th month, 1845, that the lord of the fief, Inoue Masaharu, should be moved, and as in the previous case in Shōnai, the farmers attempted appeals in Edo. The representatives of the eighteen villages of the fief divided into four groups in Edo for this purpose, presenting simultaneous

---

53. Again relying upon the figures of Numazaki, uprisings occurred as follows. 99 from 1833 to 1842, 36 from 1843 to 1852, 56 from 1853 to 1863, and finally 61 from 1863 to 1867. For the years immediately preceding the Restoration the following figures are given. 3 for 1864, 6 for 1865, 32 for 1866 and only 12 for 1867. Cf. Numazaki, *op. cit.*, Charts III and IV.

appeals directly to the palanquins of four of the *Rōju.*[54] In every case the petitions of the helpless farmers were accepted and read, but the farmers were taken into custody and turned over to their lord. Thus in spite of the people's prayers for success, as the *Bakufu* had already made its decision, the appeals had little effect, although no punishment was administered to the farmers.[55]

Interesting for the boldness of its auther, is a complaint made in 1850 by a representative of the farmers (*hyakushō-dai*) Nagatani Kanzō.[56] Born in 1770 in the Province of Kōzuke, the son of a *sake* manufacturer, he had become interested in Confucianism and especially the new movement of loyalty to the Emperor and his restoration to power. Nagatani's criticism of the government came as a direct challenge to a *hatamoto* having killed a *nanushi* who had complained of heavy taxes. This forced the *Bakufu* to order the *hatamoto* to reduce his taxes who in turn took his revenge upon the *nanushi.* Among the grievances enumerated by Nagatani were extravagances of the Shōguns in their construction of the Nikkō Mausoleums at a cost of 568,000 *ryō*, the harshness of the *daikan* over the eight eastern provinces, the unfairness attached to the custom that the villages should pay for the arrest of homeless and vagrants in their communi-

---

54. The *Rōjū* to which the farmers appealed were Makino, Bizen no Kami, Tadamasa, 牧野備前守忠雅‘ *Rōjū* from 1843 to 1857; Aoyama, Shimosuke no Kami, Tadayoshi, 青山下野守忠良, *Rōjū* from 1845 to 1848, Toda, Yamashiro no Kami, Tadaharu, 戸田城山守忠温, *Rōjū* from 1846 to 1851; and Abe, Ise no Kami, Masahiro, 阿部伊勢守正弘, *Rōjū* from 1842 to 1857, rival of Mizuno and staunch supporter of more friendly treatment towards the foreigners.

55. Cf. *Ōmi, Gamō Gunshi, op. cit.*, Vol. IV, pp. 352 *et seq.* There appears to have been an important uprising in the Province of Higo the following year, but I have been able to study only a limited amount of materials on this incident. It contained many *rōnin* and ruffians and centered around Amakusa. Five hundred soldiers were finally sent out to tranquilize the riotous group of whom 128 were arrested and the affair was settled. Its causes were opposition to the policies of the land owners and silver guilds. Cf. *Jiji Roku, Mikan Hakushu,* Vol. VI, p. 306 *et seq.* and Kokushō, *Ikki no Kenkyū, op. cit.*, p. 443.

56. Nagatani Kanzo, 長谷勘蔵 (1770–1854).

ty, the unnecessary expenses entailed in the reconstruction of the Edo castle, the despotic demands of various *hatamoto*, the decrease in rural population and finally hoarding. Although a thorough search was made for the author of such a document, seditious from the *Bakufu* point of view, he was not found by the officials and died in 1854.

Following the uprising in Kaga in the realm of Maeda Noriyasu, in 1838, more trouble was to develop as a result of a dispute between fishermen and wealthy officials of the domain, named *Zeniya,* who asked that they be allowed to reclaim land along the borders of an inland harbour. An uprising of seven villages of fishermen, fearing they would lose their only means of livelihood, was insufficient to stop the work of making new lands from which it was estimated some 2,900 *koku* would be produced. Finally in 1852 the fishermen broke into the construction camp and completely stopped the work. Consequently the fish, which it was known the fishermen would eat, were poisoned, causing several deaths. Complaints were again made to the castle at Kanazawa,[57] which immediately sent out an official to investigate. Following this, two men, Zeniya Gohei and his son, Yōzō,[58] were accused of having asked that the land be opened up for their own private use, and of having poisoned the fishermen. They were both imprisoned and condemned for their part in the scandal.

Leaving the two important uprisings in Echigo and Morioka in 1853 for treatment in the regional studies, troubles

---

57. Cf. *Supra* p. 96.
58. Zeniya Gohei, 錢屋五兵衛, (1798–1852) was a descendant of a money changer, but he himself became a boat builder, sending ships to Nambu, Tsugaru, Matsumae and Hakodate. After the crop failures of the Tempō Period (1830–1843) and the consequent uprisings like those of 1838 mentioned above he suggested better communications to alleveiate the situation and constructed two new ships. He was then given the name of Kiyomizu and soon became quite wealthy. Yōzō, 要藏, his third son, wished new lands and thus suggested the above plan of transforming the Kahoku Inlet into fields. Gohei died in prison in 1852 and his son was condemned to death the end of the next year with his accomplice. Cf. *Dainihon Jimmei Jisho, op. cit.*, pp. 994–996. Also Papinot, *op. cit.*, p. 901 who gives Gohei's death as 1855.

arose from the change of feudal benefices in Kii, in 1855. Although the reasons for the change are not clear, villages with income amounting to some 2,000 *koku* were ordered changed from direct suzerainty of Tokugawa Yoshitomi,[59] to that of one of the ministers of the Tokugawa family. As the farmers in the Kii domain had been unable to support themselves recently, they were extremely grateful for the gifts from the storehouses of the Tokugawa family. Fearing they would lose this favour if transferred, one village complained that:

> At the news of our transfer everyone in the village has abandoned their labour because of worry. Furthermore, in connection with the recent arrival of foreign ships, we have received favours from our lord [who paid for the expenses of replenishing the ships which stopped off of Kii]. Moreover, there have been unusually severe earthquakes and tidal waves recently and we cannot bear the thought ef separation from our protector. Thus we ask that our requests be carefully examined and our petition granted.
>
> Signed the 2nd day of the 4th month, 1855 by: Four hundred and seventy-two people: Joint Seal
> Ten *Kumigashira:* Joint Seal
> Three village officials: Joint Seal
> Eleven citizens wearing swords: Joint Seal.[60]

This was followed in the 4th month by twelve other villages, and in the 5th month an appeal was again made to the *Kanjō bugyō*. Though the jurisdiction of the villages was changed, it was impossible to keep the inhabitants quiet so it became necessary to reverse the decision in 1857.[61]

---

59. As already pointed out, Tokugawa Harutaka held the Kii domain until 1824. He was succeeded by Nariyuki. 齊順, (1801–1846). At his death, Narikatsu, 齊彊, (1820–1849). twentieth son of the Shogun Ienari, received the fief until his death. He was then followed by Tokugawa Yoshitomi, 德川慶福, (1846–1866), son of Nariyuki who became the 14th Shogun Iemochi, 家茂, in 1858 and whose control of the fief went to Mochitsugu, 茂承, (1844–1906).

60. Cf. *Wakayama Kenshi, op. cit.*, Vol. I, p. 252 *et seq.*

61. *Ibid*, p, 264.

Two of the provinces in isolated Shikoku, Tosa and Iyo, will be dealt with more fully later, but troubles also occurred in Awa and Sanuki, the two remaining provinces. In the latter, in 1856, a dispute arose between two villages concerning rights of ownership of a mountain forest lying between them. Appeals were sent to the local *daikan* by the village of Nakatsu which had had the privilege of cutting this timber, when it was encroached upon by the next village. The *daikan* refused to make a decision on the matter, but finally the *Kori bugyō* of the fief decided that the land had belonged to Nakatsu, but all land upon which timber had been cut by the other village should be theirs. Feeling themselves thus frustrated, the villagers of Nakatsu fled to the next province of Awa in protest.[62]

Another uprising of special significance because of its connection with the movements of the period was that in Kaga in 1858, a direct result of the unusual financial burdens placed upon the Maeda fief. Containing as it did an extended coast line, the problem of national defense was discussed by the officials of the fief who finally concluded that "because of the recent taxes of the *Bakufu* for the reconstruction of the castle at Edo, the finances of the domain have become in disorder and there is danger that the people will consequently suffer, unless strict economies are observed".[63] In 1857, however, additional taxes for coastal defense were ordered and this was met by an order from Maeda Nariyasu, lord of the fief, to borrow the necessary funds. The farmers in their turn were taxed to meet a previous loan which would soon be due, to which they objected strenuously, attacking the home of the wealthy. Edo castle burnt again in 1859 and Kaga was ordered to present 50,000 *ryō*. This added to the general financial distress so that it became necessary to borrow money continuously.[64] Such a situation resulted in continued oppression for farmers.

---

62. Cf. Ono, *Nihon Sonraku Shikō,* 1 Vol; Tōkyō, 1928, especially p. 86 *et seq.*
63. Cf. *Ishikawa Kenshi, op. cit.,* Vol II, p. 978.
64. *Ibid,* Vol. II, p. 979.

Before turning to a brief outline of some of the uprisings centering around the Meiji Restoration of 1868, two special incidents should be mentioned. The first of these occurred in the Province of Yamato in 1863. There a deputy came from Edo to collect a forced levy (*Goyōkin*) on four villages, saying that all cryptomeria and cyprus trees with a circumference greater than 3 *shaku* should be cut down immediately and the money therefrom be used for the forced levy. The farmers asked to be exempt from this and planned an uprising, but a lad of ninteen decided the best way to solve the problem would be to murder the deputy. This he did only to face imprisonment along with four of his accomplices. In 1866 he was finally killed, and the farmers received his remains and buried them with the greatest of reverence.[65] The second is that in Sanuki in the 1st month, 1868, just prior to the Restoration, an uprising resulting from the *Bakufu* ordering a certain class of people known as *ninmyō* to furnish boats and sailors for the subjugation of the rebellious Nagato fief. The *ninmyō* then transferred this order to the *monto*[66] a class of people of inferior social rank. In opposition to this, the *monto* attacked the *ninmyō* and several were killed. The whole affair was finally settled when troops were sent from the neighbouring province of Tosa and the leaders were arrested.[67]

D. Uprisings centering around the Restoration of 1868

Thus it appears that down to the years just prior to the Restoration of 1868, when the *daimyō* were lining up their allegiance either on the side of the Imperial Family or backing the old Tokugawa regime, the peasant uprisings remained a

---

65. *Naraken Udagun Shiryo*, 1 Vol.; 1917 p. 15.
66. The *ninmyo*, 人名, and *monto*, 毛人. The readings of *ninmyo* and *monto* are those given by Prof. Kokushō. It has been brought to my attention by Mr. R. Tsunoda of Columbia University, that in the province of Kōzuke the usual term for Ainu is *kenin* 毛人 and that the use of the term *monto* in Sanuki may be a linguistic proof of the existence of Ainu in Shikoku at some time, the use of the term existing long after their migration northward.
67. Cf. Kokusho, " Gyomin Sōdō", *op. cit.*, Vol. 26 No. 2, p. 142.

separate movement. Although the uprisings of this period of transition and change warrant a special study in themselves, perhaps a short account of them here is in order.[68] Following the actual unrest caused by the restoration itself, they were to burst forth in rapid succession with over 190 between 1868 and 1878, with forty-two in the year 1869–1870 alone.[69] Professor Kokushō has divided the causes of the uprisings of this period into two types, the fundamental and the immediate. Among the former he includes those derived from the general disorder attendant with the changes in Japan's whole social structure. The ignorance and obstinacy of the farmers on the one hand and the weakness of a unifying power of the early Meiji government on the other, were likewise predominant causes. Such were the forces behind the uprising of the farmers who objected to the order that their lord, Abe Masatsune be moved from his castle in Fukuyama, Bingo. On the pretext of wishing to have the prefectural governor re-installed in office, the farmers began an uprising in 1871, wrecking the houses of the *shōya* and wealthy people.[70] In other cases, there were uprisings from the disquiet among the warriors themselves who were deprived of their rice stipends and who also often acted quite arbitrarily of the central government.[71]

Included in the immediate causes of the uprisings of the Restoration, Professor Kokushō classes those of a social nature. These were the opposition arising from the law eliminating any differentiation in classes between the farmers, merchants, craftsmen and townmen, as well as the abolition of the class of

---

68. For source materials and studies on Peasant Uprisings during the early Meiji Period Cf. Ono, Takeo, ed. *Isshin Nōmin Hōki Dan,* 1 Vol; Tōkyō, 1930, 623 pp. Tsuchiya and Ono, ed., *Meiji Shonen Nōmin Sōjoroku,* 1 Vol; Tōkyō, 1921, 655 pp. For secondary material Cf. Ono, Takeo, *Isshin Nōson Shakai Shiron,* 1 Vol.; Tōkyō, 1932. 468 pp. Kokushō. I, "*Meiji Shonen Hyakushō Ikki*", in *Meiji Isshin Keizaishi Kenkyū* edited by E. Honjō, Tōkyō, 1930, 913 pp.

69. Cf. Tsuchiya, *op. cit.,* p. 3 and 653; Kokushō, "*Meiji Shonen Ikki*", *op. cit.,* p. 709.

70. Abe Masatsune, 阿部正恒, born in 1851, was lord of the castle of Fukuyama. Cf. Ono, *Isshin Nōmin Hōki Dan, op. cit.,* pp. 105 *et seq.* for materials on this incident.

71. Kokushō, "Meiji Shonen Ikki", *op. cit.,* p. 709.

"outcasts". The farmers were not only opposed to the more innocent law making coiffures for men illegal, but to the permission to eat cattle, beasts important not so much for the milk they produced as for their use as draft animals.[72] Other immediate causes included the rise in commodity prices, and the use of a diversified currency. In Chikuzen in 1873 developed an uprising throughout the entire province, including some 300,000 people, the largest during the early years of the Meiji Period. This was originally caused by the increase in price of rice and the inequalities resulting therefrom.[73]

Many of the *daimyō* refused to accept paper money as legal tender and this caused other uprisings. Taxes still remained oppressive and one of the important immediate causes for revolt; while the establishment of a universal conscription law, schools which encouraged western learning, telephone and telegraph service, and finally requirments that everyone should register, all produced their share of disorder among the peasants. In the case in Tosa the end of 1871 the people called the government's attempt to collect taxes in money not rice, the rennovation in the paper money in the fief, the restriction of the temples, the order that priests should become commoners, the raising the social status of the "outcasts", and the establishment of universal conscription, "the squeezing of the fat from them".[74] Together with the movement that Buddhism and Shintoism should be strictly isolated, a series of uprisings, religious in nature, developed. In Bungo in 1872, some 40,000 objected to the cutting down of sacred trees on the one hand and the various taxes for religious purposes, on the other. In 1873 a priest of the Shinshū sect instigated the farmers to revolt against Christianity and advocated the abolition of western learning in the schools as that was the civilization of the Christians.[75]

Thus several years must elapse before the farmer, still suffering from years of oppression during the Tokugawa

72. *Ibid*, p. 713 *et seq.*
73. Cf. Ono, *Isshin Nōmin Hōki*, *op. cit.*, p. 275 *et seq.*
75. Kokushō, "Meiji Isshin Ikki," *op. cit.*, p. 739.

Period, was to settle down to a more serene existence. With the increase in general disorder coming as an aftermath of the Restoration of 1868, Japan was spared the ordeal of a bloody revolution such as France had endured. It was fortunate, perhaps, that the farmers had been kept subjugated as a class and had never been unified within the whole country ready to forcibly revolt as a mass against the old feudalistic form of government. Communications were too poor, there was lack of an organizing leader, and they were concerned more with the immediate problems before them than with any more general or far reaching political or social changes throughout the entire country. It only remains, therefore, to treat of the uprisings in special regions where source materials are plentiful.

CHAPTER VII

REGIONAL STUDIES OF PEASANT UPRISINGS

A. Introduction

As previously pointed out, and as would be expected, uprisings were more frequent in districts away from the centers of government, isolated by mountains, rivers or distance, where it was difficult for either the *Bakufu* officials or the lords of the domains to have a real picture of the conditions of the fiefs. Poor transportation facilities, a cold climate or a mountainous country, and special regional characteristics of the people all made these remote districts more susceptible to trouble. Although the value of any regional study is largely dependent on the materials available, enough source materials have been collected in some of these more remote localities to make their special study significant. Uprisings in Echigo and Sado on the northwest coast of Japan, Nambu in the north, Shinano and Mino in central Japan, Mimasaka in the west and Tosa and Iyo in Shikoku in the south will receive brief treatment which will give a general idea of these particular localities as well as the distinctive type of uprisings they produced.

B. Echigo and Sado

The Province of Echigo on the northwestern coast of Japan, isolated from Edo and the central government by mountain ranges, subject to heavy snowfall in winter from the winds blowing down from the Japan sea, and a district where farming at best was exceedingly difficult, affords an excellent opportunity for a study of uprisings whose causes were largely maladministration of subordinate officials who taxed the farmers unmercifully. From materials thus far collected,[1]

---

1. An excellent compilation of primary sources has been made under the auspices of the Niigata Prefectural Home Office arranged chronologically in Ishii, S., ed.; *Echigo Sado Nōmin Sōdō* 1 Vol.; Niigata, 1930, 629 pp.

there were fifty-five uprisings between 1595 and 1868. The first eleven of these coming up to 1759, took the form either of a regular uprising or that of a "mob-appeal" (*gōso*), followed by general disorder. Two of these uprisings extended throughout the entire proviuce. They were, on the most part, the result of maladministration, heavy taxes or the corruption of the local officials.[2]

In Kita Kambara District,[3] following an unsuccessful appeal in 1756 of seventy villages to their *daikan* that the recent opening of new land had only caused an increase in taxation, another petition was framed in 1759, signed by the *shōya*, one or more *Kumigashira*,[4] and representatives of the farmers from seventy villages, and delivered to the *daikan.* They complained that since the survey of land in 1734–1744 their taxes had been exceedingly heavy and that many of the farmers had been without food and drink. Together with this, the sale price of rice and beans, the two main products of the district, had been so low it was imposible for them to buy necessary implements and live stock.[5] Not content with this, six representatives of twenty-six villages went directly to Edo to appeal in the 3rd month, where they arrived after nearly a fortnight's journey. Here they appealed directly to the *Kanjo Bugyō*, Isshiki Shōkō,[6] giving him a detailed account of the abuses of their *daikan.* Petitions continued in Edo and it was not until the 9th month that the last delegation of representatives of the farmers returned to Echigo. Unfortunately, how-

---

plus chronological charts and maps. Professor Kokushō has also dealt with Echigo in his *Hyakushō Ikki Shidan,* 1 Vol.; Tōkyō, 1928, especially pp. 268–290. However this work should be checked with the more recent documents appearing in Ishii's work. Cf. Numazaki, *op. cit.,* Chart II for the most recent figures on appearances of uprisings in Echigo.

2. Cf. *Echigo Sado Sōdō op. cit.,* Supplement p. 1.

3. Kita Kambara District, 北蒲原郡

4. *Kumigashira*與頭, a village official or head of group apparently used synonymously for *kumigashira* 組頭. When the group was of a military nature it is read *yogashira.* Cf. Otsuki: *Daigenkai* Vol. II p. 58.

5. Cf. *Echigo Sado Sōdō op. cit.,* p. 90 *et seq.*

6. The text gives Isshiki, Aki no Kami, 一色安藝守, who is Isshiki Shōkō, 一色政沆, *Kanjō bugyō* from 1752–1755. Cf. *Echigo Sado Sōdō, op. cit.,* p. 105 and *Dokushi Biyō op. cit.,* p. 522.

ever, documents are lacking as to the outcome of their appeals.[7]

In the year 1789, although it is not clear whether uprisings actually follwed, two important appeals were made in different districts. The first of these in Santō District, in the domain of Makino, Bizen no Kami,[8] was a complaint made by a *kumigashira*, Okumura Kenuemon,[9] for nine villages which had recently been incorporated into the Makino domain to which he strenuously objected, fearing despotic taxes. His appeal was accepted and the taxes were reduced though in 1793 he received sentence of death and gibbitting for "having transgressed the law of the fief and having planned an appeal, formed a crowd, visited the villages with a memorandum and having obtained signatures."[10] Other punishments followed, mostly for the *shōya* and *kumigashira* of the villages concerned, some of whom were banished, others deprived of their office and fined.

The second appeal in 1789 was that from nine villages in the *Bakufu* domain under the control of Matsudaira, Higo no Kami, Katanobu, lord of Aizu.[11] These villages had recently been transferred to the jurisdiction of the Matsudairas and the farmers complained twice to Edo about the taxes and the unnecessary expenses of the *ōwarimoto*,[12] or officials in charge of several villages. There were, it appears from another complaint in 1792 by the same villages, three *ōwarimoto*, each receiving 30 bales of rice yearly from the lord of the fief as stipends, together with permission to wear swords and the use of a surname. Moreover, they received from the district in

7. Cf. *Echigo Sado Sōdō, op. cit.*, p. 193.
8. Makino, Bizen no Kami, Tadakiyo, cf. *supra* p. 100 note 4.
9. Okamura Kenuemon, 岡村權右衞門, was born in 1755, had studied Buddhism and Confucianism and was well known for his interest in the welfare of the peasant.
10. Cf. *Echigo Sado Sōdō op. cit.*, p. 212.
11. Matsudaira, Higo no Kami Katanobu, 松平肥後守容頌, was eldest son of Katasada, 容貞, (1719–1750). He was born in 1743, received the fief in 1750.
12. The term *warimoto*, 割元, is an abbreviation for *warimoto Sōdai*, 割元總代, which is synonymous with *ōshoya*, or official in charge of several villages. Hence *ōwarimoto*, (大割元) would be an official in charge of an even greater number of villages.

connection with their official work the following supplementary income: 100 *koku* of rice, 8 *momme* of silver, and the proceeds from a tax on writing brushes, paper, ink, charcoal and oil.[13] The farmers likewise complained of the *ōwarimoto* who were not in possession of the official seal and stated that the officials had been full of greed and avarice during the past ten years. Thus with the administration of this *Bakufu* domain in the hands of men away from their own home fief of Aizu, it was easy for the *ōwarimoto* to avoid censure and carry on a corrupt government for their own ends.

But the peak of uprisings in Echigo was to be reached in the early summer of 1814. During the previous fall there had been an exceedingly poor harvest although the taxes had remained the same, causing seven uprisings in six different districts from the 4th to the 6th months. Of these, that in the 4th month, 1814, is of most interest. Here the farmers in the entire 30,000 *koku* domain of Hori Naokata,[14] began a destructive march towards the castle town of Muramatsu, wrecking scores of houses as they advanced. They were instigated, not only by severe taxes in spite of a poor harvest, but also by the misgovernment and avarice of one of the elder councillors of the Hori fief who had established special taxes and bureaus for their collection. The *daikan* of the fief had likewise ordered an inspection of land to be carried out by the younger brother of the avaricious councillor, to increase the taxation. This the people could not bear, so a band of 10,000 attacked the office of the *daikan*, forcing him to flee, next wrecking the houses of the *kimoiri ōshōya*, the tax offices, the places of the inspectors of new lands, the surveyors, and tree inspectors. After a week of disorderliness, Hori Naokata returned from Edo and presented 3,000 *koku* of rice to the farmers. The councillor to which the farmers objected was

13. *Echigo Sado Sōdō, op. cit.*, p. 236.

14. Hori Naokata, 堀直方, (d. 1767), was the adopted son of Naonori, 直教, lord of the fief at Muramatsu, 村松, from 1785–1787. In 1787, Naokata inherited the domain, to keep it until 1819. It was not the fief of Hori Naotaka, 堀直堯, (1715–1785) as stated in *Dokushi Biyō, op. cit.*, p. 488. Cf. *Denki Dainihon Shi, Daimyō Hen op. cit.*, p. 478–479.

dismissed, and his brother who had carried out the inspection of land was demoted. The *daikan* and his assistant were confined to their homes and then deprived of office; while a surveyor and an *ōshōya* were imprisoned. A loan of 3,000 *ryō* which was held by an official was confiscated and other officials were imprisoned. Many of those whose places were wrecked in Muramatsu seem to have deserved such treatment for they were arrested. Of the farmers, some forty were apprehended, the two leaders received death sentences to be carried out the year following.[15]

In the next month, in both the *Bakufu* domain and that of Naitō Nobuatsu,[16] thirty-four villages in Kambara and Iwafune Districts,[17] distributed a letter stating that:

> "Because of the crop failures, the small farmers have become destitute. This year the price of rice has become painfully high, yet the rich people along the coast purchase it, ship it elsewhere and receive high prices and profit from it. Because of the famine, the small farmers and even the poorest peasants, (*mizunomi*)[18] plan to meet tomorrow . . . . . One person from each house should come armed with an implement. We have no grievances against our lord but only those rich men on the coast. Come even though you have not time for preparation and if you do not, we will burn your village."
>
> Signed: the 23rd of the 5th month, 1814.[19]

15. Cf. *Echigo Sado Sōdō, op. cit.*, p. 240–252.
16. Naitō Nobuatsu, 内藤信敦, (1777–1825), was the eldest son of Naitō Nobuyoshi, 内藤信凭, (1743–1781). Nobuatsu, received the fief of 50,000 *koku* at Murakami, 村上, in Echigo, in 1781 from his father. Matsudaira Sadanobu recognized his abilities and wished to use him for the reformation of the central government. His appointments included *Jisha-bugyō* from 1813–1817, *Wakadoshiyori* (assistant councillor) 若年寄 from 1817–1822) Kyōto *Shoshidai* from 1822–1825. During this period he attempted reforms within his own fief, eliminating extravagances, building a school, encouraging fishing, sericulture and agriculture. In this connection, let it be noted the present uprising was the last to be recorded in the Naitō realm. His actions are in striking contrast to those of the Makino family, as will soon be apparent.
17. Kambara and Iwafune Districts, 蒲原 and 岩船.
18. Mizunomi, 水呑, "water drinkers".
19. *Echigo Sado Sōdō, op. cit.*, p. 298.

For the next three days, about 2,000 farmers continued their house-wreckings until 1,000 soldiers were dispatched from a nearby *daikan's* office and they were tranquilized. After a trial held during the summer months under the supervision of officials sent from Edo, the prisoners were transferred to Edo and the following rewards and punishments were announced. A fine of 4 *ryō*, tattooing and whipping with fifty strokes for some; a fine of 215 *kamme* for farmers of thirty-three villages; a scolding for those who gave food to the mob or took part in the purchase of rice at low prices for their own profit; a fine of 3 *kamme* for the representatives of the farmers (*hyakushō-dai*), the banishment of the *kumigashira*. Rewards were as follows: 5 *ryō* for not having entered the uprisings; 3 pieces of silver for helping to apprehend a prisoner; 1 piece of silver for helping during the examination. In 1816, at the 200th anniversary of the death of Ieyasu, everyone's punishment was lightened one degree.[20]

As six of the fourteen uprisings in Echigo between 1828 and 1868 are to fall in the fief of the Makino family, let us turn to the conditions in the domain centering around Nagaoka. Makino Tadakiyo (b. 1760), lord of this 70,000 *koku* domain, spent much of his time carrying out official duties of the Edo government, having been *Jisha bugyō* in 1787, Kyōto *Shoshidai* in 1798 and *Rōjū* in 1801.[21] Thus it was necessary that his fief be run by a substitute, leaving room for corruption and graft. In 1828 taxes were increased throughout the domain, extending even to such objects as charcoal and paper. The farmers, however, planned an uprising against this situation, called out a representative from each house, and guarded the exits of the home of the *daikan* with the intention of starving him out. Troops were soon dispatched from Nagaoka and the leaders captured finally being banished from the province. In the meantime, however, the *daikan* and ten

20. *Ibid.* p. 316 *et seq.*
21. Cf. *Supra* p. 100 note 4

officials were censored, but to little avail.[22] Another uprising in the same fief, whose causes were not clear, arose in 1832, the year Makino Tadamasa took over the domain which he held until his death in 1858. Like his father he spent much of his time in Edo, holding official positions from 1836 when he was appointed *Jisha bugyō* until 1857, when he resigned from *Rōjū*.[23] Neglecting the conditions of his own fief, the situation became such that the farmers again petitioned in 1853 against their heavy taxes and the arbitrary action of their village officials. They should, they claimed, be exempt from taxes of beans and sesame seed, a seed from which oil was extracted and which was used for food, released from the obligation to pay money for certain officials, while the question of the purchase of charcoal for official use should be satisfactorily settled. The fief officials, after various house-wrecking and destruction of the houses of the merchants and *shōya* by the farmers, refused to reduce the taxes, but deprived those whose homes had been wrecked of their duties. However, no one was accused of having started the uprising. This was followed the next year, 1854, by an even more widespread disturbance. Farmers from eighty-six villages, allying themselves with the towns-people, objected to the revenue tax on charcoal, and the monopolization of the purchase of pongee at a price unfavourable to the farmers who produced the silk. The houses of four heads of the villages were wrecked, as well as rice, sake, salt and pongee shops. The leaders of the uprising escaped, but others were fined and banished. This time, however, rice and money were given to those whose places had been wrecked.[24] Thus while the lord of Nagaoka held one of the highest positions in the Edo government, his fief was in the hands of corrupt officials and an ideal setting for uprisings developed.

Again in 1866, six villages objected to the fact that they

---

22. *Echigo Sado Sōdō, op. cit.*, p. 377 and Kokushō, *Ikki Shidan, op. cit.*, p. 277.
23. Cf. *Supra* p. 100, note 4.
24. Cf. *Echigo Sado Sōdō, op. cit.*, pp. 422 and 431 *et seq.* also, Kokushō, *Ikki Shidan, op. cit.*, p. 278 *et seq.*

had recently been transferred from the *Bakufu* domain to that of the Nagaoka fief where they received unfair treatment from the *shōya*. When the officials of the fief arrested the leaders who drafted this complaint, the people rose in revolt, demanding the release of the prisoners, which was granted. The objectionable *shōya* was also ordered into retirement.[25] Two years following this, 2–3,000 farmers objected to the increase in taxation attendant with the Restoration of 1868, and again wrecked the homes of the wealthy. Thus in spite of, or perhaps because of, the high positions in the government held by the Makino family, uprisings frequently broke out in the domain, largely the result of heavy taxes imposed by unscrupulous officials. Obvious it is that if the *daimyō* were unable to cope with the situation within their own fief, they were poorly equipped for the more difficult task of ruling the whole country.

The Island of Sado, off the coast of Echigo, affords even better opportunity for a study of uprisings resulting from the action of corrupt officials. Sado, famous for its silver mines, was a *Bakufu* domain, controlled by the *Sado bugyō* who lived at the principal city, Aikawa. The tasks of this office, first established in 1603, included the collection of taxes, the direction of the silver mines and patrolling against possible incursions of foreign ships. As will be seen from the accompanying chronological chart, the eight uprisings in Sado[26] from 1603 to 1837 were all the result of heavy taxes, six of them extending over the whole island. As a result of an uprising of more than two hundred villages in 1749 the farmers were allowed a fifteen years exemption on half of a new tax

---

25. Cf. *Echigo Sado Sōdō, op. cit.*, pp. 453–463. Makino Tadayuki, 牧野忠恭, was lord of the fief from 1858–1866. He was an adopted son of Tadamasa, was *Jisha bugyō* from 1862 to 1863, then becoming *Shoshidai* for a year, *rōjū* from 1863–1865. He was followed by Tadatsuyo, 忠毅, who held the fief in 1868.

26. Sado 佐渡, Cf. *supra* p. 12 note 41. From Chart I of the appendix it will be noticed that Numazaki gives fourteen uprisings in Sado, but I have not seen material on the other six nor are they mentioned in *Echigo Sado Nōmin Sōdō*.

recently imposed upon them. In 1767 it is reported the whole island revolted, even killing the *Sado bugyō*, so intense was their hatred of the officials.[27] As a result of a mob-appeal of the entire island in 1847 against the evil administration of the officials, both the *Sado bugyō* in Edo and that in Sado were dismissed from office and confined to their homes.[28] Among the farmers the punishment was more severe. Eighteen were sentenced to death and to have their heads exposed, eighteen given an ordinary death sentence without exposure, twenty-eight exiled, probably to Hachijō Island, south of Edo, and over a hundred and fifty received orders to be exiled to varying distances from their homes. Others were banished, handcuffed, or fined.[29] Thus Sado was an ideal place for officials to act as they pleased, isolated from the central authorities, until they had oppressed the peasants to the point of revolt, thus forcing a change of officials, only to have the whole process repeated after a lapse of years.

ECHIGO UPRISINGS CHRONOLOGICAL LIST[30]

DATE	DISTRICT	FIEF	CAUSES	FORM
1592	Kita-Kambara	Takanashi	Harsh government.	Uprising

27. Cf. *Echigo Sado Sōdō, op. cit.*, pp. 571 *et seq.* and 595 *et seq.* Professor Tsuji reports that a court nobleman of Kyōto wrote in his diary that this occurred in the 8th month, 1768. Cf. Tsuji, *Tanuma Jidai, op. cit.*, p. 141.

28. In 1603 a *Sado bugyō* was appointed by the *Bakufu* with an income of 1500 bales of rice and enough to support 100 men: including 2 *kumigashira*, 30 *yoriki*, and 70 *dōshin*, as his guard. Two *bugyō* were appointed in 1712, the number returning to one in 1862.

29. Cf. *Echigo Sado Sōdō, op. cit.*, p. 610 *et seq.* The uprising referred to in *Ukiyo no Arisama* as occurring in 1838 when the farmers drove away the inspector sent from Edo, probably refers to the above. Cf. *Ukiyo no Arisama, op. cit.*, Vol. IV, p. 209.

30. The following tables on Echigo and Sado are based on those in *Echigo Sado Sōdō, op. cit.*, Supplement, p. 1–4. Thus the discrepancies between the uprisings listed and those mentioned below in Chart I, Appendix II. The "Form" these uprisings took are those given in the original chart. The terms *bōdō* 暴動 and *sōran* 騷亂 have been rendered as "uprising"; *fuon* 不穩 as "disorders"; *esso* as "appeal"; *gosō* 强訴 as "mob-appeal" and *uchikowashi* 打毀 as "house-wreckings." Cf. *supra* p. 16 note 5 and p. 58 note 86.

DATE	DISTRICT	FIEF	CAUSES	FORM
1596	Santō	Takanashi	Harsh government.	Mob-appeal
1599–1600	Entire Province		Transference of lord of the fief.	Uprising
1621 7 mo.	Koshi	Makino	New government Heavy taxes.	Mob-appeal
1690 10 mo.	Koshi	Makino	Method of collecting taxes.	Mob-appeal
1710 2 mo.	Kambara	Matsudaira	85 villages complain of change from *Bakufu* jurisdiction to that of private domain.	Appeal, disorders.[31]
1711	Minami Kambara	Mizoguchi	Evil government of *Ōshōya* and friction between them and the *nanushi*.	Disorders
1722	Entire Kubiki District	*Bakufu*	Quarrel over leased land with *Bakufu* officials.	Appeals Uprisings
1724 2 mo.	Naka Kambara	Yanagiwara	Dispute between private and *Bakufu* realm over woodland and water source.	Uprising
1729 8 mo.	Kambara	Mizoguchi	Not clear.	Mob-appeal
1736 12 mo.	Kita-Kambara	Mizoguchi	Inequality in reference to taxes on new fields.	Mob-appeal
1759 3 mo.	Kita-Kambara	*Bakufu*	Mis-government of *daikan*, survey with wrong assessment causing unfair, heavy taxes.	Mob-appeal
1767	Near Niigata	Makino	Heavy taxes because of forced levy by *Bakufu*.	Mob-appeal
1778	Minami-Kambara	Mizoguchi & *Bakufu*	Not clear.	House-wrecking
1783 3 mo.	All of Province		Not clear.	Not clear

31. Arai Hakuseki advised the Shōgun to grant the farmers their demands which was done, though the land remained in the fief of Matsudaira Terasada. Cf. Knox, *op. cit.*, p. 128 *et seq.*

DATE	DISTRICT	FIEF	CAUSES	FORM
1789 1 mo.	Santō	Makino	Transfer of villages to Makino fief and heavy taxes.	Mob-appeal
1789 1 mo.	Minami-Uonuma	*Bakufu* under care of Matsudaira.	Mis-government of *ōshoya* and bad management of finances of villages by officials.	Mob-appeal
1806	Naka-Kambara	Not clear	Not clear.	Not clear
1814 4 mo.	Naka & Minami Kambara	Entire fief of Hori	Bad harvest, heavy taxes, oppressive officials.	Mob-appeal House-wrecking
1814 5 mo.	Kita-Kambara	Matsudaira	Bad harvest.	Mob-appeal
1814 5 mo.	Kita-Kambara & Iwafune	*Bakufu* & Naito	Bad harvest.	Mob-appeal
1814 5 mo.	Minami-Kambara	*Bakufu*	Bad harvest.	Mob-appeal
1814 5 mo.	Naka-Kambara	Matsudaira	Bad harvest.	Mob-appeal
1814 6 mo.	Santō	Makino	Bad harvest.	Mob-appeal
1814 6 mo.	Koshi	Makino	Bad harvest.	Mob-appeal
Before 1817	Naka-Kubiki	Not clear	Bad harvest.	Mob-appeal
1828 8 mo.	Koshi	Makino	Tax on pongee and collection in silver.	House-wreckings
1829	Naka Kambara	Mizoguchi	Change of status of villages.	House-wreckings
1830	Niigata City	*Bakufu*	Townsmen and farmers suffer from bad crop.	House-wreckings
1832 6 mo.	Nishi-Kambara	Makino	Not clear.	Mob-appeal
1837	Naka-Uonuma	Matsudaira	Bad crops.	House-wreckings
1837 6 mo.	Kariwa	Matsudaira	Bad crops.	House-wreckings
1848	Naka-Kambara	Not clear	Wealthy people asked that new lands be opened.	Uprising

DATE	DISTRICT	FIEF	CAUSES	FORM
1853 8 mo.	Koshi	Makino	Heavy taxes.	Mob-appeal and house-wreckings
1854 6 mo.	Koshi	Makino	Heavy taxes and monopoly on purchase of pongee.	Mob-appeal and house-wreckings
1861	Higashi-Kubiki	*Bakufu*	Increase in price of rice.	House-wreckings
1863	Minami-Kambara	Not clear	Dispute between *Bakufu* and private fiefs over broken dykes.	Uprising
1865	Kita-Uonuma	*Bakufu*	Taxes on cotton goods.	Mob-appeal
1866	Kariwa	Makino	Change in status of villages from *Bakufu* to Makino fief.	Disorder
1868 4 mo.	Nishi-Kambara	Makino	Bad crops, evil administration of *shōya*.	House-wreckings

SADO UPRISINGS CHRONOLOGICAL LIST

DATE	REGION	FIEF	CAUSES	FORM
1603 7 mo.	All of Sado	*Bakufu*	Heavy additional taxes.	Appeal
1627	All of Sado	*Bakufu*	Change in taxes.	Appeal
1632	All of Sado	*Bakufu*	Methods of tax collection and affairs concerning the silver mines.	Mob-appeal
1710 5 mo.	All of Sado	*Bakufu*	Increased taxes and evil administration of officials.	Mob-appeal
1749 11 mo.	207 villages	*Bakufu*	Heavy taxes and evil administration of officials.	Appeal and disorder
1761	58 villages	*Bakufu*	Heavy taxes	Appeal
1767 11 mo.	All of Sado	*Bakufu*	Heavy taxes	Mob-appeal
1837	All of Sado	*Bakufu*	Heavy taxes and evil officials.	Mob-appeal

Note: Sano Gaku, in his *Nōson Mondai*, p.115 states that

there was a peasant uprising in 1768, including 70,000 men, at which time *Bakufu* officials and the *Sado bugyō* were killed. This is probably that of 1767. [Ishii's note.]

C. Nambu

Although not so isolated geographically as either Echigo or Sado, the fief of the Nambu family, centering around Morioka in Rikuchū, affords interesting material for detailed study due to the fact that it was under the control of the same family from the first uprising in that domain in 1617 until the eighty-fourth in 1870. The Nambu family, whose early ancestors fought with Yoritomo in the 12th century, was first established in Morioka in 1600.[32] The central organization of the fief was composed of a "Head of the Guard of the Central Castle",[33] in charge of all police and military duties. There were also seven to fourteen *Goyōnin*,[34] or managers, a Finance Minister,[35] with a dozen assistants called *Kanjō bugyō*, and various other officers with special duties such as the *daikan*, each of whom had charge of one of the thirty-three *tōri*,[36] or administrative sections. The domain was rich in resources, gold, copper and iron being the most important minerals and horses and rice being the most profitable farm products. In 1682 it is reported there was a rice crop of 249,000 *koku* for a population of 307,000 people; while even in 1780 there was an average of two horses for every household. Gold was mined some sixty different times between 1600 and 1740, but after 1688 the gold production began to decline and bad harvests and

---

32. The Morioka Castle, 盛岡, was built in 1600 by Nambu Toshinao, 南部利直, (d. 1632), who controlled a fief of 130,000 *koku*. In 1664 the Hachinohe, 八ノ戸, branch of the family was established with 20,000 *koku*. The fief received some 148,000 *koku* of new land up to 1716 and by 1804 it was definitely recognized as a fief of 200,000 *koku*.

For a study, not only of the peasant uprisings in the Nambu realm, but also the financial and economic situation of the fief, Cf. Mori, K., ed. *Kyū Nambu Han ni okeru Hyakushō Ikki no Kenkyū*, 1 Vol.; Saitō Foundation, Sendai, 1935 364 pp.

33. He was called the *Nakamaru Gobangashira*, 中丸御番頭.

34. Goyōnin, 御用人.

35. Ōkura Daijin, 大蔵大臣.

36. Tōri, 通. Cf. Mori, *Kyū Nambu Ikki, op. cit.*, p. 2 *et seq.*

famine were common. Fields were abandoned and the people and horses starved to death. By the beginning of the 18th century it is reported the fief carried a loan of 100,000 *ryō* and the finances had become completely insolvent. To this was added the fact that there were seventy-nine complete or partial crop failures between 1617 and 1870 so it is not surprising to find uprisings plentiful. It is said that after the middle of the 18th century innumerable persons perished throughout the years of famine and pestilence, while the survivors freely practiced abortion, infanticide and other negative methods of birth control to keep down the population.[37]

Rather than give a detailed account of the various uprisings throughout the Nambu fief, the accompanying chronological list gives a general outline of their frequency of occurrence, their causes and results. There are, however, thirteen uprisings recorded for the year 1853, the most important of these being well worthy of special attention. During the years 1847–1849, when Nambu Toshiyoshi controlled the fief, the government was well run, but the ministers who held the favour of his retired father, Nambu Toshitada, slandered the young ruler and forced him to live in retirement in Edo. His successor was his younger brother, Toshihisa, while the actual government was carried on by corrupt ministers and the retired father, Toshitada.[38] Among these ministers was one Ishihara who was a tobacco merchant and who allied himself with Toshitada through marriage. He is reported to have been avaricious, luxurious in his demands and a favourite of the old lord. As a result, new taxes were imposed, and monopolistic control of all markets was established under the control of wealthy merchants, and Ishihara

---

37. *Ibid*, p. 8 *et seq.* and p. 21 *et seq.* 49,594 are reported to have died in 1755.

38. Nambu Toshitada, 南部利濟, had resigned from head of the fief in 1847 in favour of his son, Nambu, Iga no Kami, Toshiyoshi, 南部伊賀守利義. He was forced to resign in the 9th month, 1849 in favour of his younger brother, Mino no Kami, Toshihisa, 美濃守利剛. Unfortunately no exact dates for these men are given. Cf. *Kokushi Daijiten,* Vol. IV, p. 1930 *et seq.*

was raised to the rank of a warrior with a yearly income and complete freedom over the finances of the fief.[39] Thus troubles began to break out early in 1853 when some 600 farmers decided to appeal to the neighbouring domain of Sendai against corruption in their fief, and if that failed, to carry their complaints to Edo. It was not, however, until after a fencing master who had been spying for the farmers reported in the 5th month of the same year,[40] that, "there were evil ministers assisting both Toshitada and his son, who increased the luxuries and who were responsible for the distress among the people by their additional taxes." After that the real trouble was to develop.[41]

On the 21st of the 5th month, 99 villages sent a formal protest against the forced resignation of their former lord, Toshiyoshi. Word was then circulated about by the farmers that they were to assemble at Noda Village on the 27th of the 5th month, the farmers in the meantime had asked wealthy men for contributions to defray the expenses of their proposed plans, and had received an offer of 10,000 *ryō* from a sympathizer. A *daikan* was immediately sent from the castle at the signs of disorder, accompanied by 200 soldiers, but he was informed by the farmers that they would not appeal to Morioka, but were going to another domain to work or to become indentured servants. The officials were slandered who attempted their arrest, one fell off his horse, and some of the mob of 10,000 gladly bound him in the net he had brought, then hung him upside down on a tree. As the mob increased in size and distructiveness, they demanded 200 to 500 *ryō*

---

39. Mori, *Kyū Nambu Ikki, op. cit.*, p. 214 *et seq.*

40. Cf. *Tōno Toni Nemonogatari*, an account of the uprisings of 1853 by a contemporary, Senryūken Nanseki, whose identity remains unknown. The author, because of fear of the authorities, often uses arbitary terms for proper names. Thus the first disturbance is reported as occurring in Sannohe District, 三ノ戸, really Sannohe, 三邊. Morioka is referred to as Moriyama, Edo as Kamakura. The text is printed in Ono, Takeo, *Tokugawa Jidai Hyakushō Ikki Sōdan*, Vol. 1, p. 384–444. It is likewise treated in detail in Mori, *Kyū Nambu Ikki, op. cit.*, pp. 213–298.

41. Cf. *Tōno Tōni Nemonogatari, op. cit.*, p. 394 *et seq.*

from the wealthy in return for not wrecking their houses. Thus they began their southern journey to the neighbouring fief of Sendai, undaunted by the natural barriers between them and the border, or a thousand soldiers sent out to stop them.[42]

Of a total crowd of some 25,000, nearly half that number reached the frontier and crossed into the Sendai domain. They were then met by the *Kōri bugyō* and other officials from Sendai to whom they presented the following:

"1. All the people in our province [of Rikuchū] desire that Lord Iga [Nambu Toshiyoshi], who is now living in Edo, return and become lord of our domain.
2. Beginning with ourselves, all the farmers of Sannc' District desire to become farmers of your fief.
3. We demand that the abuses related in our petition of fifty-two demands be rectified."[43]

They then asked that any one of these three requests be granted but the Sendai officials refused them. They presented, however, their petition of fifty-two articles. Officials from their own fief of Morioka were not only ridiculed by the farmers when they appeared, but blamed by the Sendai officials for their neglect of duty. "If in the Sendai fief", the officials said, "There was an uprising of 10,000 or even 20,000 people, and we the officials of Sendai with a guard of 20 gens d'armes allowed a single person to pass, we would commit sucide because of our shame." Finally the farmers were instructed to leave forty-five men behind as representatives and the remainder were persuaded to return home while the Sendai officials examined their requests and priests from temples in Sendai acted as intermediaries.

The farmers then asked that they be allowed to become farmers of either the Sendai or *Bakufu* domain and that their grievances be met. The articles of complaint having been received by the priests who presented them to the Morioka

---

42. Cf. *Ibid*, p. 395 *et seq.*
43. Cf. *Ibid*, p. 407–408.

officials, the farmers returned home in the 9th month. Although various texts give a few discrepancies in these famous fifty-two articles, though some of them are lost, and the meaning of some is obscure, nevertheless as the officials of the fief carefully examined these and presented their reply on the 9th of the 10th month, both the demands and replies are valuable for the picture they give of the economic life of Nambu. They are as follows:[44]

1. Request:

   We regret the recent offer to increase our taxes and to collect them in money when the price of rice is disadvantageous to us.

   Reply:

   Having previously determined the price of rice, [it will continue to be the same].

2. Request:

   We object to the custom of having "commissioners for all kinds of things" since about 1820.[45]

   Reply:

   The request is granted for the dismissal of the new officers [commissioners] who have been appointed [to take charge of these matters].

3. Request:

   We object to the purchase of large beans and cotton by the authorities at a low price.

---

44. For two different sets of these articles Cf. *Tōno Tōni Nemonogatari, op. cit.*, p. 420–424 and 431–434. For a correlated list of ten different texts of these articles Cf. Mori, *Kyū Nambu Ikki op. cit.*, p. 244–255. The same reference gives the replies of the Nambu fief officials on the 9th of 9th month, on p. 275–277. The requests and replies have been given together here to make it of more interest. The order of the requests is that given in *Tōno Tōni, op. cit.*, p. 430 *et seq.*, but compared with those given in *Kyū Nambu Ikki,* and translations made from the clearest texts.

45. The text reads: *Shoshiki ukeoi,* 諸色受負 "having commissioners for all kinds of goods". *Ukeoi* is defined as, "taking financial responsibility for".

Reply:

Large beans shall be bought at a higher price. As for cotton, your demand is not clear [and without grounds].

4. Request:

We object to the increased expenses due to the growth in number of *daikan* from one to four.

Reply:

There shall be two *daikan* and two assistants [only].

5. Request:

We object to the extraordinary taxes [or services or *corvee*] which did not exist [formerly]. For the last twenty years we have had to pay an extraordinary tax several times a year, but last year ten times, and this year, a large amount of money twice.[46]

Reply:

It is not easy to reply [concerning this] and we will report our answer later.

6. Request:

We complain of the increase in the number of the "mountain supervisors" (*yama bugyō*) to six and their expenses, whereas the office was formerly held by the *daikan*.

Reply:

This shall be as formerly with the *daikan* taking charge of the duties of this office.

7. Request:

Formerly there were two assistant officials [who were warriors] in each village. We object to their having increased to four.

---

46. Cf. Mori, *op. cit.*, p. 244 and *Tōno Tōni* p. 421 which gives the following: "We object to the extraordinary taxes or services or *corvee* (*Gojō yaku*), 御定役, which did not exist previously. Twenty years ago we paid 10 bales of rice a year, now we pay 11 bales thrice yearly [of extraordinary taxes].

Reply:
Their numbers have been reduced.

8. Request:
We complain of the increase in clerks from one to three.
Reply:
Their numbers have been reduced.

9. Request:
We complain of the increase in the examiners of live stock from one to four officials.
Reply:
Their numbers have been reduced.

10. Request:
We complain of the increase in horse officials[47] [to examine the horses for taxation purposes].
Reply:
Their numbers have been reduced.

11. Request:
Previously there had been no inspection of horses in foal [for tax purposes]. We complain of the expenses from this yearly inspection.
Reply:
The request shall be granted.

12. Request:
We complain of the expenses for feasts for officials as well as those for paper and notebooks.
Reply:
The request shall be granted.

13. Request:
There has been an increase in each of the following officials from one to two: *metsuke, Kanjo bugyō*, and horse inspector.
Reply,
The number of officers shall be equal to those formerly.

---

47. *Uma kimoiri*, 馬肝煎.

14. Request:
    Formerly the inspection of three-year-old colts took place at the town horse office. Recently a *metsune* and *jōyaku* have been appointed to do this to which we object [because of the increased expenses].

    Reply:
    The number of officials shall be equal to those formerly.

15. Request:
    We object to the sale of horses being transferred from Sendai Market to Morioka [where the prices are lower].

    Reply:
    Two-year-olds, old horses or poor horses are permitted to leave the fief.

16. Request:
    We complain of having to hand over even the skin of a dead horse to the "commissioners".

    Reply:
    This shall be stopped.

17. Request:
    We complain of the purchase of raw silk at a low price by "commissioners".

    Reply:
    This shall cease.

18. Request:
    We wish the management of three villages to be as formerly under the jurisdiction of the capital.

    Reply:
    This is difficult to concede.

19. Request:
    We complain of the recent increase in certain taxes.

Reply:
This matter must be examined further [after which] we will notify you.

20. Request:
We object to the increase in "sailor inspectors" from one to four.
Reply:
Their numbers have been reduced.

21. Request:
We wish to receive daily wages as previously.
Reply:
Your demand is not clear [and without grounds].

22. Request:
We object to the monopoly in the handling of seaweed and bone powder used for fertilizer.
Reply:
This shall cease.

23. Request:
We object to the monopoly on tunny and fish nets.
Reply:
This matter must be examined further [after which] we will notify you.

24. Request:
We object that the price of fish for food has failed to decline.
Reply:
Your demand is not clear [and without grounds]

25. Request:
We object to the cash-tax on fire-wood and nets.
Reply:
This shall cease.

26. Request:
We object to the double in taxes of goods entering and leaving Morioka.
Reply:
This shall be as formerly.

27. Request:
    We object to the increase in salt tax from 2 *mon* per *shō* to 8 *mon* per *shō*.
    Reply:
    This shall be as formerly.
28. Request:
    We object to an increase in tax on rice from 2 *mon* per *shō* to 4 *mon* and a tax on small beans.
    Reply:
    This shall be as formerly.
29. Request:
    [A settlement of the question of] labourers required for the iron mines.
    Reply:
    They shall be paid as much as possible.
30. Request:
    We object to the paper money used at the fish market.
    Reply:
    Your request shall be granted.
31. Request:
    In consideration of the extremely severe control of the price of rice and the land tax which was collected in money with the value of a *koku* of rice being estimated above the actual rice exchange price, we object to the sale of stored rice at a high price.
    Reply:
    Your demand is not clear [and without grounds].[48]
32. Request:
    We object to the monopolistic purchase of silk and hemp.

---

48. The text of this request, like many others is extremely abbreviated but can perhaps be translated as above.

Reply:

Your demand is not clear [and without grounds].

33. Request:

We object to the increased levy of cows for use in transportation in requisitions of copper mines and the shipment of copper.

Reply:

This cannot be granted.

34. Request:

There is an unfair tax on salt pots.

Reply:

Your demand is not clear [and without grounds].

35. Request:

We object to the supplying of wood for the fires in making gunpowder from saltpetre.[49]

Reply:

This cannot be granted.

36. Request:

We object to the evils connected with the footmen leading horses.

Reply:

[None given in the text].

37. Request:

We object to the tax on lacquer plants.

Reply:

This shall be granted.

38. Request:

We object to the increase in taxes on dog-tooth violets [from which starch is made].

Reply:

This shall be granted.

39. Request:

We object to the various costs in reference to documents.

---

49. The details of the text on this point are completely omitted and further research is required before this point is fully clarified.

Reply:

This matter must be examined further [after which] we will report to you.

40. Request:

We object to the various services which are required.

Reply:

[None given in the text].

41. Request:

We object to the tax on "cloudy wine" [which was used by the farmers in contrast to the clear wine used by the townsmen].

Reply:

This has been granted.

42. Request:

We object to the monopoly on timber.

Reply:

This cannot be granted.

43. Request:

We object to the special forced levies seven or eight times a year.

Reply:

This request shall be granted.

44. Request:

We object to the heavy bribery of postillions and others.

Reply:

[Not given in the text].

45–52. [Lost].

Though the original demand that their previous lord, Toshiyoshi, be returned from Edo, was not granted, nevertheless nearly all of the specific demands were approved by the authorities. This was the result, perhaps, of the officials realising that if 12,000 farmers could travel to the next domain without being stopped they were in earnest and they would desert again unless their requests were granted.

For the other uprisings in Nambu fief, the following chronological list will suffice:

NAMBU CHRONOLOGICAL LIST

DATE	SECTIONS (*TŌRI*)	CAUSES	FORM	SUCCESS	NUMBERS
1627	?	Against new lord.	Disorder	No	
1695 8 mo.	1	Famine and heavy taxes.	Mob-appeal	Yes	
1731 3 mo.	3	New taxes.	Mob-appeal	Yes	1,000
1744 2 mo.	1	Opening new land.	Mob-appeal	Yes	2,000
1754	1	Forced levy	Mob-appeal	No	Several hundreds
1754 12 mo.	1	Desired postponement of date of tax collection	Appeal[50]	No	
1764	1	Forced levies.	Mob-appeal	No	
1777	2 uprisings in 2 sections	Money tax on salt.	Mob-appeal	Yes	580
1793	1		Appeal	No	
1794	1	Demand for fees for services of lackies.	Appeal	No	
1795	6 uprisings in 23 sections	Heavy taxes.	Mob-appeal	Yes	Several thousands
1796	5 uprisings in 2 sections	Heavy taxes.	Mob-appeal	Yes	Several thousands
1796	5 uprisings in 2 sections	High price of rice.	House-wrecking & appeal	Yes & No	Several thousands
1797	1	Heavy taxes.	Appeal	Yes	Several hundreds
1801	2	Desired loans to pay for taxes yearly.	Mob appeal-	No	Several hundreds

50. The term *shūso*, 愁訴 is used in the text for "appeal" in all but three cases, when *esso*, 越訴, is used.

DATE	SECTIONS (*TŌRI*)	CAUSES	FORM	SUCCESS	NUMBERS
1803	1	Desired reduction of taxes, chastisement of warriors & village officials.	Appeal	Yes	Several hundreds
1804	2	Desired loans to pay for taxes yearly.	Appeal	No	Several hundreds
1804	1	Heavy demands for lackies.	Appeal	No	Several hundreds
1805	1	Heavy demands for lackies.	Appeal	No	Several hundreds
1811	1	Heavy demands for lackies.	Appeal	Yes	Several hundreds
1814	2 uprisings in 2 sections	Heavy taxes & selection of village officials.	Mob-appeal	Yes & No	Several hundreds
1815	2 uprisings in 5 sections	High price of rice and division of villages.	Mob-appeal	No	Several thousands
1819	Over 2	Heavy taxes, desired loans to help pay for taxes.	Mob-appeal House-wrecking.	Yes & No	Several hundreds
1822	1	Attack of village officials.	House-wrecking.	Yes	Several hundreds
1823	1	Opening of new fields	House-wrecking.	Yes	Several hundreds
1824	1	High price of rice and desired loans for taxes.	Mob-appeal	No	Several hundreds
1825	1	Monopoly of salt.	Mob-appeal	Yes	Several hundreds
1827	1	Forced levies	Mob-appeal	No	Several hundreds
1832	1	Heavy taxes	Mob-appeal	Yes	Several hundreds
1833	1	Lackies services	Mob-appeal	Yes	Several hundreds
1834	2 uprisings in 3 sections	Heavy taxes	Mob-appeal	Yes & No	2,000
1835	2	Inspection of land	Mob-appeal	No	Several hundreds

DATE	SECTIONS (*TŌRI*)	CAUSES	FORM	SUC-CESS	NUMBERS
1836	1 district (*kōri*)	Heavy taxes paper currency	Mob-appeal	No	Several thousands
1836	1 district (*kōri*)	Grievance over management	Mob-appeal	Yes	Several thousands
1836	3 uprisings in 3 districts	Monopoly and evils of wealth.	House-wrecking	1 No 2 Yes	Several hundreds
1836	1	Desired exemption of taxes.	House-wrecking	Yes	Several hundreds
1837	1 district	Breach of contract of authorities	Appeal	No	Several thousands
1846	1	Promotion of village head.	House-wrecking	Yes	
1847	3 uprisings in 5 sections	Heavy taxes.	Mob-appeal	1 Yes 2 No	1,600
1849	2	Evil *Daikan*	Appeal	No	Several hundreds
1853	1	Heavy taxes.	Mob-appeal	No	Several hundreds
1853	3	Heavy taxes.	Appeal	No	25,000
1853	11 uprisings in 11 sections	Heavy taxes and influence of above uprising.	Mob-appeal & House-wreckings	6 Yes 5 No	Several hundreds
1854	5 uprisings in 13 sections	Collection of loans, export tax.	House-wreckings and mob-appeal	Yes	Several hundreds
1866	6	Heavy taxes.	Mob-appeal	Yes	Several thousands

D. Shinano

Shinano, in the modern prefecture of Nagano, an extremely mountainous province in central Japan, affords interesting material for study, with some twenty-five uprisings occurring between 1670 when the farmers first violently objected to a heavy increase in taxation, and 1868 when the populace, influenced by riots in the neighbouring province of Kōzuke, wrecked the houses of the wealthy in their protest against the high price of rice.[51] The first important disturbance of Shinano occurred, however, during the last month of 1761 at Ueda.[52] This town with some 1500 houses,[53] and fifteen temples, was the centre of the domain of Matsudaira, Iga no Kami, Tadayori, with a fief of 58,000 *koku.*[54] This fief was divided into seven administrative groups and was controlled by five elders with an income of about 650 *koku* each, who supervised the work of twenty-two assistants including the treasurers, the *daikan,* and their subordinate officers.[55]

On a night of the 12th month, 1761, two or three hundred farmers from the village of Shijiri gathered in front of the castle gate. They were then confronted by two *Kōri bugyō,* who ordered the farmers to make any complaints they might have through the regular channels of the village officers. To this the farmers replied that they had appealed as a mob because all their petitions to the village officers had been neglected. "Though we may be killed by you," they continued, "because of our continued distress due to levies of advance taxes and special 'forced levies' in recent years, we have decided to petition before the castle. Moreover, in the rice

---

51. For a detailed study of peasant uprisings especially in the southeastern part of Shinano, Cf. Kobayashi, H., *Inanōmin Sōdō Shi, op. cit.*, 1 Vol.; Iida, 1933, 291 pp. Numasaki gives fifty-five uprisings in Shinano and has obviously found new material.

52. The following material is taken from *Ueda Ryōnai Sōdō,* a MS. in the Shiryō Hensanjo of Tōkyō Imperial University which gave the author free use of this material. The original MS. is owned by Katsura Takateru of Echigo. As the only other mention of this uprising is in Kobayashi, *op. cit.*, p. 7, where materials are taken from another source, it seems justifiable to present somewhat in detail the materials given in the *Uyeda Ryōnai Sōdō* MS.

53. Cf. *Kyōhō Hōreki Kammonsho,* another MS. in the *Shiryō Hensanjo.*

54. Ueda Castle, 上田城, had been under the control of Saneda Nobufusa, 眞田信幸, at the time of Ieyasu, a domain of 90,000 *koku.* In 1622 it was transferred to Sengoku Tadamasa, 仙石忠政, whose descendants remained at Ueda until 1706. The lord of the Ueda Castle in 1763 was Matsudaira Tadayori, 松平忠順, (1726–1783). Called Iga no Kami, he inherited the fief of 53,000 *koku* in 1750. In 1763 he was appointed *Sōshaban* 奏者番 officer who introduced the *daimyō* to the Shogun, and *Jisha bugyō* 1764. In 1775 he was appointed *Wakadoshiyori* which post he held until his death.

55. Cf. *Uyeda Ryōnai Sōdō,* p. 15.

market it has been ordered that the price of rice shall be 1 *koku* 4 *to* per *ryō* of gold instead of 1 *koku* 8–9 *to*."[56] The two officials were then forced to flee within the castle gate, followed by the farmers who smashed down the gate with their bamboo spears and fire hooks, and then retired in front of the castle wall. That night they built fires and the priests in the town sounded the fire alarm. At this 17–18,000 farmers appeared before the castle. They then demanded that the two officials who had just admonished them be turned over to them together with the produce market official, the treasurer, and the official of the cereal stores.[57] An assistant elder minister and *Kōri bugyō* acted as intermediary and promised in writing that the demands of the farmers would be presented to the lord of the domain in Edo. The intermediary, together with another official, then departed.

In the meantime, the farmers divided into two parties, wrecking the homes of two *warimoto*, one *ōshōya* and two others, clearing out everything in their homes as well as the contents of their storehouses. One place was burnt down but the farmers kept the fire from spreading by laying watersoaked mats on the roofs of the neighbouring houses.[58] They next wrecked the property of a townsman of the rank of one who carried a sword and who received a stipend of ten men's rations. They brought out all the cotton goods he had for sale but left untouched the pawned articles in his godown. Of the merchants in the town they demanded wine and rice

---

56. *Ibid*, p. 2. It is interesting to note here the beginnings of a transfer from a strictly rice economy to a money and its subsequent complications and hardships upon the peasant.

57. *Kaisho yakunin*, 會所役人. An official in charge of the produce market. In some localities it was the officials in charge of the office where the village heads gathered. In many cases this would be "The produce market." *Okura bugyō*, 御藏奉行, is translated as "the official in charge of the cereal stores". In Edo he was an official under the *Kanjō bugyō* who had charge of storing rice and cereals and their distribution to the officials, hence a type of paymaster of cereals. In the present domain the produce market official and office of treasurer (*Kanjō bugyō*) were held by the same person.

58. Cf. *Uyeda Ryōnai Sōdō* pp. 3–5.

under the threat of wrecking their places and moved on to clear out half the merchandize of a haberdasher because of the insults he had given them. Sugar was confiscated from the four pharmacies in the town and eight *sake* shops were destroyed. Eight additional properties of *warimoto* and *koshōya* were then wrecked, from which the register books and household effects were taken to make fires to warm the mob during the night.[59]

Upon the return of the intermediary from Edo on the 22nd, he called the priests to the castle and asked them to protect the four officials the insurgents desired. To this the priests consented provided the leaders of the farmers be exempt from any investigation or sentence when the affair was settled.[60] The intermediary then summoned five representative farmers from each of the seven groups to the castle and reported that the "forced levies" and money taxes would be returned to them at the rate of 2 *koku* of rice for each *ryō*. Among the further requests made by the farmers were the following: the distance for the transportation of tax rice be shortened, the collection of taxes be made in unhulled rice, new lands be exempted from yearly taxes, mountain lands likewise be exempted, and that there be exemption from repair work on the castle and there be no further additional taxes. They asked for permission to use guns and that the question of giving feasts to various officials and free boarding to travelers be settled. Objections were raised to the custom of changing the *shōya* and *warimoto* of the villages every five years. Although no record remains of the results of these latter demands, the following punishments were ordered: two *Kōri bugyō*, "the produce market official" the treasurer and four *daikan* all be deprived of their offices. Thus the affair was settled quite amicably for the farmers although a small uprising is recorded for one day in the next month.

---

59. According to Kobayashi, the side hair on the heads of the householders were cut off, others were stripped naked and tied, beaten and covered with human excrement. Cf. Kobayashi, *op. cit.*, p. 7.

60. Cf. *Ueda Ryōnai Sōdō* p. 6.

In spite of the uprising coming at the end of the year with its attendant hardships upon the merchants and artisans, the New Year's festivities were ordered to be continued. From the town of Ueda, complaints were made for the loss sustained from wood stolen by the farmers and the increase of daily wages of workers from 52 *mon* to 72 or 86 *mon*. Following this, the outraged townsmen were given 200 bales of rice and 200 horseloads of firewood, after which the question of wages was settled.[61]

The remaining uprisings in Shinano, with no particular justification for their detailed description, should not be completely omitted. Hence a somewhat extended chronological list follows.

Chronological list of Shinano Uprisings after 1761

1762–Ina District, near the castle town of Iida, in the fief of Hori Chikanaga.[62]
 Causes: Tax of 2 *ryō* per month on 1000 people imposed by *shōya* and other officials.
 Form: House-wreckings, mob appeal of 18,000.
 Result: Special tax suspended, Elder minister left office, leaders of uprising who were imprisoned later pardoned.[63]

1769–Nishi Chikuma District.
 Causes: Not clear.
 Form: Mob-appeal.
 Results Not clear.

61. Cf. *Ibid*, pp. 9–12.

62. Hori Chikanaga, 堀親長, (1752–) inherited the fief at Iida with 15,000 *koku* in 1746, and retired in 1779. He was likewise called Yamato no Kami after 1753.

63. The following incidents will be based on Kobayashi, *op. cit.*, pp. 8 *et seq.* unless otherwise designated. The majority of uprisings in Shinano will appear to occur in Ina simply because that is the only district so far having received special study.

1775–Village of Kishima in Shimo-Takai District.
Causes: Not clear.
Form: Mob-appeal before office of garrison chief.
Result: Leaders arrested and the uprising tranquilized.[64]

1777–Takai and Minochi Districts.
Causes: Demands for extension of date of collection of taxes refused.
Form: Attack upon *daikan's* house.
Result: Two leaders killed, six exiled. An order in the 9th month stated that henceforth those making an appeal would receive severe punishment.[65]

1781–Minami Atsumi District,
Causes: Unjust land inspection.
Form: Mob-appeal.
Result: Not clear.[66]

1783–Eastern districts of Shinano, Ina and Saku.
Causes: Eruption of Mt. Asama, bad harvest and uprisings in neighbouring province of Kōzuke.
Form: Mob-appeal of 1,000.
Result: Numerous arrests and order from *Bakufu* that records should be kept of any such uprisings in the future and that neighbouring villages should arrest the leaders or else report the nearest officials.[67]

1787–Ina District.
Causes: Poor crops and increase in price of rice.
Form: Mob-appeal.
Result: Not clear.

1790–Ina District.
Causes: Misconduct of elders of domain.
Form: Appeal.
Result: Not clear.

---

64. Cf. *Atomi Gusa op. cit* , p. 683.
65. Cf. Tsuji, *Tamura Jidai op. cit.*, p. 149.
66. Cf. Kokushō, *Ikki Kenkyū, op. cit.*, p. 430.
67. Cf. Kobayashi, *op. cit.*, and Tsuji, *op. cit.*, p. 150.

1796–Ina District.
Causes: Levy of *sukegō* tax of horses and men.[68]
Form: Not clear.
Result: Not clear.

1809–Imata village in *Bakufu* realm in Ina District.
Causes: Establishment of wholesale paper shop, tax on paper 1 *momme* above other fiefs.
Form: Appeal, house-wreckings.
Result: Wholesale house abolished, tax money refounded to village and leaders who survived imprisonment released.

1813–Matsushiro and *Bakufu* realm.
Causes: Bad crops and high prices of rice.
Form: House-wrecking and mob appeal.[69]

1823–Ina District–Five villages in domain of Naitō Yoriyasu.[70]
Causes: Continued bad crops made fief finances precarious. Extra taxes included 100 *ryō* for any one building a gate, 100 *ryō* for anyone wishing an official position with which came the privilege of a name and the right to wear a sword. Tax of two pair of straw sandals daily from each boy above 15; one bolt of cotton cloth monthly from each girl.
Form: Disorder.
Result: Leaders arrested, minister responsible for new taxes dismissed, new taxes abolished.

1825–Nagano Mob of 10–30,000.
Causes: Bad crops, monopoly of wholesale purchase of hemp.
Form: Disorder and house wreckings.
Result: Not clear.

---

68. The last three incidents appear in Kokushō, *Ikki Kenkyū op.* cit., p. 453.

69. *Ibid,* p. 436.

70. Naito Yoriyasu, 内藤頼寧, received the fief of Takatō, 高遠, of 33,000 *koku* in 1820. He retired in 1860. Having official duties in Ōsaka his fief was run by ministers.

1835–Kami-Ina District.
Causes: Crop failure due to destruction by wind storms.
Form: Disorder.
Result: Not clear.

1836–Minami Atsumi District.
Causes: Succession of bad harvests resulting in high price of rice.
Form: Disorder.
Result: Not clear.[71]

1837–Minochi District.
Causes: Not clear.
Form: Appeal of farmer's representative to castle.
Result: Demand of farmers granted.

1850–Four mountain villages of Ina District.
Causes: Villages allowed privilege of cutting timber and fire-wood for city of Iida. In 1850 trees sold and officials came to cut them down.[72]
Form: Disorder.
Result: Not clear.

1859–Thirty-six villages in Ina District.
Causes: Recent transfer of status from *Bakufu* to private domain. *Daikan* changed method of collecting taxes and raised levy. Money demanded for repairs of waterways. Imprisonment of farmers.
Form: Disorder and mob appeal, but *no* house wrecking.
Results: *Daikan* dismissed from office, villages refunded 200 *ryō* of taxes, four leaders arrested but later pardoned.

---

71. For the last two uprisings Cf. Kokushō, *op cit.*, p. 440–441.
72. Hori Chikayoshi, 堀親義, was lord of the fief from 1845 to 1868, a direct descendant of Hori Chikanaga. Cf. *supra* p. 161 Note 62.

1863–Shimo-Takai District.
Causes: Water dispute.
Form. Disorder.
Result: Not clear.[73]

1866–One uprising in each of following: Chikama, Azumi and Kiso Districts.
Causes: High prices of rice and scarcity of food due to natural calamities.
Form: Disorder.
Result: Not clear.

1868–Saku District.
Causes: Spread of Kōzuke uprising over high price of rice.
Form: House-wreckings and disorder.
Result: Not clear.

E. Mino

The peasant uprisings in the Province of Mino have as their underlying causes three distinct facts. In the first place, it was a province divided into innumerable small fiefs and separated from the direct surveillance of the various domains through absentee ownership. This also carried with it the financial difficulties peculiar to all small fiefs and the evils of government by absentee officials and lords. Secondly the people of Mino were of an unusually virile and belligerent disposition and were easily instigated to revolt, so that many modern tenancy struggles still center there. Thirdly, Mino is crossed by several rivers which flood easily, this being especially true of the Kiso River[74] separating the two provinces of Owari and Mino. As the Owari dykes were unusually well constructed, they only forced the waters over into Mino and caused continual floods in that country, so several of the uprisings were a direct result of this situation.

The first uprising to draw our attention is that in 1758

73. Cf. Kokushō, *op cit.*, p. 445.
74. Kisogawa, 木曾川.

in the fief of Kanamori Yorikane.[75] Here continued troubles had arisen from the methods of determining taxes and the farmers had presented their petitions and objections to the maladministration of the fief before the authorities in Edo. The *Shōgun* finally decided to confiscate the fief due to the lord's inability to control his domain.[76]

Beginning in 1788, uprisings developed over the question of floods and the repairs of dykes. At that time, the farmers refused to build the dykes along the Nagara River in one domain, while those across the river took the opposite stand. Appeals to the nearby *bugyō* were useless as he had already been bribed to oppose the peasants.[77] In 1798 floods caused the farmers to attack the officials in charge of the dykes in the Kano domain,[78] and at the end of the year the farmers revolted against taxes levied because of heavy losses in the first place and the order that they should repair the dykes in the second. In 1813 the farmers of Atsumi District, on the other hand, appealed for repairs of the old dykes and that new ones be constructed.[79] Again in 1835 an uprising resulted from floods due to neglect and maladministration of the officials in charge of the canals for irrigation and for carrying off flood waters. The home of the *daikan* responsible for this was wrecked as were fifteen other places, making it necessary to call out troops from the Owari domain to bring about order.[80] The next year, 1836, new floods revealed the fact that the *dai-*

75. Kanamori Yorikane, 金森頼錦, was exiled to Nambu in 1759. His dates have not been found.

76. Cf. Takekoshi, *Economic History, op. cit.*, Vol. III, p. 136. For an account of this as well as Mino uprisings in general Cf. Kokushō, *Hyakusho Ikki Shidan, op. cit.*, p. 290 *et seq.* For a detailed primary source on the uprising of 1758 Cf. *Nōhoku Hōreki Giminroku*, 1 Vol.; Sanuki, 1929, 205 pp.

77. Cf. Kokushō, *Ikki Shidan, op. cit.*, p. 298.

78, Kano, 加納, was a 36,000 *koku* domain of the Nagai family, 永井氏, from 1756–1868. Nagai Naotada, 永井直弼, (b. 1782–) became the adopted son of Naohisa, 直旧, (1768–1790) in 1790 and inherited the fief the same year.

79. Cf. Kokushō, *Ikki Shidan op. cit.*, p. 299.

80. Cf. *Nagoya Shishi*, Seiji Hen, *op. cit.*, p. 570 *et seq.*

kan had kept 2,000 of the 3,000 *ryō* collected for repairs of the dykes and thus had completely neglected his duties. He, along with many other avaricious officials, was arrested and taken to Edo.[81] These few examples, therefore, of the twenty-five uprisings in Mino, serve to show the distinctive characteristics and causes presented by uprisings in that province.

F. Mimasaka

In the west, in the Province of Mimasaka, two distinct types of uprisings developed; those of a decidedly rebellious nature accompanied by house-wrecking and general disorder on the part of the farmers, and the tranquilization by gun fire and loss of life on the part of the soldiers. The second type were uprisings of a quiet and negative nature taking the form of orderly appeal or desertion from their land. In either case, Mimasaka uprisings were motivated by the fact that it was a mountainous country with many of the people being forced to labour outside the province. Its population was 20% more male than female, and the inhabitants increased nearly 25% during the Tokugawa period as opposed to a decrease in most regions. With mountains dividing the various fiefs, most of the disturbances were disconnected and isolated, and it was extremely difficult for the entire province to unite at one time into a general uprising.[82]

The following chronological treatment of these uprisings will make these characteristics apparent.[83]

1. 1st month, 1673 in Tsuyama Fief.[84]

---

81. Cf. *Ukiyo no Arisama, op. cit.*, Vol. II, p. 338.
82. Cf. Kokushō *Hōken Shakai no Tōsei, op. cit.*, p. 316 *et seq.*
83. For primary sources for uprisings in Mimasaka Cf. *Sakushū Hyakushō Ikki Sōsho* in which contemporary accounts of uprisings in 1698, 1726, 1739, 1866, and 1868 are given. It is printed in *Kinsei Shakai Keizai Sōsho, op. cit.*, Vol. X, pp. 3–162. For a secondary source based mostly on this material Cf. Kokushō: *Hōken Shakai no Tōsei, op. cit.*, pp. 268–374.
84. Tsuyama, 津山, was the residence of the Mori Family, 森氏, from 1604–1697. In the 1st month, 1673, lord of the fief was Mori Nagatsugu, 森長繼, (1610–1698) who retired in the 4th month in favour of Nagatake, 長武, (1653–1686).

Causes: Survey of timber land for taxation purposes and levy of a 60% tax.
Form: Desertion under pretext of going to Ise on a pilgrimage.
Result: Tax reduced to 50%. People returned.[85]

2. 11th month, 1698 in Tsuyama.
Causes: Mori family without an heir in 1697 so fief transferred to Matsudaira Nobutomi in 1698.[86] Nobutomi increased taxes from 50% to 60%.
Form: Mob-appeal.
Result: Eight leaders put to death.[87]

3. 3rd month, 1726 Seventeen villages of Katsuminami District.
Causes: Bad crops.
Form: Appeal to *daikan* for aid. Two representatives appealed in Edo.
Result: Aid sent by 8th month.[88]

4. 12th month, 1726 in Tsuyama.
Causes: Farmers resented powers of warrior class. Lord of fief without heir and realm reduced to to half. Date of collection of taxes advanced.
Form: Appeal.
Result: Matsudaira Nagateru appointed lord of half former domain.[89]

5. 3rd month, 1739 in *Bakufu* domain in Katsukita District.

---

85. Cf. Kokushō *Hōken Shakai no Tōsei, op. cit.*, p. 314.

86. In that year, Matsudaira Nobutomi, 松平宣富, became heir to 100,000 *koku* at Tsuyama.

87. Cf. *Sakushū Hyakushō Ikki op. cit.*, p. 19–29 and Kokushō, *Hōken Shakai no Tōsei, op.* cit., p. 305.

88. *Ibid*, p. 313.

89. It was Matsudaira Asagoro, 松平淺五郎, (b. 1713) who followed Nobutomi, who died in 1726 without an heir. Matsudaira Nagateru, 松平長熙, (1716–1732) was then given the fief. Cf. Kokushō, *Hōken Shakai no Tōsei, op. cit.*, p. 305 *et seq.* and *Sakushū Hyakushō Ikki, op. cit.*, p. 34–115.

Causes: Famine and lack of food stimulated by recent robberies.

Form: Mob-appeal. Two self-appointed leaders agitated for mob-appeals among the farmers of thirty-five villages.

Result: Local officials unable to settle affair. Troops dispatched from Tsuyama and fired on farmers who were making preparations to resist them. *Ōsaka Machi bugyō* investigated affair. Leaders taken to Ōsaka and killed. Twenty-four banished.[90]

6. 1746 in a village in Katsuminami District.

Causes: Heavy taxes imposed by *shōya.*

Form: Desertion and abandoning section of land producing 40 *koku.*

Result: Not clear.

7. 2nd month, 1769. Several Villages in Kumenanjō District.

Causes: Not clear.

Form: Robbery aud plundering of wealthy.

Result: Arrests.

8. 12th month, 1786.

Causes: Not clear.

Form: Unrest checked by *ōshōya.*

9. 6th month, 1798 in 228 villages in *Bakufu* domain.

Causes: Change in method of collection of the tax of which one-third was paid in money, calculations made from the 10th month price of rice in Tsuyama market.

Form: Four farmers petitioned in Edo.

Result: Old methods of collection of taxes restored.

10. 12th month, 1825. Several villages in *Bakufu* domain

---

90. Cf. *Sakushū Hyakushō Ikki, op. cit.,* p. 115–124; Kokushō, *Hōken Shakai no Tōsei, op. cit.,* p. 308.

in Katsukita District and in Matsudaira domain in Tsuyama.

Causes: Not clear.
Form: Violent disorder.
Result: Not clear.[91]

11. Winter 1833.

Causes: Poor crops.
Form: Disorder.
Result: Not clear.[92]

12. 11th month, 1866. 2–3,000 farmers in Higashi Kitajō District in Tsuyama fief.[93]

Causes: Bad crops and lack of food.
Rice merchants monopolized purchase of rice and manipulated the market. Bought rice at 10% reduction and shipped it to Ōsaka for sale when food needed in Mimasaka.
Form: Farmers divided into two parties, one to attack rice supplies, the other to enter Tsuyama on the 25th of the 11th month. A diary of a school teacher of Tsuyama reports as follows:

At about 8 A.M. there came the report that a barrier gate had been broken down as well as houses of two men. At the same time we heard noises of the "riot call" bells at other barriers. A couple of hours later the farmers assembled at the big bridge over the Miya River and raised their battle cry. We heard the report of twenty small guns a little later. I remarked: 'They are shooting off blanks to menace the mob.' However, my friend Matsutane came running by and reported: 'At the Big Bridge Barrier four or five of the petitioners have been shot.' I was greatly alarmed at this and returned home, meeting various soldiers dragging cannon in front of the school. The same day many of the

91. For the last five incidents Cf. Kokushō, *Hōken Shakai no Tōsei op. cit.*, p. 309, 313, 314, and 315.
92. Cf. Kokushō, *Ikki no Kenkyū, op. cit.*, p. 440.
93. Lord of Tsuyama in 1866 was Matsudaira Yoshinori, 松平慶倫.

soldiers of the fief went into the castle to protect it. When 5–600 of the mob came to one of the barriers a *monogashira* tried to admonish them but was driven back with stones. The mob advanced on him and surrounded him. However, his followers checked them, unsheathing their swords and one person was killed.... The mob defiantly climbed up on the balcony of the gate before the castle and faced the soldiers jeering, 'Try and shoot us.' The soldiers, hating to shoot fellows from the same domain as themselves, fired upon them none the less, for the sake of preserving the peace and shot down four or five of them.... Returning home by mid-afternoon I heard that the farmers had been tranquilized and given gruel. Again a "war cry" was heard over the Big Bridge. It seems the petitioners had just arrived from the east, wearing big straw hats and armed with bamboo spears. I do not know how many of them there were....

Someone came and reported that 13,000 bales of rice had been presented as relief, which was announced on placards, but still the farmers refused to return home ....As things were quite agitated throughout the town, I stationed two of my men at the gate with the instructions to reply: 'We will come out,' if the mob demanded it.... Late to-night the *Bangashira* and *Machi bugyō* and warriors were sent out and guarded the town with naked spears. They arrested some twenty or thirty of the insurgents. Therewith the mob that came from the east returned to their villages and the castle town was again quiet. It is reported that seventy-four houses were destroyed.[94]

Result: Leader who made appeal and six others beheaded, and four men who took advantage of uprising and robbed, banished.

94. Cf. *Sakushū Hyakushō Ikki*, *op. cit.*, p. 124 *et seq.*

G. *Iyo and Tosa*

Isolated geographically from the main island of Japan, and further retarded in their development by numerous mountains, Iyo and Tosa, in the island of Shikoku, were centers not only of numerous uprisings of the usual type, but also of those of a negative type, namely, desertion from the villages or fief to the neighbouring domain or province. In Iyo the majority of the fifty-one uprisings between 1587 and 1873 were desertions,[95] the effectiveness of many of these resulting from the small size of the fiefs and the ease with which the farmers could slip through the mountains into the adjoining fief. They were instigated, moreover, by the fact that Iyo was famous for its production of paper, which the authorities of the fiefs were quick to monopolize in order to enhance their finances. This fact will become apparent from a study of the uprising of 1793, but prior to this, cursory mention must be made of those preceding it. Between 1587 and 1741 ten uprisings occur whose causes were largely economic and which presented no new characteristics in either their form or results.[96] During the next period, 1741 to 1793, of the sixteen uprisings, five took the form of desertions, resulting largely from maladministration of the fief and heavy taxes.[97]

In the Yoshida domain of Date Murayoshi,[98] an extremely mountainous region, the officials in charge of administering the

95. Unfortunately, with the exception of the uprising in 1793, the primary source materials on the Iyo uprisings are still in MS. form, having been collected by Saionji, Gento in *Iyo Hakushō Ikki Kiroku,* to be published upon the completion of Professor Kokusho's work on source materials of Japanese peasant uprisings. The majority of these are discussed, however, in Kokushō, *Hōken Shakai no Tōsei, op. cit.*, pp. 449–480.

96. Their dates are as follows: 1587, 1600, 1605, 1615, 1629, 1630, 1648, 1664, 1672, and 1732. Cf. Kokushō, *Hōken Shakai no Tosei, op. cit.*, pp. 451–454.

97. *Ibid,* pp. 454– 456. They occur as follows: 1741, 1742 (two incidents), 1747, 1751, 1753, 1754, 1770, 1786, 1787 (2 incidents), 1788 (3 incidents), 1789 and 1793.

98. Yoshida, 吉田, was the castle town of the 30,000 *koku* fief of a branch of the Date family, 伊達氏, since 1614 Date Munezumi, 伊達宗純, (1636–1708), received the fief in 1657 from his father, Hidemune, 秀宗,

domain had little idea of what a fair tax should be and the farmers were treated practically as slaves. Bribery became rampant, continual appeals for aid had been useless, so a farmer named Musaemon spent three years secretly plotting among the peasants to unite and rise in opposition to their oppression. Finally in 1792, after those holding a monopoly in the paper industry had lent capital to the farmers to aid them in manufacturing paper, and later had purchased the finished products at an extremely low price, the farmers decided to sell their goods elsewhere. This was forbidden by the authorities who ordered an inspection of all the houses in the domain, when the inspectors confiscated any paper found, keeping 70% for themselves and turning 30% over to the paper guild.[99] After numerous complaints on the part of the farmers and the ineffectual admonitions for leniency towards them by the elder minister of the fief, an arbitration board came to the following conclusions on the 1st month, 1793:–

1. As the policy of the paper wholesale merchant to lend money at high interest and to purchase manufactured paper at a low price is a natural business proceeding, it is not a crime.
2. Even though the management of the officials of the paper guilds has been excessively harsh, as they were fulfilling the duties of their office, they are not to be blamed.
3. It is unreasonable to say that the farmers cannot endure the taxes they have born up to the present time.[100]

(1591–1658), lord of Uwashima, 宇和島, with 100,000 *koku*. Date Murayoshi, 伊達村芳, (1775–1816) became heir to the Yoshida domain in 1789 and received the fief in 1791. He spent his entire time in Edo and consequently knew little of the administration of the fief. He was followed by Munemoto, 宗翰, who held the fief until 1843. Cf. *Musaemon Okinaden*, in Ono *Hyakushō Ikki Sōdan*, Vol. I, pp. 451–453 and *Denki Dainihon Shi*, *Daimyō Hen*, *op. cit.*, pp. 433–434.

99. For a primary source Cf. *Musaemon Okinaden, op. cit.*, pp. 447 *et seq.*

100. *Ibid*, p. 456.

Upon hearing this Musaemon issued the following:

> You peasants of the Yoshida realm who are oppressed to death by unjust merchants must overthrow them and open up your own path of life. Ye who have courage arise![101]

To this appeal, 10,000 farmers started towards the Uwashima domain, being instructed by Musaemon that they should not harm the officials as the object was the reform of their own government. After arrival at Uwashima, where they were given gruel, the elder minister of their own fief appeared before them saying:

> I am the elder minister of the Yoshida domain, Andō by name, I alone am responsible for any mis-management in the government of the fief. You are mistaken in hating your lord. As there is no word of thanks for me, the cause of this uprising, I hereby clarify my responsibility. Present your appeal quickly, receive your lord's approval, and return to your villages and begin again your labours.[102]

So saying, he committed suicide. The farmers, after presenting their memorandum and seeing Andō die at his own hand, returned to their own villages, to have many of their demands accepted, but to lose their leader, Musaemon, who was beheaded and to whose memory they later erected a shrine.

The following eleven articles were agreed upon by the lords and officials as concessions to the demands presented by the farmers:

1. The office controlling paper shall be discontinued and the district office (*gunsho*)[103] shall be responsible for the paper mulberry as previously. The capital or principal of loans [of the farmers] shall be repaid this spring by the money received from selling remanufactured paper.

---

101. *Ibid*, p. 457.
102. *Ibid*, p. 464.
103. *Gunsho*, 郡所, the district office.

2. As for the question of the price in silver of large beans: Heretofore the price of large summer beans has been determined by the sales price at Ōsaka. Henceforth it will be determined by the transactions at Uwashima.
3. As for the question of making up for the shrinkage in large beans: Henceforth we decree that this [making up of the shrinkage] shall not [be practiced] so care must be taken in drying and shipping beans [to avoid loss in transport].
4. As for the weighing and measuring of goods for regular and special supplementary taxes (*komononari*):[104] Henceforth it is intended to examine this as below(?).
5. The question of weighing the *aohiki*:[105] [a certain kind of silk cocoon]: As we have heard that the methods of handling the silk cocoons have not been satisfactory, the previous laws regarding this must be followed.
6. The sojourn in the harbour before leaving port: There shall [always] be a collection of shelter expenses, even on rainy days.
7. In reference to the measurement [of a bale] of rice being transported [to Ōsaka]. Heretofore it has been decided that 1 *shō* 5 *gō* of rice shall be presented to make up for the loss in transportation (*sashi mai*)[106] for each bale, and a bale shall equal 4 *to*.
8. The question of rice-rations in time of famine or distress or those to be used for loans (*bujiki*): In Uwashima it has been decided that there shall be 4

---

104. *Komononari*, 小物成.

105. Aohiki, 青引.

106. *Sashimai*, 差米. As there was a loss of rice in transportaion, it was ordered to make up for this deficiency by means of *sashimai* prior to the shipment of the bales. A bale, equal to 4 *to* of rice or 4 *koku*, was usually taxed 1 *shō* or 1/40 the total contents of a bale for this shrinkage. Cf. Ono, *Nomin Goi*, *op. cit.*, p. 178.

gō 3 *shaku* 3 *sai* per person, but as it is difficult to determine what this amount [should be] because of the age conditions [of the farmers] 2 *gō* [2 *shaku*] shall be added so that there shall be 6 *gō* 7 *shaku* 3 *sai.*[107]

9. As for paying in silver the year's redemption on old loans [granted by] the paper control office: Its collection shall be postponed for five years after which the affair must be settled.
10. Though there was a tax in silver on the amount of paper mulberry trees sold elsewhere than [in the fief] in the past few years, henceforth there shall be a tax in silver on trees sold elsewhere than [in the fief] as it existed [originally].
11. As for the request for the prohibition of the manufacture of *sake* in Yamaoku: This shall be granted for the present.

As for the following twelve articles, though we the fief authorities cannot grant them [immediately] we will investigate them:

12. In reference to the measurement [of a bale] of rice which is to be sold outside [the domain]: Although it has been decided that [a bale] shall equal 4 *to,* if the recipient complains of shortage, an examination should be made.
13. The question of giving rations for materials and labour for the [construction of] ships: Previously it has been decided that each man shall receive 5 *go* of rice rations for work on the Hachiman maru [a boat] and for its equipment. Then this work was interrupted and recently the workers have been given

---

107. The text appears to contain a mistake of the copyist which has been corrected in the translation. A "six" has been interchanged with a "four". *Bujiki,* 夫食, was rice stored for lean years or the distress of the farmers, collected by the officials of the fief for that purpose. It likewise termed *gisōmai.* Cf. *infra,* p. 177. A *shaku,* 勺, equals 10 *sai,* 才; 10 *shaku* equal 1 *go* or .318 pints.

the amount as before. If in the case of construction or repairs of boats special villages are assigned special tasks, they shall be paid accordingly.

14. The question of rations for people of Igawa: Though they have been discontinued for several years, henceforth there shall be added 2 *gō* 5 *shaku* each to that already decided upon.
15. The perpetual examination [for taxation purposes] of paper coming in and going out of [the province]: Since the office controlling paper has been abolished, its inspection shall be entirely in the hands of the district office as before.
16. The selling elsewhere [other than in Yoshida] of firewood held in common by the local population and of various cereals along the coast: If a [yearly] request is made and there is a frequent examination then there is no objection to this.
17. The storing of rice for lean years (*gisōmai*):[108] During the hardships of 1787 [rice] was distributed to all the people of the villages. Since that time, by exerting their utmost effort, there are those who have gradually returned [this rice]. Most of them have not returned half [of this amount]. Henceforth without ordering the inspectors about [the collection of the *gisōmai*], it will be left to the discretion of the villages.
18. There be a reduction of 500 bales of wheat borrowed from the "cereal store house"[109]. Heretofore this wheat and other [wheat] has been given through the auspices of the *shōya*. The same policy should be followed with the wheat as the rice stored for lean years.

---

108. *Gisōmai*, 義倉米. Often called *Bujiki* cf. *supra* p. 176.

109. *Shasō*, 社倉, Cereal storehouses: Cereal was collected by the authorities which the people could borrow at a small rate of interest. In this case the farmers apparently wished part of their previous loans of wheat to be cancelled although the text is very vague.

19. The question of the sawyers and carpenters: In cases where the head of the carpenters is ordered to make repairs in the villages, if there is an obstacle preventing the official carpenter from carrying this out, then an order must be sent from the office of the fief to the head of the carpenters for labourers to come from elsewhere.
20. Presenting of bribes in the sea-coast villages:....The officials must have the exact work that is to be done [marked on paper] with their seals attached and carry this with them when they go to the fields [on official inspection].
21. The question of [supplying] large pillars, (*otoko hashira*).[110] As it is reported that the recent increase in [supplying these pillars] has caused great inconveniences, care must be taken to follow all previous rules concerning this matter.
22. Transportation rates for a pack-load of charcoal: An examination shall be made into increases ordered in these rates and a decrease in their despatches.
23. Presents(*shimmotsu*)[111] from the sea-coast [villages]: Except in the case of succession to the domain and an audience, there shall not be any presents made, even of light articles such as vegetables and pickles.

We order that all the farmers comply to these articles.[112]

Of the uprisings that remain in Iyo, most of them are small, several took the form of attempted desertions which failed because of the interference of the authorities, and none of

---

110. *Otoko hashira*, 男柱, were the main supporting pillars used in buildings or bridges.

111. *Shimmotsu*, 進物.

112. For the above articles, cf. *Museamon Okina Den*, Ono, *Hyakushō Ikki Sōdan*, *op. cit.*, Vol. 1, pp. 468–473.

them have anything new to add to the situation as it existed in 1793.[113]

In Tosa, the whole province being under the control of the Yamanouchi family, ten uprisings are reported between 1603 and 1871, largely the result of the methods of monopolistic control of local products by the fief authorities, with practically no demands on the part of the peasants, that their taxes be reduced. These uprisings especially after 1755, were of a negative nature, taking the form of desertion to Iyo.[114]

Their occurrences are as follows:

1. 11th month, 1603 at Motoyama.
   Causes: Heavy taxes.
   Form: Disorder.
   Result: Leaders fled.
2. 1663. Joint action of farmers and townsmen.
   Causes: Monopolistic control of products.
   Form: Appeal.
   Result: Methods slightly mollified.
3. 6th mo., 1751 in domain of minister of Yamanouchi Family.
   Causes: Not clear.
   Form: Sixty men made appeal.
   Result: Not clear.
4. 11th month, 1755.
   Causes: Monopoly of purchase of paper and tea at low prices by wholesale merchant.

---

113. Uprisings were as follows: 1798, 1816, 1823 (2 incidents), 1826, 1827, 1830 (5 small incidents), 1857, 1862, 1863, 1864, 1865, and 1866 (2). Cf. Kokushō, *Hōken no Tōsei,* pp. 458–465. He estimates there were fifty-four altogether, while Numazaki lists fifty-one. Cf. *Infra* Appendix II, Chart I.

114. As a result of the aid given at the battle of Sekigahara, Yamanouchi Kazutoyo, 山内一豊, (1546–1605) received a fief of 182,000 *koku* and moved to Kōchi, 高知, in 1600) when the fief was later increased to 242,000 *koku.* His descendants remained there until 1868. For an account of the Tosa uprisings cf. Kokushō, *Hōken Shakai Tōsei, op. cit.,* pp. 481–508. Numazaki lists thirteen uprisings as having occurred there. Cf. *Infra,* Appendix II, Chart I.

Form: Appeal, threatened mob-appeal or desertion.
Result: Merchant condemned to death.[115]

5. and
6. 2nd month, 1787 in Agawa District and Moriyama.
Causes: Famine and bad crops. Purchase of paper at 1 *momme* 5–6 *fun* [10 *fun* equal 1 *momme*] and its being sold at 2 *momme* 3–4 *fun*. Necessity to pay rice tax to wholesalers.
Form: Desertion of 700 farmers to Iyo.
Result: In spite of officials' attempts to make a secret settlement to prevent the lord of the domain[116] in Edo from learning of the incident, priests had to intervene. Exposure of despotic government officials resulted. Lord Toyonobu became worried over the government of the fief and the evils of monopolistic control were abolished. There ensued a long period without uprisings.[117]
7. 10th month, 1797.
Causes: and other details not clear.
8. 7th month, 1842. Nanogawa in Agawa District.
Causes: *Ōshōya* official neglected duties and oppressed *Koshōya* who stirred up the people.
Form: 300 farmers, each carrying a sword escaped to Iyo.

115. For these four incidents cf. Kokushō, *op. cit.*, p. 482–486.
116. Lord of Kōchi Castle in 1787 was Yamanouchi Toyonobu, 山内豊信, (1747–1789). He received the fief in 1768. In 1789 he supplied 20,000 trees for the construction of the Imperial Palace in Kyōto.
117. For a primary source cf. *Ikegawa Yōkyō Hijō Daiyō Kiroku* in *Kinsei Shakai Sōsho, op. cit.*, Vol. XI, pp. 31–94 and for a secondary source cf. Kokushō, *Hōken Shakai no Tōsei, op. cit.*, pp. 501–508.

Result: 450 warriors sent to arrest farmers. Afraid of them for the first time.[118]

9. 11th month, 1860. Eight villages of Tsunoyama.
Causes: Question of date of collection of taxes. With decline in price of local products there had been a rise in price of hulled rice. Order for payment of taxes in silver. Indirectly affected by general disturbances concerning opening of country.
Form: Appeal to office of *Kōri bugyō.*
Result: Demands granted.

10. 1871–1872.
Causes: New laws of Restoration of 1868.
Form: Uprising.
Result: Leader condemned to death.

Thus from a glance at the above local studies, it is obvious that peasant uprisings varied in their characteristics as well as frequency in the different regions of Japan. The more remote the domain the easier for corruption to enter the administration of the fief and to result in uprisings. In the north, in Echigo, Sado, and Nambu, as well as in Shinano, frequent crop failures added their impetus to the hardships of the peasants. In Mimasaka, floods and the belligerent disposition of the populace caused frequent unrest, while in Tosa and Iyo desertions were frequent in opposition to the monopolistic control of the purchase and sale of local products.

118. For a primary source cf. *Nanogawa Gōmin Tōsanki* in *Kinsei Shakai Sōsho, op. cit.,* Vol. XI, pp. 1–31.

APPENDIX I

SELECTED BIBLIOGRAPHY

A. Primary Sources.

Manuscripts

The following manuscripts are all in the library of the Shiryō Hensanjo of Tōkyō Imperial University.

Hyakushō Sōdō Ikken; 百姓騒動一件; "A peasant Uprising", an account of the uprising in 1783 in the province of Izumo.

Izumo Shishi; 出雲私史; "Private history of Izumo", part 12 of this manuscript contains accounts of the uprising in 1783 in Izumo.

Kyōhō Hōreki Kammonsho; 享保寳暦間聞書; "History of the Kyōhō and Hōreki Periods"; with accounts of uprisings in 1761 in Shinano and in 1750 in Iwashiro.

Matsudaira Kafu, Izumono Kuni, Hirose Jōshu; 松平家譜出雲國廣瀬城主; "Genealogy of the Hirose branch of the Matsudaira family of Izumo."

Matsudaira Kafu, Izumo Kuni, Matsue Jōshu; 松平家譜出雲國松江城主; Genealogy of the Matsue branch of the Matsudaira family of Izumo.

Temmei Sankyōsaku Ichizu; 天明三凶作一途; "An account of the three years of bad crops following 1781"; and an uprising of 1783.

Ueda Ryōnai Hyakushō Sōdō Bunsho; 上田領内百姓騒動聞書; "An account of a peasant uprising in the Ueda Fief" in Shinano in 1761.

Printed Materials

Abeno Dōjimon; 安部野童子問; in *Kinsei Shakai Sōsho,* Vol. XI., pp. 187–296. A description of an uprising in Bingo in 1786.

Akita Suginao Monogatari; 秋田杉直物語; in *Rekko Shimpi Roku* pp. 455 *et seq.* "An account of an uprising in Akita" in 1755.

Asakawa Sōdō Kembun Roku; 淺川騷動見聞錄; in Ono, *Ikki Sōdan,* Vol. II, pp. 177–184. "Reports of the Asakawa Uprisings in 1798" in Iwaki province.

Atomi Gusa, 後見草; in *Shiseki Shūran,* Vol. 17, Tōkyō, 1903. "Reflections", a contemporary account of conditions during the latter part of the 18th century with references to uprisings in 1764, 1775, and 1781, written by Sugita Gempaku, 杉田玄伯.

Etchū Shiryō; 越中史料; 4 Vol.; Toyama, 1918. "Historical materials of Etchū", arranged chronologically. Vol. III deals with uprisings from 1755 to 1858.

Gunnai Sōdō; 郡內騷動; in Ono, Ikki Sōdan, Vol. II, pp. 280–355. "The uprising of Gunnai" or Kai in 1836.

Hida Kuni, Ōno Gunshi; 飛彈國大野郡史; 3 Vol.; Takayama, 1925. "History of Ōno District of Hida Province"; with accounts of uprisings in Hida after 1747.

Higashi Yamanashi Gunshi; 東山梨郡誌; 1 Vol.; 1916, "History of Higashi Yamanashi District" of Kai Province containing an account of the uprising there in 1836.

Hokkaidō Shi; 北海道史; 1 Vol.; Tōkyō, 1918, 958 pp. "History of Hokkaidō".

Iishi Gunshi; 飯石郡誌; 1 Vol.; 1921. "History of Iishi District" of Izumo Province containing not only accounts of uprisings in Izumo but also a list of special terms with explanations.

Ikegawa Yōkyo Hijō Daiyō Kiroku; 池川用居非常大要記錄; in *Kinsei Shakai Sōsho,* Vol. XI, pp. 31–94. "An account of the desertion of 1787 of Ikegawa" in Tosa.

Ishii, Seikichi, editor, *Echigo Sado Nōmin Sōdō,* 1 Vol.; Niigata, 石井淸吉編越後佐渡農民騷動; 1 Vol.; Niigata, 1930, 629 pp., charts and maps. "Peasant disturbances in Echigo and Sado", chronologically arranged covering some fifty incidents from 1595–1872.

*Ishikawa Kenshi;*石川縣史; 3 Vol.; Kanazawa, 1928. "History of Ishikawa Prefecture" with accounts of uprisings in the Province of Kaga.

Iyo Yoshida Han Sankan Sōdō; 伊豫吉田藩三間騷動, in *Kinsei Shakai Sōsho,* Vol. XI, pp. 97–187. "A desertion in the Yoshida fief in Iyo in 1870"

Jiji Roku, Mikkan Suihitsu Hyakushū; 事々錄未刊隨筆百種, 23 Vol.; 1927, expecially Vol. 6. "General Affairs from 1831–1849".

Kinsei Shakai Keizai Sōsho; 近世社會經濟叢書; Honjō, E. and Kōkushō, I, editors; 12 Vol.; Tōkyō, 1927. "A collection of materials on recent sociology and economics", of which Vol. I, X, and XI contain materials concerning peasant uprisings.

Kishū Ikki Oboegaki, Shiseki Shūran; 紀州一揆覺書史籍集覽; 33 Vol.; 1900, especially Vol. 16. "Reminiscences of an uprising in Kii in 1823."

Kōya Ryōmin Ikki Shimatsu,; 高野領民一揆始末; in *Kinsei Shakai Sōsho,* Vol. X. "Details of the uprising of the peasants of the Kōyasan fief," a contemporary account of the uprisings of 1776.

Miyoshi Gunshi; 三好郡誌; 1 Vol.; 1924. "History of Miyoshi District" in the province of Awa, describing a border dispute between Awa and Sanuki.

Musaeman Okina Den; 武左工門翁傳; in Ono, *Ikki Sōdan,* Vol. 1; pp. 447 *et seq.* "A biography of Musaemon", the leader of the peasant uprising in Iyo in 1792.

Nagoya Shishi; 名古屋市史; Seiji Hen, 10 Vol.; Nagoya, 1916. "A history of the city of Nagoya, Administrative section," giving documents concerning uprisings in 1835 and 1836.

Nanogawa Gōmin Tōsanki; 名野川鄉民逃散記; in *Kinsei Shakai Sōsho,* Vol. XI, pp. 1–27. "An account of the desertion of villagers of Nanogawa" in 1842 in Tosa Province.

Naraken Udagun Shiryō; 奈良縣宇陀郡史料; 1 Vol.; 1917. "Historical materials of Uda district in Nara Prefecture".

Nōhoku Hōreki Gimin Roku; 濃北寶曆義民錄; "An account of the people in northern Mino", and the uprising there in 1758.

Nuno Kuma Gunshi; 沼隈郡誌; 1 Vol., Matsue, 1923, 1163 pp. "History of Nuno Kuma District" in Bingo Province, containing accounts of the Fukuyama domain's uprisings in 1753, 1786, 1787 and 1871.

Omi Gamō Gunshi; 近江蒲生郡誌; 4 Vol.; 1922. "History of Gamō District in Ōmi Province," especially Vol. IV for an account of the uprising in southwestern Ōmi in 1842.

Ono, Takeo, *Tokugawa Jidai Hyakushō Ikki Sōdan;* 小野武夫; 徳川時代百姓一揆叢談; 2 Vol., Tōkyō, 1927. "Materials on Peasant Uprisings during the Tokugawa Period." This collection contains valuable materials on the uprisings throughout the entire period.

Rekko Shimpi Roku; 列候深秘錄; 1 Vol.; Tōkyō, 1914. "A collection of secret records of all great lords", containing accounts of the uprising in 1754 in Kurume, Chikugo; in 1755 in Akita and others.

Sakushū Hyakushō Ikki Sōsho; 作州百姓一揆叢書; in *Kinsei Shakai Sōsho,* Vol. X, pp. 1–163. "Collection of materials on peasant uprisings in Mimasaka Province.

Seji Kemmon Roku; 世事見聞錄; in *Kinsei Shakai Sōsho,* Vol. I, "Ideas on affairs of the world", written in 1816. The introduction is signed by Buyō Inshi, 武陽隱士.

Shiga Kenshi; 滋賀縣史; 3 Vol.; Tōkyō, 1928. "History of Shiga Prefecture", containing accounts of uprisings in Ōmi Province.

Shimane Kenshi; 島根縣史; 10 Vol.; 1930. "A History of Shimane Perfecture", containing an account of the Matsudaira fief in Izumo Province and the revolt of 1783.

Tango no Hyakushō Ikki; 丹後の百姓一揆; in Ono, *Ikki Sōdan,* Vol. II, pp. 20–177. "A peasant uprising in Miyazu, Tango."

Tempō Gimin Roku; 天保義民錄; in Ono, *Ikki Sōdan,* Vol. I, pp. 267–387. "An account of the people of the Tempō Era"; a description of the uprising in Ōmi in 1842.

Tempō Kaikyo Roku; 天保快擧錄; in Ono, *Ikki Sōdan,* Vol. I, pp. 33–186. "The valiant uprising of the Tempō Era", an account of the uprising in Shōnai of 1840–1841.

Tōbu Hyakushō Ikken; 東武百姓一件; in *Kinsei Shakai Sōsho,* Vol. X, pp. 265 *et seq.* "The uprising of the farmers of Tōbu", or an account of the uprising in 1764 in the three provinces of Kōzuke, Musashi and Shimosuke.

Tōmin Ryūsetsu; 黨民流說; in Ono, *Ikki Sōdan,* Vol. II, pp. 359–458. "Stories about the mobs", a contemporary account of uprisings in Bungo and Buzen in 1811 and 1812.

Tōno Tōni Nemonogatari; 遠野唐丹寢物語; in Ono, *Ikki Sōdan,*

Vol. I, pp. 384–444. "Tales of Tōno Tōni", a contemporary account of the desertion of the farmers of Nambu to Sendai in 1853. The author probably lived in Nambu as he conceals the identity of the uprising by using proper names arbitrarily chosen.

Ukiyo no Arisama; 浮世ノ有様; 6 Vol.; in *Kokushi Sōsho,* 國史叢書, Vol. 37–42. "Conditions of a fleeting world", a work probably written by an Ōsaka physician, recording the various calamities, local happenings and affairs from 1806–1840.

Wakayama Kenshi; 和歌山縣誌; 2 Vol.; 1924. "A history of Wakayama Prefecture", containing accounts of the Kii uprising of 1823.

Yōrō Gunshi; 養老郡志; 1 Vol.; 1924. "A history of Yōrō District", in Gifu Prefecture giving a description of the uprising in Mino in 1769.

Yume no Matsukaze; 夢の松風; in Ono, *Ikki Sōdan,* Vol. II, pp. 185–279. "Wind in Pine Trees of a dream", an anonymous account, written in story form, of the uprising in Matsu in 1770, 1775 and 1784.

B. *Japanese Secondary Sources*

Abe, Makoto, "Nōgyo Keizai", *Sekai Rekishi Taikei,* 阿部眞琴; 農業經濟; 世界歴史大系; Vol. 13B. "Agricultural economics", a brief account of agricultural economics of the Tokugawa Period.

Honjō, Eijirō, *Kinsei Hōken Shakai no Kenkyū;* 本庄榮治郎; 近世封建社會の研究, 1 Vol.; Tōkyō, 1928.

"Studies in Recent Feudal Society", in which Professor Honjō traces the impoverishment of agricultural communities, the development of towns, the population question, changes in social classes, and the collapse of feudal society.

________________, *Kinsei Nōson Mondai Shiron;* 近世農村問題史論; 1 Vol., Tōkyō, 1935.

"Historical discourses on recent agricultural problems", especially during the Tokugawa Period, including the problems of taxation, population, leases and peasant uprisings.

________________, *Meiji Isshin Keizaishi Kenkyū,* 明治維新經濟史研究; 1 Vol.; Kyōto, 1930.

"Studies in economic history of the Meiji Restoration of 1868."

________________, *Tokugawa Bakufu no Beika Chōsetsu,* 徳川幕府の米價調節; 1 Vol.; Kyōto, 1924.

"The regulation of Rice Prices by the Tokugawa Government."

Kawaguchi, Sonjirō, *Hida no Shirakawa Mura,* 川口孫治郎, 飛彈の白川村; 1 Vol., 1934.

"Shirakawa Village in Hida Province", a study of folklore in a remote village in Hida.

Kimura, Seiji, *Nihon Nōmin Sōtō Shi;* 木村靖二; 日本農民爭鬪史; 1 Vol.; 1930.

"A history of Japanese peasant struggles" from feudalism, through its downfall and up to the establishment of capitalism.

Kobayashi, Hirosane, *Ina Nōmin Sōdōshi*; 小林郊人; 伊那農民騷動史 1 Vol.; Iida, 1933.

"A history of agricultural uprisings in Ina," in Shinano.

Kokushō, Iwao, "Gyomin Sōdō", *Keizai Ronsō,* 黑正巖; 漁民騷動; 經濟論叢 Vol. 26, No 2.

Fishermen Uprisings

________________, *Hoken Shakai no Tōsei to Tōsō,* 封建社會の統と鬪爭 1 Vol.; Tōkyō, 1928.

"Unity and strife of feudal society". Professor Kokushō devotes the first half of this work to economic studies of feudal societies, the second half to uprisings in Mimasaka, Fukuyama, Kōyasan, Shōnai, Iso and Tosa.

________________, *Hyakushō Ikki no Kenkyū,* 百姓一揆の研究 1Vol.; Tōkyō, 1928.

"Studies in Peasant Uprisings". This excellent study deals with over five hundred uprisings in the Tokugawa Period.

It treats of their causes, forms, condition of growth and their nature of propagation. The work is filled with valuable charts and a chronological table of uprisings with bibliographical references.

________________, *Hyakushō Ikki Shidan,* 百姓一揆史談 1 Vol.; Tōkyō, 1928.

"Historical talks on peasant uprisings" in Echigo, Mino, Mimasaka, Fukuyama, Kōyasan and Shōnai.

Kurita Genji, *Edo Jidai, Sōgō Nihonshi Taikei*, 栗田元次; 江戸時代 綜合日本史大系 Vol. 9, Tōkyō, 1926.

"The Edo Period", an excellent monograph on the earlier half of the Tokugawa Period.

Mori, Kahei, *Kyū Nambu Han ni Okeru Hyakushō Ikki no Kenkyū*, 森嘉兵衞; 舊南部藩に於ける百姓一揆の研究 1 Vol.; Saitō Gratitude Foundation, Sendai, 1935, 364 pp.

"Studies in peasant uprisings in the old Nambu Fief", an analytical study of some eighty-four uprisings in Nambu from 1657 to 1870, together with a discussion of the general economic situation in the fief and its administration.

Numazaki, Hidenosuke, *Hyakushō Ikki Chōsa Hōkokusho*, 沼崎英助; 百姓一揆調査報告書 Kyōto, 1935.

"Report and investigation of Peasant Uprisings", a pamphlet containing the most recent charts on uprisings.

Ono, Takeo, "Hyakushō Ikki ya, kinnōgunya", 小野武夫; 百姓一揆乎勤王軍乎 *Shakai Keizaishi Gaku*, Vol. 6, No. 4, 1936.

"Peasant Uprisings and the Royalist Movement."

________________, *Isshin Nōmin Hōki Dan*, 維新農民蜂起譚 1 Vol.; Tōkyō, 1931.

"Talks on peasant uprisings of the Restoration Period", containing accounts of eleven different incidents, with bibliography.

________________, *Nihon Sonraku Shikō*, 日本村落史考 1 Vol.; Tōkyō, 1931.

Historical studies of Japanese Villages". A general discussion of the growth of the farmers and their villages during the Tokugawa Period, the famines in Nagato, uprisings in 1856 and tenancy problems.

________________, *Nōmin Keizaishi Kenkyū*, 農民經濟史研究 1 Vol.; Tōkyō,

"Studies in agricultural economic history", referring especially to modern tenancy disputes and tenancy problems.

________________, *Nōson Shakaishi Ronkō*, 農村社會史論講 1 Vol.; Tōkyō, 1835.

"Historical discussions on rural society", a description of feudal society, a study of peasant uprisings, tenancy problems and other features of Tokugawa agricultural society.

Tamura, Eitarō, *Ikki Kumosuke Bakuto* 田村榮太郎; 一揆雲助博徒 1 Vol.; Tōkyō, 1933.

"Uprisings, palanquin bearers and gamblers", containing accounts of uprisings in Shirakawa in 1720 and Kōzuke in 1781.

____________________, *Hōken Seika no Nōmin Ikki*, 封建制下の農民一揆 1 Vol.; Tōkyō, 1833.

"Peasant Uprisings under feudalism", with special references to those in Dewa in 1747, Echigo in 1837 and Shōnai in 1847.

Tsuchiya Takao and Ono, Michio, editors, *Meiji Shonen Nōmin Sōjō Roku*, 土屋喬雄, 小野道雄編, 明治初年農民騒擾錄, 1 Vol. Tōkyō, 1931, 665 pp.

"Peasant disturbances of the early Meiji Period", source materials geographically arranged on uprisings after 1868.

Tsuji, Zennosuke, *Tanuma Jidai*, 辻善之助; 田沼時代, 1 Vol,; Tokyō, 1915.

"The age of Tanuma", An account of the latter half of the 18th century centering around the life of Tanuma Motosugu, 田沼意次, (1719–1788).

C. *Western Bibliography*

Asakawa, K. "Some aspects of Japanese feudal institutions", *Transactions Asiatic Society of Japan*, Vol. 46, pt. 1, 1918.

____________________, "Notes on village government in Japan after 1600", *Journal American Oriental Society*, Vol. 30 & 31, 1910–1911.

An excellent study with copious and bibliographical references.

____________________, "The origin of feudal land tenure in Japan", *American Historical Review*, Vol. 20, 1914.

Bramsen, William, "Japanese chronological tables", *Transactions Asiatic Society of Japan*, Suppl. Vol. 37, 1910.

De Visser, M. W., *The dragon in China and Japan*, Amsterdam, 1913, 242 pp.

De Wolff, W. J.J., Von Ende, editor, *Herinneringen uit Japan*, 1 Vol., Brussels, 1890.

Droppers, Garret, "The population of Japan in the Tokugawa Period", *Transactions Asiatic Society of Japan*, Vol. 22, 1894.

Gubbins, J. H. "The 100 articles and the Tokugawa Government", *Proceedings and Transactions of Japan Society of London*, Vol. 17, 1920.

Haga, J. *Indonesische en Indische Democratie*, 1 Vol.; The Hague, 1924.

Hall, J. C., "Japanese feudal laws", *Transactions Asiatic Society of Japan*, Vols. 34, 36, 38 & 41.

Honjō, Eijirō, *The social and economic history of Japan*, 1 Vol.; Kyōto, 1935. An excellent brief account of Japan's social and economic history.

Miyashita, Koichi, *Beitrage zur Japanischen Geldgeschichte*, 1 Vol.; Vienna, 1931.

Murdoch, James, *A history of Japan*, 3 Vol.; London, 1926, especially Volume III.

Nakamura, Kichiji, (abstracted by E. O. Reischauer), "Popular Uprisings and *Tokusei* during the Onin and Bummei Periods (1467–1486)". *Abstracts of articles appearing in current Japanese periodicals*, Washington, 1935.

Rahder, J.; "Record of Kurume Uprisings", *Acta Orientalia*, Vol. XIV.

Ramming, M. "Die Bodenreform der Meiji Jahre", *Mitteilungen des Seminars fur Orientalische Sprachen*, Vol. 36, 1933.

Sawada, Shō, (translated by Hugh Borton), "Financial difficulties of the Edo Bakufu", *Harvard Journal of Asiatic Studies*, Vol. 1, No. 3.

Scott, J. W. R., *The foundations of Japan*, 1 Vol. London, 1922.

Smith, N. S,, ed., "An introduction to some Japanese economic writings", *Transactions Asiatic Society of Japan*, 2nd series, Vol. XI.

Takekoshi, Y. *The economic aspects of the history of the civilization of Japan*, 3 Vol.; London, 1930, especially Vols. II & III.
Takizawa, M. *The penetration of money economy into Japan and its effect upon social and political institutions*, 1 Vol.; 1927.
Von Siebold, Fr., *Nippon: Archiv zur Beschreibung von Japan*, 1 Vol.; Leyden, 1832.
Yanagisawa. Y. "Histore critique des travaux statistique au Japon depuis 1 anti Jusqu'a la restauration imperial", *Bulletin de l'Institut International de Statistique*, Tome 19, 1911.

D. *Reference, bibliographies, dictionaries*

Couvreur, F. S., *Dictionnaire classique de la langue Chinoise*, 1 Vol.; Ho Kien Fou, 1911.
Dai Hyakka Jiten, 大百科事典, 26 Vol., Heibonsha, 平凡社, Tōkyō, 1934.
"Great Encyclopedia", valuable for biographical references.
Daijiten, 大辭典, 25 Vol.; Heibonsha, Tōkyō, 1933.
"Complete Dictionary."
Dai Nihon Jimmei Jisho, 大日本人名辭書, 1 Vol.; Tōkyō, 1903, 2244 pp.
"Biographical Dictionary of Japan", excellent for those included in the work, but limited in scope.
Dai Nihon Kokugo jiten, 大日本國語辭典, 5 Vol.; Tōkyō, Ueda Bannen, editor, 上田萬年編.
"Dictionary of Japanese." an excellent dictionary, especially for terms of the Tokugawa Period.
Denki Dai Nihonshi Daimyō Hen, 傳記大日本史大名編, 1 Vol.; Tōkyō, 1933.
"Japanese history in biography," the *daimyō*, with a biographical index of most of the *daimyō*.
Dokushi Biyō, 讀史備要, 1 Vol.; Tōkyō, 1932, 2154 pp., edited by Tōkyō Imperial University, Shiryo Hensanjo.
"Essential Correlated tables to Japanese History," An extremely valuable work for the Japanese his-

torian with chronologies, charts, lists of names etc. The following have been especially useful: *Chronology*, including chief officials of the Tokugawa *Bakufu*, pp. 231–253; a *catalogue* of the *daimyō*, pp. 475–494; *catalogue of chief officials of Bakufu*, pp. 495–532; *catalogue of provinces and districts* pp. 551–610, lists of deaths of important persons, pp. 1935–2118.

Honjō, Eijirō, *Nihon Keizaishi Bunken*, 本庄榮治郎編, 日本經濟史文獻, 1 Vol.; Tōkyō, 1933.

"Bibliography of Japanese economic history". An excellent bibliography giving author, title and resume of each work quoted. It also contains a full index, list of prefectural and district histories and European bibliography on Japanese economic history.

Keizai Gaku Jiten, 經濟學字典, 6 Vol.; Tōkyō, 1932.

"Dictionary of Economics".

Kōji Ruien, Heiji Bu, 古事類苑兵事部, 1 Vol.; Tōkyō,

"Encyclopedia of Ancient Things".

Kokushi Daijiten, 國史大辭典, 6 Vol.; Tōkyō, 1927.

"Japanese historical dictionary."

Ono, Takeo, *Nihon Nōminshi Goi*, 小野武夫; 日本農民史語彙, 1 Vol.; Tōkyō, 1926.

"A glossary of Japanese agricultural history."

Papinot, E. *Dictionnaire d'histoire et de geographie du Japon*, 1 Vol.; Tōkyō, 1906.

Yoshida Tōgo, editor, *Dai Nihon Chimei Jisho*, 吉田東伍編, 大日本地名辭書, 4 Vol.; Tōkyō, 1900.

"Japanese geographical dictionary."

GLOSSARY

Aohiki, 青引; a kind of silk worm.

Bakufu, 幕府 :"Tent government", but referring to the government of the Tokugawa Period with its centre at Edo, after the establishment of the Tokugawa *Bakufu*, of Ieyasu.

Bakumatsu, 幕末 : The end of the Bakufu or Tokugawa Period. A term used by historians to denote the period following the reforms of 1786,

Benshi, 辨指 : An assistant official in charge of a group (*kumi*) in Bungo.

Bōdō, 暴動, An uprising.

Bu, 分; A unit of length equal to 1/10 *sun* or 1/100 *shaku*, or .12 inches.

Bu, 歩: A monetary unit for gold or silver coins, equal to 1/4 *ryō*.

Bu, 歩: A unit of square measure equal to a square *ken*, or 1/30 *se*; 3.95 sq. yds.

Bugyō, 奉行: An official in charge of a specific district as the *Kori Bugyō*, or a town as the *Machi Bugyō*.

Bujiki, 夫食: Rice stored by the fief officials for lean years. See *Gisomai*.

Bushi, 武士: Warriors or *samurai*, a term applying to the whole warrior class of society who wore two swords.

Chōbu, 町歩: A unit of measure, an area equal to 2.45 acres, composed of 10 *tan*.

Chōnin, 町人: Townsmen, as opposed to the farmers, who lived in the villages, and the *bushi* who had the privilege of wearing two swords.

Chūkoshō, 中小姓: A special class of pages of the castle.

Daikan, 代官: The deputy in charge of the domain; an intendant. There were originally forty *daikan* in charge of the public domains of the Tokugawa *Bakufu*. But the term was later applied to officials of the *daimyō*.

Dōshin, 同心: A type of policeman or soldier, sent on expeditions to quell riots, under the supervision of the censors or *metsuke*. Lictors.

Dōshin metsuke, 同心目付: Same as *dōshin*.

Edo, 江戸 : An old name for present Tōkyō.

Edo *Bakufu*, 江戸幕府: Same as *Bakufu*.

Esso, 越訴: An appeal usually made through the usual channels of officials, as opposed to *gōso*. See also *shūso*.

Fumai, 夫米: A tax or duty of villagers to pay in rice or money for the expenses of laborers in the lord's mansion in Edo or Kyōto. These services had originally been carried by men from the lord's fief, but coming from the country they did not readily enter into city life so a tax of rice or money was substituted.

Fuon, 不穏: General "disorders" or unrest.

Fushinyaku, 普新役: Assistants of the *kanjō kata* or treasurer. They may also have been officers in charge of repairs.

Fuyaku, 夫役: Labour requisitioned for various public works.

Ginsatsu metsuke, 銀札目付: Censors superintending the proper circulation of silver certificates as in the province of Bungo in 1786.

Gisōmai, 義倉米: Rice stored for lean years, often collected in the form of a tax. See *bujiki*.

Gō, 合: A unit of capacity equalling 1/1000 *koku* or .318 pints.

Gokanjō kata, 御勘定方: See *kanjō kata*,

Gonin kumi, 五人組: Five-men groups or the smallest administrative division of a village. Punchayets.

Gosada yaku, 御定役: Extraordinary services or taxes.

Ooshiire yaku, 御仕入役: Officials in charge of storing goods for merchants or other officials.

Gōso, 强訴: A "mob-appeal", having the meaning of forming a mob, and forcibly placing an appeal before the authorities in contrast to regular appeals, *esso*.

Goyaku gomen, 御役御免: To be deprived of one's office or official position.

Goyōkin, 御用金: Special "forced levies" on rich merchants, *daimyō*, and later, farmers, to meet the financial demands of either the central or local governments. They were used by the *Bakufu* to collect funds for the reconstruction of the palaces after fires or earthquakes.

Goyōnin, 御用人: A chamberlin in a *daimyō's* court. A managerial type of officer or assistant to the treasurer.

Gun, 郡: See *kōri*.

Gundai, 郡代: An official of a *daimyō* or the *Bakufu* in charge of administration of a district.

Gunsho, 郡所: The district office.

Hatamoto, 旗下: Standard bearers; direct retainers of the Tokugawa *Bakufu*.

Hiki, 疋: A bolt of cloth 30–35 feet long.

Hissoku, 逼塞: A type of imprisonment or confinement within one's home for 30–50 days.

Hyakushōdai, 百姓代: Elders of the village who oversaw the actions of the other village officials. They were representatives of the farmers and chosen from among the most respected peasants.

Hyakushō ikki, 百姓一揆: A peasant uprising.

Hyō, 俵: A bale of rice, containing .4 of a *koku*.

Ikki, 一揆: "A group", band, usually referring to a peasant uprising or *hyakushō ikki*.

Jisha bugyō, 寺社奉行: An official in charge of shrines, temples and priests, created during the Kamakura Period and revived in 1613. In 1635 there were three of these officials of the *Bakufu* government, each taking charge of the office for a month in rotation.

Jishu, 地主: A landholder.

Jitō, 知頭: Office or officer in charge of administration of a fief.

Jōchu, 常厨: Officer in charge of finances of a fief. It may refer to an ordinary (*jō*) steward as opposed to the chief (*shu*) steward.

Jōmenhō, 定免法: The settlement of the tax rate on the average taxes of a whole crop for a period of five to twenty years and keeping it fixed for that period regardless of the harvest.

Kaisho yakunin, 會所役人: An official in charge of the produce market. In Shinano it was an office held simultaneously by the Treasurer.

Kaizaku bugyō, 改作奉行: An officer in charge of the re-assessment of land for taxation purposes in Kaga, established in 1651 to relieve the stress from bad crops.

Kammai, 缺米: Supplementary rice tax to pay for loss in transport, usually amounting to about 3% of total rice shipped. See *sashimai.*

Kamme, 貫目: A weight used for money equal to approximately 3.75 kilograms, composed of 1000 *momme.* It was used especially for silver.

Kanjō bugyō, 勘定奉行: Minister in charge of the finances of the Tokugawa government, a type of finance minister. Also used for similar posts in the fief of the various *daimyō.*

Kanjō kata 勘定方: One who collects imposts and taxes.

Kanjō kata rusuyaku, 勘定方留役: "Representative of the *kanjō kata.*" Officials sent from Edo to participate in the judicial examinations following an uprising in Ōmi in 1842.

Kayaku, 課役: Service required of peasants for repairs of dykes, roads and bridges.

Kemmihō, 檢見法: Examination of the crop and the establishment of the taxes every year by taking a sample of one section of the standing crop in each type of field, in contrast to the *jōmenhō,* or settlement of tax for a number of years.

Ken, 間: A unit of length, equal to 6 *shaku* 1 *bu* in Tokugawa Period. Its present length is 6 *shaku* or 1.99 yards.

Kenchi yaku, 檢地役: Officer in charge of examination, inspection or surveying of land to determine the total taxable crop.

Kenda, 檢斷: A village chief, another term for *shōya,* one of the three chief village officials. It was used especially in Shinano, Dewa and Mutsu.

Kimoiri, 肝煎: A village head or chief, a term used instead of *shōya* in the north and in Kaga.

Koban, 小判: A small coin equal to approximately 1/10 the *Ōban* diminishing in value as the period progressed but equal approximately to one *ryō*.

Koku, 石: A unit of capacity for measuring rice equal to 4.96 bushels. It is composed of 100 *shō* and 2½ bales or *hyō*.

Komononari, 小物成: An additional special tax levied for various services usually collected in money.

Kōri, 郡: A district several of which made up a province.

Kōri bugyō, 郡奉行: Official in charge of administration of a district.

Kosaku nin, 小作人: A tenant farmer.

Koshōya, 小庄屋: An assistant village officer, an assistant to a *shōya*.

Kuchi mai, 口米: An additional rice levy assessed as a tax to defray the expenses of administration of the villages under the jurisdiction of a *daikan*. It sometimes amounted to 6–8% of the usual tax.

Kumigashira, 組頭: A village official, selected from among the peasants, an assistant of the *shōya*. A head of a group or *kumi*.

Kumigashira, 與頭: A village official or head of a group, apparently used synonymously for *Kumigashira* (組頭) in Echigo. When the group was of a military nature, it is read *yogashira*.

Kurakata kumigashira, 藏方組頭: Superintendent of the store keepers or those in charge of receiving and giving out rations. See *Okura bugyō*.

Machi azuke, 町預: To be confined within the limits of a *machi*, a town or block of a town or village, and to be placed on parole with the obligation of reporting at stated intervals to the officials. The officials in charge of the culprit were liable to punishment if he committed a crime during the period of his parole. See *mura azuke*.

Men, 免: The literal meaning of *men* is to exempt, pardon relieve from office, i.e. dismiss. It came to be used for the tax one paid in order to exempt oneself from further taxation; then used for the tax itself. Thus *yatsu men*, 八ツ免: meant an 80% tax.

Metsuke, 目付: An official acting as public censor or policeman for the authorities, sometimes rendered as spy.

Mizunomi, 水呑: "Those who drink water", hence the poorest type of farmers, also used for "hired man."

Mokuba, 木馬: "Wooden horse," a type of torture in which the culprit was placed on a wooden horse over a fire and roasted until he confessed.

Momme, 匁目: A weight equal to 3.765 gramme. 1,000 *momme* equal 1 *kamme*.

Mon, 文: A cheap coin like a farthing.

Monogashira, 物頭: A superintendant or official in charge of general business affairs of the *Bakufu* or a fief.

Monoto, 毛人: An inferior class of fishermen or sailors of Sanuki. Possibly a term derived from its use referring to the Ainu.

Mura azuke, 村預: To be placed on parole within one's village. See *machi azuke*.

Mura yokome, 村横目: Censors or police of the village.

Myōden kosaku, 名田小作: Tenancy of land belonging to the landowner and not covered by a mortgage. See *shichiji kosaku*.

Nanushi, 名主: One of the three chief village officials and head of the village, appointed by the fief. A term used in the eastern region for *shōya*. It had an earlier origin than *shoya* and was probably derived from *myōden-shu*, 名田主.

Nimmyō, 人名: A social class in Sanuki. A type of fishermen above the *monto*.

Ōban, 大判: A gold coin of early Tokugawa days worth about 7½ *ryo*.

Okage mairi, 御蔭参: A pilgrimage every sixty-one years to the Ise Shrine for offering thanks for good harvests, the first having taken place in 1705. It originally took the form of individual secret pilgrimages.

Okura bugyō, 御藏奉行: An official in charge of the cereal stores, under the control of the Treasurer. He had charge of the storing of rice and cereals and their distribution to the officials as salary.

Ōkura Daijin, 大藏大臣: Finance Minister.

Ōmetsuke, 大目付: Head of the *metsuke*, censors.

Osabyakushō, 長百姓: A village official, often called *toshiyori* or *Kumigashira*. He was a village elder selected from among the influential peasants.

Ōshōya, 大庄屋: Village officer in charge of several *shōya*, usually having ten villages under his jurisdiction.

Ōwarimoto, 大割元: Another term for a village officer in charge of a number of villages.

Rōjū, 老中: A councillor of the *Shōgun*, an elder minister of a fief. For the *Shōgun* they were chosen from among the *daimyō* with an income over 25,000 *koku*.

Rōnin, 浪人: "Wave men", warriors who had lost their lord and who wandered about the country with no one to whom they paid allegiance.

Ryō, 兩: A monetary unit for gold coins equal to 60 *momme* of silver and about ¥1.00 in 1868. 1 *ryō* equals 4 *bu*, equals 16 *shu*.

Ryōke, 領家: A seignior.

Sai, 才: A dry unit of measure, 10 *sai* equal 1 *shaku* 100 *sai* equal 1 *gō*.

Sakujikata, 作事方: An officer in charge of general public works and repairs. He had an income of 50 *koku*. "Manager of public works."

Sakunin, 作人: A cultivator.

Sankin kōtai, 參勤交代: The system of alternate attendance of feudal lords to Edo and the requirement that they leave their families there as hostages when they returned to their home fiefs.

Sashimai, 差米, Tax to make up for the shrinkage or loss in shipment of rice, payable in advance amounting to 1 *shō* per bale or 1/40 of the total. Also called *Kammai*.

Se, 畝: A square measure, a hundredth part of a *chōbu*, equal to .0245 acres.

Shaku, 勺: A unit of capacity equal to 1/10 *gō* or .388 pints.

Shaku, 尺: A unit of length equal to .994 feet, composed of 10 *sun*.

Shasō, 社倉: Common cereal collected by the authorities from which the people could borrow at a low rate of interest.

Shichiji kosaku, 質地小作: The tenancy of mortgaged land.

Shichimotsu, 質物: An indentured servant or one who is pledged.

Shinya shitayaku, 新家下役: Assistant officers in charge of new buildings.

Shitashirabe yaku, 下調役: A temporary judicial examiner.

Shō, 升: A dry measure equal to 3.18 pints.

Shōen, 莊園: A private manor of the middle ages.

Shoin Ōbangashira, 書院大番頭: Chiefs of the various palace libraries of the *Shōgun*.

Shoshidai, 所司代: *Bakufu* representative in Kyōto in charge of the supervision of the Imperial Palace.

Shoshiki ukeoi, 諸色受負: "Commissioners for all kinds of things" in Nambu fief.

Shōya, 庄屋: One of the three main village officials together with the *toshiyori* and *hyakushōdai*. The *shōya* was a village chief selected from one of the leading farmers by the lord or the fief officials. The term was used in western Japan as synonymous with *nanushi*.

Shōya tōdori, 庄屋頭取: A chief or head of the *shōya*.

Shu, 朱: A small unit of gold or silver coin, the value varying from 1/8 to 1/16 of a *ryō*.

Shūso, 愁訴: An appeal made in the approved fashion through the channel of the village officials, as opposed to *gōso* or mob appeal.

Sōbugyō, 総奉行: A supervisor of the fief or officer in charge of the various offices and duties of the fief.

Sōran, 騷亂: An uprising.

Soroban, 算盤: A type of torture in which slabs of stone were piled on the culprits legs. An abacus.

Sōshaban, 奏者番: Officer of the *Shōgun's* court whose duty it was to arrange for audiences and to introduce the *daimyō* to the *Shōgun* at festivals and at the New Year.

Sukegō, 助郷: A tax in horses or service of men levied on villages along the main highways for trips of Korean envoys to Edo or *Bakufu* officials to the Nikkō mausoleums.

Sun, 寸: A unit of length equal to 10 *bu* and 1/10 a *shaku*.

Sunshimai, 寸志米: Special additional rice tax levied in Izumo and Bingo.

Takamen, 高免: "High exemption", that is, high taxes in order to be exempt. See *Men*.

Tan, 段: A square unit equal to 1/10 *chōbu* or .245 acres.

Tedai, 手代: Representatives of a *daikan* or assistant managers under his jurisdiction.

Tokugawa Bakufu, 徳川幕府: The government of the Tokugawa Period. See *Bakufu*.

Tonya, 問屋: A wholesale commissioner.

Tōri, 通: An administrative section of the Nambu fief.

Toshiyori, 年寄: Elders, heads of the village. One of the three officers of the village along with the *shōya* and *hyakushōdai*.

Totō, 徒黨: Any kind of rebellious league, band or mob. They were usually formed by the peasants in the process of an uprising.

Tsuchi ikki, 土一揆: Uprisings of the soil, common before the Tokugawa Period. They were composed of *rōnin*, priests, miners and farmers.

Tsuriage, 釣上ゲ: A type of torture in which one was suspended by one's arms tied behind the back.

Uchi kowashi, 打毀: "House-wrecking", or forceful demolition of property usually of the officials or wealthy persons, by a mob either in the villages or towns.

Uma kimoiri, 馬肝煎: Horse officials who seem to have examined the horses for taxation purposes. The term was common in the Nambu fief.

Wakadoshiyori, 若年寄: Assistant councillors of the *Shōgun*.

Warimoto, 割元: A head of a village, a term used for *shōya* in Shinano.

Yama bugyō, 山奉行: Mountain officials.

Yokome, 横目: See *mura yokome*.

Yōmai, 用米: Rice paid in lieu of wages.

Yoriki, 與力: An officer under the *bugyō* similar to the *dōshin* with police and military duties, a kind of gens d'armes.

Zeni, 錢: A cash, a copper or iron coin of little value.

Zōshiki, 雜色: A general "handy man" or messenger.

APPENDIX II.

Chart I.

Density and re-appearance of uprisings according to provinces, (1603-1867).[1]

Number of Occurrences	Names of Provinces	Number of Provinces
None	Iga and Iki	2
1	Shima, Satsuma, Ōsumi	3
2	Kwachi, Awaji	2
3	Izu, Awa (Tōkaidō), Oki, Bizen	4
4	Sagami, Shimōsa	2
5	Yamashiro, Owari	2
6	Izumi, Suruga, Shimo-zuke, Noto, Aki, Chikuzen	6
7	Tōtōmi, Wakasa, Inaba, Matsumae	4
8	Kazusa	1
9	Yamamoto, Chikugo	2
10	Ise, Izumo	2
11	Kai	1
12	Tango, Tajima, Hizen	3
13	Hitachi, Iwaki, Rikuzen, Mutsu, Iwami, Tosa	6
14	Sado, Nagato	2
15	Settsu, Ugo, Bingo, Buzen	4
16	Bitchū	1
17	Kii	1
18	Musashi, Hida, Kaga, Sanuki	4

1. Cf. Numazaki, *op. cit.* Chart 2.

Number of Occurrences	Names of Provinces	Number of Provinces
19	Etchū, Hōki, Tamba, Mimasaka	4
20	Harima, Suwō	2
24	Mikawa	1
25	Higo	1
27	Kōzuke	1
28	Mino	1
30	Awa (Nankaidō)	1
32	Hyūga	1
34	Iwashiro, Bungo	2
35	Ōmi	1
41	Uzen	1
42	Echizen	1
51	Iyo	1
54	Rikuchū	1
55	Shinano, Echigo	2

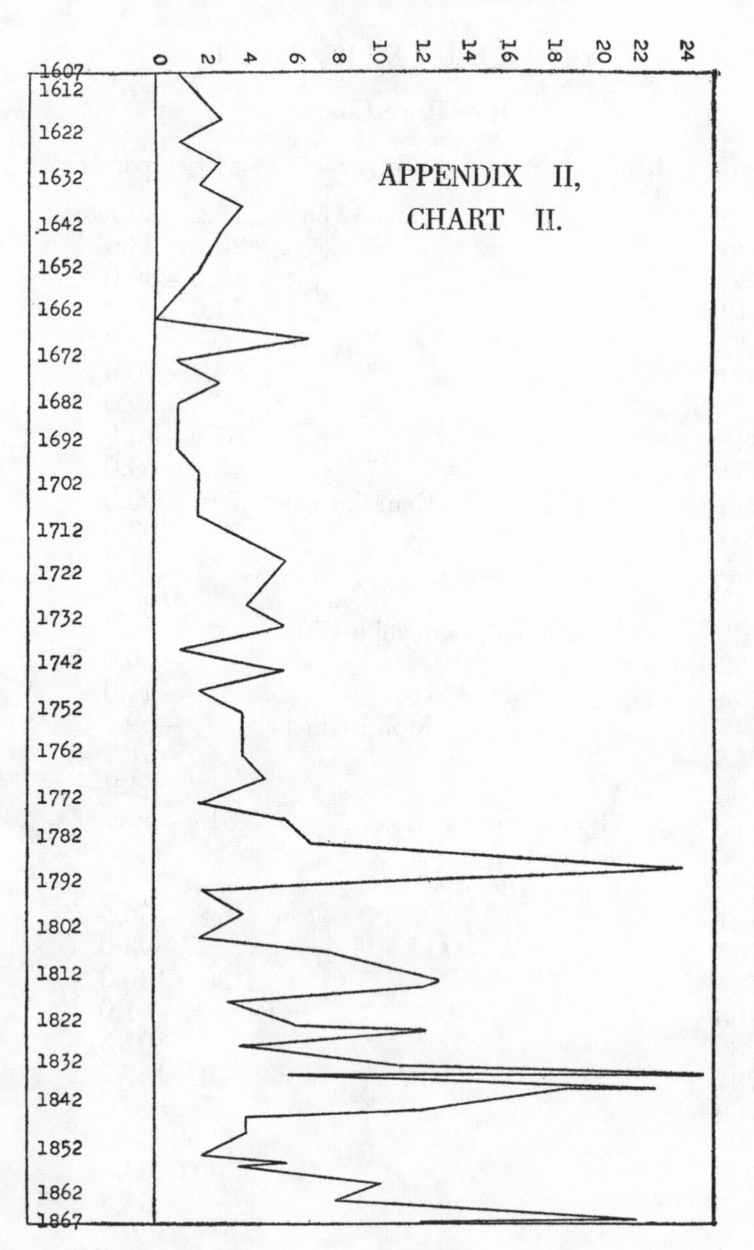
0
2
4
6
8
10
12
14
16
18
20
22
24
1607
1612
1622
1632
1642
1652
1662
1672
1682
1692
1702
1712
1722
1732
1742
1752
1762
1772
1782
1792
1802
1812
1822
1832
1842
1852
1862
1867
APPENDIX II,
CHART II.

APPENDIX III, Chart I

Rice Price Chart

Year	Kind of Rice	Silver	Price per *koku*
1616		Keichō Gin	18.2 – 20 *momme*
1626		”	20. – 23.6 ”
1636		”	43.0 – 50.0 ”
1642		”	54.0 – 60.0 ”
1647		”	24. – 26.0 ”
1660		”	69. – 70.0 ”
1670		”	56. – 59.0 ”
1680		”	67.0 – 70.0 ”
1694		”	65. – 69.0 ”
1695	Higo	Genroku Gin	70. – 80.0 ”
1703	”	”	92. – 93.0 ”
1705	”	”	– 41.0 ”
1713	”	Hōji Gin	–155.0 ”
1725	Hiroshima	Kyōho Gin	– 50.3 ”
1732	”	”	67 – 90.0 ”
1735	”	”	31 – 41.0 ”
1745	”	Monji Gin	– 69.7 ”
1755	”	”	– 81.3 ”
1765	”	”	– 64.9 ”
1775	Higo rice used as standard henceforth.	”	51 – 56. ”
1781	”	”	54 – 56. ”
1783	”	”	– 98.0 ”
1784	”	”	130 –140.0 ”
1785	”	”	– 61.0 ”
1786	”	”	101.5 ”
1787	”	”	181–187 ”
1788	”	”	66.0 ”
1798	”	”	58–60.0 ”
1808	”	”	80.0–83. ”
1818	”	”	54.5 ”

1830	Higo	Shimmonji Gin	88.5	*momme*
1833	"	"	119.9	"
1836	"	"	155.7	"
1837	"	"	250–94.0	"
1840	"	"	63.4	"
1848	"	Hōji Gin	89.8	"
1849	"	"	100.1	"
1850	"	"	147.9	"
1851	"	"	81.2	"
1857	"	"	106.3	"
1858	"	"	131.5	"
1859	"	Seiji Gin	203.0	"
1860	"	"	142.0	"
1862	"	"	100.0	"
1863	"	"	325.0	"
1864	"	"	530.	"
1865	"	"	1300.	"
1866	"	"	590.	"

1. The above table is taken from Honjō, E., *Tokugawa Bakufu Beika Chōsetsu op. cit.* pp. 407–415.

INDEX OF PROPER NAMES

DATE DUE

5/2			
AUG 8			
DEC 1 3 1978			